Janet Reger
HER STORY

Janet Reger
HER STORY

JANET REGER
WITH SHIRLEY FLACK

CHAPMANS

Chapmans Publishers Ltd
141–143 Drury Lane
London WC2B 5TB

First published by Chapmans 1991
This paperback edition first published by Chapmans 1992

© Janet Reger and Shirley Flack 1991

The right of Janet Reger and Shirley Flack to be
identified as the authors of this work has been asserted
by them in accordance with the Copyright, Designs
and Patents Act, 1988

ISBN 1 85592 575 3

Printed and bound in Great Britain by
Clays Ltd, St Ives plc

For Peter
who made it all happen

Illustrations

Preface

Recently an American customer in Beauchamp Place said: 'I'm so pleased to find the shop still here. It doesn't belong to her any more, does it?'

My daughter Aliza was wrapping the customer's purchase. 'It most certainly does. Mrs Reger owns the shop.'

I happened to be checking stock. My ears pricked up.

'But isn't she dead?' He seemed confused. 'I thought Janet Reger died some time ago and somebody else bought the shop.'

Aliza replied: 'I assure you Janet Reger is most certainly alive and well.'

And standing behind you, she could have added. But she didn't; we aren't in the business of embarrassing our customers.

I am alive. I didn't 'go bankrupt'. I didn't sell my name to Berlei.

Over many years as a designer attracting epithets such as 'The Queen of Luxury Lingerie', I built up a business that, it seemed for a time, couldn't do a thing wrong. It was only after it crashed that I learned business is not about design; it is about finance.

I went into liquidation like a lamb to slaughter because I thought everybody else knew best. Not any more.

Anyone who has been through liquidation and receivership has experienced the humiliation of failure. There was a moment, in January 1983, when, as the *Daily Express* put it: 'The world mourns the passing of lingerie queen Janet Reger', while at the same time the queues outside my shops stretched the length of Bond Street and Beauchamp Place and the doors were locked to supervise the crowds.

That same week, trying to keep my spirits up, cheered by the rush to buy Janet Reger underwear before it was too late, I asked one of the officials monitoring the takings the question most often asked by any shopkeeper of the person on the till: 'What have we taken so far today?'

'Don't ask me that, I'm not allowed to tell you,' he replied. That was when I realised I'd lost the business.

Today I control a successful and expanding enterprise. My lingerie is as much in demand as ever; my ideas flow as always, and I suspect I will always be referred to as 'Janet Reger who went bankrupt and began again'. All in one sentence. Liquidation isn't uncommon in the fashion business. Many big names have been through it more than once. But because my personal story seems to occupy a special place in the public's imagination, read on . . .

1

I always felt I had a charmed life and nothing terrible would ever happen to me. I grew up with that belief and retained it right through my teens and adult life until a few years ago. My sister Barbara felt the same and still does. It must be something to do with our upbringing.

At the beginning we lived in Jubilee Street, in the East End of London. I was nearly four when World War II's blitz began, and my little sister, Barbara, had just been born. All that first week of bombing we slept in the air-raid shelter in the garden.

One afternoon as I played hopscotch in the street, the sirens sounded and my father snatched me from my game and ran with me in his arms to the shelter. We scrambled down the steps as the first bomb fell, a screaming sound that made me put my fingers in my ears. And then the explosion, worse than anything we had heard before. My father had closed the curtain across the entrance, so we lay in the dark, listening to the planes, the bombs, the guns. It was hours before the all clear and we emerged to see the gaping holes in our house, the entire street a scene of devastation.

My father, a decisive person, packed his little family into the car with a few essentials and, making only a small detour to collect his parents, drove out of London, through the burning and smouldering streets of the East End, and headed for Reading, where Aunt Becky, my mother's sister, lived.

I awoke as we arrived, fumbling through black-out darkness into the huge Victorian house and to welcoming grown-up arms, hot cocoa and biscuits. That night we slept on mattresses on the attic floor – as exciting to us as camping out – and next day our pleasure increased when we learned that there were numerous young cousins to play with, for Aunt Becky already had a house full of relatives escaping from the blitz. The attic was our temporary domain.

Zaida, my paternal grandfather, found a house just along the street and we moved in to No. 52 Tilehurst Road, a big white building standing in a wonderfully wild and overgrown garden hidden from general view by a brick wall. This was to be my home for the next eight years. Today I cannot think of that house without smiling at the memory of Grandfather and Grandmother Phillips (Zaida and Booba) presiding over us all: my parents, my sisters, the aunts and uncles, cousins and friends. My father was one of six children: three sons, three daughters, all, like their parents, very volatile and quarrelsome. There has never been a time in living memory when all six were on speaking terms. There were so many people in that one house.

At Aunt Becky's and Uncle Alf's, where my maternal relatives lived, the atmosphere was less excitable. Mother, too, was one of six children but, like her, all of them were gentle.

Gradually as the men were called up into the services, both households became predominantly female and buzzed with domesticity and chatter. Coming upon one of these elbows-on-the-table-gathered-around-the-teapot sessions in either house we children were given a *Kuchen* and sent on our way.

There was total intermingling of Phillipses and Levenes. The two families had known each other for years. I have a picture in my mind of Grandmother Levene in the scullery at Aunt Becky's house, peeling potatoes and speaking Yiddish. Born in Poland, she never learned English, was widowed young and left with six children to raise.

At first my Grandfather Phillips commuted to work from Reading; then he found a warehouse and was able to relocate his textile business. My grandmother helped him there, her main function, it seemed to us children, to serve as unofficial tea lady to the Reading transport workers whose bus depot was close by the factory. She and her husband had great faith in the restorative powers of a never-ending supply of tea.

My grandfather had a curious habit on a bus journey of retaining his fare money until his journey was over, then pressing the coin into the conductor's hand, saying in a penetrating stage whisper, 'Don't give me a ticket, buy yourself a cup of tea.' This was a source of terrible embarrassment to my mother, who feared he would be caught, arrested and bring disgrace on the family.

Zaida's real surname was Chabinsky. This was hard to pronounce, so people called him by his first name, Philip. In time this became Mr Phillips, which he eventually adopted by deed poll. He escaped to England from Kiev as a boy of eighteen in order to avoid being drafted into the army, which was in effect a death sentence. Young Jews were rounded up in the ghettos and conscripted to serve twenty years. The conditions were so appalling the conscripts were unlikely to live long enough to complete their term of service. It was a way of controlling the Jewish population.

My grandfather had been told of someone, a fellow Ukrainian, who might help him in London. That someone was Grandmother's brother, and she and Zaida fell in love. The older I get, the more I appreciate what an amazing character Booba was. She still spoke English with a strong mid-European accent, had never learned to read or write, but had tireless energy. She ran the house, bossed everyone, helped in the business and later, as my father and his brothers went into the army, took their place at work.

My mother never really got on with her in-laws and I can understand why. For a start it was their house, and Zaida was its head, the only resident man until the war ended. He and Booba shouted a great deal, though never at the grandchildren. Their rows erupted out of the blue, and usually cooled fast. In serious cases of affront, Booba would withdraw to the morgue-like dining-room and lock the door, refusing to speak or accept food or drink until she was satisfied Zaida was truly contrite. Depending on the severity of the offence, he could spend a whole day on his knees pleading with her through the keyhole. He referred to her as 'my pretty little girl', which we children found ridiculously funny.

It all added spice to my life, and never threatened my security. Mother, who is gentle and patient and almost never raises her voice, strove to make peace. Dominant Booba must have been a most difficult mother-in-law. I was the eldest of their grandchildren and they showered a very special affection and attention on me, took me out and about with them, even on holidays.

Booba taught me to swim. I don't know anybody with a Jewish grandmother of that age, class and background who can make

3

such a claim. When I think of where she came from – the restrictions of her sheltered life in the Kiev ghetto, not to mention the years as a young girl in the East End of London – I am still amazed. It was during a holiday in Brighton. She took me into the sea and showed me what to do. When it started to rain, she continued the lesson at the King Alfred Baths. I began with water wings, and then Booba took the wings away and made me swim without them. Such was her authority and my faith in her that I did. Booba stood there shouting 'Breathe, breathe, breathe.' I breathed. I stayed afloat. I was very proud of myself.

From my first memory of that house in Tilehurst Road, celebrating my birthday sitting at the 'big' table in the dining-room around a spread of cakes and sandwiches, all my recollections are of a happy, safe refuge for us children. There was no such thing as pocket money, and we were rarely given toys (though books could be scrounged if you went about it the right way), but the whole house was an adventure playground of rooms and staircases, cellars and cupboards, and a garden where there was nothing to damage and everything to be explored. Several times in recent years I've passed by and been tempted to knock on the door but something always holds me back. Perhaps it's a good thing, for nostalgia is heady stuff and who knows if I would even recognise what is left inside the house by now.

When we required a change of scene and company an even larger assortment of cousins resided at Aunt Becky's house. All I had to do was let myself in through the back door to become immediately engulfed in the hubbub of children, aunts and uncles (leave permitting), cooking, eating, talking about life and death, right and wrong, rationing and the good old pre-war days. Grandmother Levene, stationed at the potato pile, took no part in these discussions and emerged from the scullery only on Friday nights for the Sabbath supper.

Because of what was said at home, I was aware from the start that being Jewish made us different, in some way set us apart. 'Jewish people don't do this . . . we aren't allowed to do that.' Cloistered with my family, my nearest and dearest, I didn't need to seek out the company of neighbouring children although we sometimes played together. My real life was within our family group, the permanent household and the visiting relatives, coming and going with their children. They would stay for a year, have a huge row with Booba or a sister and leave.

When I started school and began mixing in a wider circle, my new friends came as a big surprise. I hadn't known what to expect but, to my five-year-old mind, it was a revelation to discover that these mysterious non-Jewish children were human beings. I had been brought up with such a strong sense of being in some way special, that I was amazed to find the girls at school exactly like me in every way. Nor did they seem to think there was anything out of the ordinary about me.

Anti-Semitism, when I eventually met it, was just stupid. After a night air-raid (we experienced few in Reading) one of the children came to school next morning to announce: 'My dad says Hitler knows all the Jews are moving to Reading and that's why he's bombing the town. It's all the Jews' fault.' Even at that age I knew what she was saying was absurd: there were only about one hundred Jewish families in the whole of Reading. Neither did the occasional jibe, 'Jew girl', hurt – though later I learned to be more sensitive. The children given to making these taunts were rather inadequate, even I could recognise that, which reinforced the sense of superiority my Jewishness imparted. We lived well. My grandfather had his own business. We were well cared for, nicely dressed, and had a lady who came to help clean the house and we generally enjoyed a standard of living superior to my classmates at Battle Council Primary School, who were mainly children of factory workers and employees performing other menial jobs. At another time, in another environment, I might have felt guilty for being privileged, but not then. I felt to be Jewish was a very nice way to be born, thank you very much.

My grandfather went every Saturday to synagogue. He was something of a big noise in the community and enjoyed arguing with the rabbi, putting him right on various matters of Jewish law. Although never fanatically religious, he was knowledgeable and confident, certain that he knew everything better than anybody else, and usually he did.

When we were old enough he insisted we attend Hebrew classes on Sunday mornings. Later, when I was about ten years old, I organised the Truant Club, persuading our little group, mainly of cousins, and my sister, Barbara, to pool the sixpences we had been given for synagogue and roam free. The bus ride into Reading town centre cost a ha'penny and we would buy whatever we could find and visit the recreation park, which was usually out of bounds. We were caught out when my father came to meet us at synagogue and we were missing. Thus ended our activities.

Every Saturday at synagogue my grandfather collected the American servicemen stationed near Reading who needed a nice Jewish meal and brought them home to lunch. It was a tiny community and any stranger was immediately conspicuous and was pounced upon. Not that they objected. Friday nights and all Jewish holidays always included GIs at the dining table, and Passover, the most important – from the children's point of view – meant thirty people might be rounded up. Uncle Alf and Aunt Becky did the same.

The GIs brought us chewing gum, candy, tinned food (including syrupy peaches, a treat we never saw in the normal course of events), powdered egg, which I hated and, occasionally, nylon stockings for my mother and aunts.

They seemed like old men to us, but most were no more than boys, all from traditional Jewish homes and grateful to be part of family life, albeit briefly. They were a colourful part of my childhood and we each had our favourite; some stayed in touch after the war, continuing to write for a few years.

Booba loved visitors, and the challenge of producing a meal whatever the occasion. Zaida wouldn't eat margarine and was spared the indignity of having to, until it was discovered that actually he couldn't tell the difference. However, we always had butter in the house. My grandmother was adept at doing deals with neighbours, swapping our bacon ration for their butter. Butter was too expensive for the average working family and many had never acquired the habit, even before rationing; but to have a bit of bacon in the house meant a meal for those families.

By the same methods she obtained precious sweets and chocolate for us children, never sufficient to satisfy. When sweet rationing ended and Barbara and I hurried to Woolworth's with the money we had been saving for a binge, the shelves were already empty of everything except dolly mixtures so we gorged ourselves on those. I often wonder if all we middle-aged chocoholics are the product of wartime chocolate deprivation. Booba knew everybody and had contacts everywhere and by some unspoken rule, her little extras were not discussed. She once, years later, gave herself away. She and my mother were talking about the price of butter having just gone up. 'My God, the butter's so expensive, it's nearly as dear as it was in the war,' said Booba.

'Don't be silly,' said my mother, 'it was much cheaper in the war.'

'Not from Mr Johnson it wasn't,' said Booba, mentioning a name from the distant past. So now we knew why Mr Johnson used to call so frequently and was so warmly welcomed.

Booba's chickens occupied four runs in the large uncultivated garden and lived on peelings (vegetables were scrubbed and their peelings saved scrupulously) and scraps from the table. Nothing was wasted that could be recycled through the chickens. She would feed them herself, collect the eggs, and chase them when they escaped the run, swearing at them in Yiddish. So there were plenty of eggs and, unfortunately for any hen that wasn't laying, poultry for the table. When the chickens were laying well, the surplus eggs were preserved in a tub, which stood in the corner of the pantry.

A man came every Friday to kill a chicken. It was horrible. We children used to hide. The chicken would squawk sometimes, and then we refused to eat it. A chance remark at the supper table, 'nice young chicken this', would send me off in floods of tears, 'young' being the evocative word. I attribute my latent vegetarianism to those traumatic scufflings in the chicken run. Not that I was fond of the hens. They were vicious creatures, who pecked each other mercilessly and attracted rats.

My cousin Julian was bitten by one of the rats when we were playing in the wood near the chicken runs. He shot it with his homemade bow and arrow but didn't kill it (he was amazed even to have struck a target). It revived and bit him and he had to be rushed to hospital for an anti-tetanus jab.

We were playing a game based on a wonderful brave hero called Paul Valiant in a book we had read, who survived in the forest on what he could catch and eat, hence my cousin's bow and arrow. The heroine in the story was a miserable, wimpish girl who was always having to be rescued. That was my role. Julian was a few months younger than me, the second grandchild and the first boy. We were very close and always had a great empathy. Sadly he was killed in a car accident just before his fortieth birthday.

The most enduring game of my childhood was paper dolls. I created whole fashion parades of these chubby-faced creatures from the stiffest paper I could find, coloured them fleshy pink and dressed them in a rich variety of ballgowns, day dresses, suits, hats and handbags. Sometimes exasperated by the mess of paper trimmings littering every surface in the kitchen and on the floor, my mother would drive me outside. I continued to play paper dolls long after I should have outgrown the habit but used the excuse that I was entertaining Barbara.

Like all children we adored dressing up. Left to our own devices and without fear of interruption, Barbara and I would sneak into my mother's room and ransack her wardrobe. We revelled in the evening dresses that smelt of mothballs, and screeched with laughter as we pulled on Mother's hats and paraded in her high-heeled shoes, splashing ourselves with the perfume she carefully stored in a dark place 'for special occasions'. Best of all were the silky things in her lingerie drawer, folded in tissue paper, camiknickers and French knickers in ivory satin trimmed with lace. Mother was a great hoarder. She never wore these; they were far too precious.

The happiness generated within the family masked for us children the fear of what was happening in the war. We had escaped the blitz, but could see the sky lit up at night by distant fires, hear the sound of guns and bombs. I remember once asking when the family gathered around the wireless to listen to the News: 'When the war's over there won't be any News any more, will there?'

The grown-ups did not include the children in their conversations about the war, except to say, as no doubt did thousands of others at mealtimes: 'Eat it up. Don't waste food. Think of the poor children in the concentration camps.' Long after the war, when in my travels I met people from Germany of my age or older who said that they were unaware of what was happening in their country, that the existence of the camps was a total secret, I was puzzled that they should have been unaware of what was common knowledge in Reading.

My father served with the Signals Corps in Egypt. They let him drive a train once (fulfilment of a boyhood dream). The war ended, and we kept asking 'When's Daddy coming home?' and Mummy would reply, 'Soon, soon,' for she didn't know the answer.

One day somebody came running up and banged on the door. 'Is there a Mrs Phillips here?'

What had happened?

'Your husband's down at Reading West station. They're not allowed off the train.'

Reading West was a branch line a few streets away, but it was unheard of for a train to stop there. Now apparently one had halted, by accident or intent, carrying soldiers, and one of them, my father, recognising the locality, had alerted a passer-by. Mother grabbed Barbara and me and we rushed to the station. By the time we got there, the train had gone. We hadn't seen him for four years. Gloria, who was born just before he went overseas, couldn't remember him at all.

We knew children whose fathers had been killed in action, but I never doubted for a minute that Daddy would come home; it was just a matter of time. Years later Barbara and I discussed our being blessed with good fortune, and in general events have borne that out. We had eight uncles in the army, two in the invasion forces, and every one of them came through. When we grew up, we both married the men of our choice, had healthy children, made a good living . . . Understandably, we had the confidence of charmed lives. Perhaps if you believe that firmly enough, it works out that way.

We knew now that Father was back in England, and eventually he sent word of his arrival. Mother took Barbara and me to Reading General station to wait for him; we were so excited we couldn't stop jumping up and down. All our photographs showed him as a pale sandy-haired man and, suddenly, there he was, this soldier with a sun-reddened face striding towards us. My mother was rushing towards him and throwing her arms around him, and expecting us to do the same, to this stranger.

We took him home to celebrations, for which Booba had been cooking for days. He had brought me a silver bracelet with mosaic charms, which I treasured for years. And a mosaic box for my mother, which eventually fell to bits, all the mosaic pieces dropping out.

I thought I would burst with joy at having Father back with us, but anti-climax followed swiftly. Within a few days it was back to real life, and 'Run along, I want to talk to your mother.' After only a few days he went back to work and life returned to normal. Each day the men came home to lunch and all talked business, so the novelty of having a father around soon wore off.

In a way, my father's homecoming, which should have sealed the perfect happiness I had known so far, formed the benchmark of change. Where life had once been total bliss, I was now prone to lurking fear and insecurity which would sneak up on me.

The fear took root the day I read my first newspaper. I was nine and came home from school to find everyone talking about the front-page story, the bombing of Hiroshima. 'Oh well, the war will end now,' they were saying. 'They'll surrender.' I picked up the newspaper lying on the kitchen table and read the front page. Then I turned inside and read more. I felt sick. Like most people of my generation, I grew up a pacifist. Nothing was worth a war.

There was fear, too, in growing up. When I was a small child, I believed that I was the perfect little girl, probably because I was always surrounded by adoring relatives. Everybody loved me, except a few nasty people at school, but that was their mistake; there was nothing wrong with me. Once I reached an age of understanding, I began to worry that I wasn't pretty enough. I became aware that my younger sister, Barbara, was better looking than me. People started to say, 'What a beautiful child!' as she came into the room. She still is very beautiful.

My nose was too big. Pretty children had blond curls like Shirley Temple. I had dark straight hair, and it didn't go curly until much later – and then I hated it! As I gradually became aware that I wasn't perfect, I desperately wanted to be grown up and beautiful, to be famous and know everything, fervently believing that all my problems would be remedied by age.

As my teens approached I grew neurotic about my appearance. I had spots; my hair stopped being straight and went frizzy; I became plump. I felt miserable with myself, convinced I was so ugly nobody would ever love me, and that my mother only pretended to do so.

I escaped often into a private fantasy world where I was either famous and adored or the heroine of whatever book I was reading. I read avidly, mainly Enid Blyton, in particular the doings of the Fifth Form at St Clare's, which is odd considering how much I hated school. The ritual team choosing for netball was mortifying. Nobody ever selected me for I was truly appalling at games. (I fared better when they picked sides for a quiz: I knew a lot!) But I had a small circle of very close friends, of whom my best was Yvonne Eggers, perfect in every way except for her habit of coming top of the class.

For a bright child – I could read before I started school – I was a poor achiever. It was the hare and the tortoise. I did nothing, so the other children caught up and overtook me. In the nick of time I was saved by the arrival of Miss Harris, who understood me, inspired my enthusiasm for work and propelled me through the eleven-plus examination and on to the Kendrick Grammar School.

The promise was short-lived. From being among the top three in class, it wasn't long before I had slipped to average, only hanging on there because I did well in art. I was never happy at school, and saw it as a waste of time. I wanted to get on with growing up; school was a delay.

It became obvious to me that Daddy was not the knight in shining armour I had pictured all the years he was away. There were endless rows, sometimes in response to an innocent remark of my mother's, or at mealtimes, involving the entire family. Mostly the shouting was about money, money, money. I listened and I learned that at the root of all this was his gambling.

My father was a man of extremes. Despite the chronic smoker's cough caused by smoking sixty cigarettes a day, he was immensely strong and had great stamina. This made him a wonderful companion for outings and games and we children adored him when he was in a good mood: an emotion which became love–hate in my case as I learned to resent the distress he caused my mother.

Like most gamblers he was generous when he won, and I acquired conflicting impressions about the value of money. It seemed that sometimes there was more than enough; next day to ask for a few pennies was to create a huge furore. To the end of his life he was the supreme optimist, always on the brink of success, pretending he had not a care in the world. 'Impossible is not a word in my vocabulary,' he would boast, always at his best when a friend was in the middle of a crisis.

I understand my father's philosophy now. Then I fantasised about leaving home to find fame and wealth away from him and the sordid fights which were all his fault.

Life returned to normal after the war. The aunts and uncles left gradually to go back to their old homes or to set up new ones, and No. 52 seemed increasingly empty, shabby and lonely. Without the bustle it was just a big old house in need of repair, but permits for such work were hard to get. The two huge ancient furnaces took a lot of feeding and fuel was in short supply. It wasn't long before we too moved out, to a more manageable house in Caversham, in time for the arrival of sister Sandra. Barbara, Gloria and I were immensely relieved the new baby wasn't a boy.

As I approached fifteen, school-leaving age, my mother's ambitions for her first-born becoming a doctor (the dream of every Jewish mother) faded with my deteriorating school reports. Never mind, she said, I could train to become a secretary. I had planned on becoming a famous writer but had recently found myself leaning more towards acting, seeing myself as the successor to Margaret Lockwood. I said I thought I might try drama school.

Father had different ideas. Since the end of the war, he had, out of necessity, introduced changes into the family business. Textiles were in short supply; he had turned his attention to waste fabrics, in particular offcuts of the new rayon materials. Mother was set to work designing something, anything, that could be made from these small scraps. She came up with a bra.

There was one style, in a variety of prints and colours, and, with a large order from Littlewoods, Father hit the jackpot. This was his finest hour, the zenith of his career. Not only did he make his mark on the bra business, he achieved a social coup and was invited by the Littlewoods bosses, the Moore family, to accompany them to Aintree races. Mother had a new outfit for the occasion and looked superb, though blew the image (and Father's) by stipulating a two-shilling limit when she placed her bet.

Believing his future success in bras to be assured, Daddy suggested Leicester College of Art and Technology would be just the place where I could learn the rudiments of corsetry and underwear design, then take my place in his business.

I was interested in clothes. Art was one of my better subjects at school. Acting was a precarious life, and in any case I could always turn to it later. Likewise there was nothing to stop me writing a bestseller in my spare time. Leicester College of Art and Technology offered the thing I most desired at that moment: escape from home and from Reading.

The years ahead were to provide all the drama I would ever want.

2

September 1951, and the drive to Leicester – four hours in those days before the M1 – was passed in happy anticipation of my being about to begin adult life. Daddy deposited me at the hall of residence in the elegant Stoneygate district and the warden took me to the room where four girls who were to be my room-mates for a year were unpacking.

One of the objectives I had set myself for my new life was to overcome an innate shyness, to be open and not let myself be inhibited by others. Helen, Barbara, Jennifer and June were suitably responsive to – if not overwhelmed by – this breezy, garrulous approach, and by next morning we had become friends.

Enrolling and queueing at the college shop for supplies of pencils, notebooks, paper, drawing board, I listened to other students grumbling about costs and inadequate grants and realised my own good fortune at being well funded by my parents. As well as paying for all my materials, they covered my expenses at the hall to include breakfast and dinner, provided lunch tickets, bus money and an additional thirty shillings a week. In contrast, most of the students were making sacrifices to attend the college. Only the foreign students were better off. One Greek boy even had his own sports car . . . described in the vernacular of the day as natty. Where I came from, it was unheard of for a boy to have his own car – just to be allowed occasional use of his parents' made him something of a catch!

A group of only three students were doing the full diploma course, of which Make Up, as it was called, the actual putting together of the garment, formed a large part. I had been taught to sew and loved handiwork, but the sight of the sewing machines was unnerving, and it was several lessons before I could cope – I've never had the upper hand.

14

Design and Pattern Cutting were the province of a visiting teacher, Mrs Redlich, who was the single most important influence on my career as a designer. She taught me first and foremost how to let my surroundings inspire ideas, how to look at things, how not to look at what other people were doing. If you are painting a carrot, she suggested, don't look at someone else's painting of a carrot, look instead at another's painting of a flower or a tomato. Similarly, if you are designing a shoe, don't look at other shoes. A design must be fresh and original or the work has no life of its own. Her advice has proved sound in so many areas. I learned from her to co-ordinate cloth with cut, line with fit, style with practicality and comfort. I eagerly looked forward to her classes. She was to become part of my life, for various reasons, for many years.

I certainly did not look forward to the mornings of Book-keeping and Business Skills, passing the time daydreaming and, by year two, not bothering to attend. It seemed a total waste of time to me, and played no part in the work of a designer. Had I only known . . .

Compared with other students, my standard of drawing was merely passable, which was a surprise after being considered good at school. But it proved irrelevant. The test was in the ability to transfer ideas to paper and through to the finished garment. And I could do that. Today, as an employer, I avoid being mesmerised by brilliant sketching. I look for the underlying idea and, most important of all, like to see a garment, how it is cut and made.

From the start I found myself designing co-ordinated garments, which at that time was unheard of in underwear. Why should a woman careful to co-ordinate shoes with bag, blouse with skirt, be happy to wear black panties with a white bra?

There *was* only black and white, except for an unappealing shade of salmon popular for corsets. My father, with his strange little bras made from oddments, had been ahead of his time in introducing a multi-colour option; and he was losing ground fast with the fashion for more professional American-style bras, which were contoured, uplifted, twin-peaked.

For my final diploma I presented a matching set of bra, panties and suspender belt in white satin with white chiffon inset panels, embroidered with fleurs-de-lys in deep olive green. The college used it in the end-of-year fashion show and it excited much comment. I was quite proud of my effort, and wore the set until it fell to pieces. How I wish I had kept it.

Mrs Redlich told me I had talent and that, once I had a few years' experience behind me, could expect to earn as much as £1,000 a year – £19 a week! Four pounds ten shillings was about average at that time; clearly I was destined for a life of luxury. Naïve as I was about money and its value, even I knew that travel and beautiful clothes, the two things I craved above all others, were expensive. And I wanted these before the arrival of Mr Right, with whom I would share a life of beauty, art, glamour and unending romance.

I was going to miss Leicester. It had been a happy time, and I had enjoyed the companionship, especially the endless discussions with my four room-mates. The main topics were clothes and sex, or rather boys, reporting back after the weekends at home on current or planned flirtations. Sex was a mystery; only one of us had actually done IT, and she was a fund of information and worldly wisdom.

By some miracle – I certainly don't remember doing anything about it – I had lost weight. In photographs of myself at fifteen I am fat and awkward, and in those taken when I was eighteen I am very slim. My mother didn't believe in diets. One of her rules was that growing girls need to eat. But she did hide the biscuits from Barbara, who got very plump at one time. Barbara always found them.

My hair was still a bugbear. It was always curly when it was fashionable to have straight hair. In later years blow drying smoothed my hair, but when I was at college you had your hair set on rollers, then baked it under the dryer, and, in my case, the next day it frizzed up.

By the time I left college, my father's brassière business had plummeted from the pinnacle of success to near oblivion. I was not disappointed, and looked forward to working where I could revolutionise the underwear world with my vision of how a woman should look, undressed.

Initially I was offered two jobs: one in Ipswich, and the other in Market Harborough. Manufacturers had their showrooms in London, factories and workrooms elsewhere. But I *had* to be in

London, and on that my mother and I, for once, were in complete agreement. With a London job, she reasoned, I would be able to live at home, find myself a nice Jewish boy and settle down. I knew I wouldn't find the magic I sought in Ipswich or Market Harborough.

I soon found a job in Margaret Street, heart of the rag trade, as sole designer and pattern cutter, for which, theoretically, I was qualified, at £6 a week. The firm made bras, panties, swimsuits, sun tops and anything else the owner thought he could sell. It was fun but provided no opportunities for learning; the sum total of expertise in the place was negligible. On the day the cutter failed to turn up, the boss asked me to take over with the electric knife. I was terrified, having never even seen one before, but looking at the boss's chewed attempts on the table, felt I could hardly do worse. Stifling my initial fear I managed, neatly if somewhat ponderously, to operate the powerful rotary knife without bloodshed.

One lesson learned, it was time to move on, this time to a manufacturer producing for Marks and Spencer. The company was based in Somerset and about to transfer the design room to its showroom in Savile Row, where I was to work alongside their highly experienced designer. He, it seemed, had plans to go abroad shortly, so not only would I be fulfilling my ambition to work where I could gain some real experience, but there was a good chance I would step into his shoes when he left.

It was a surprise on my first day at work to discover that the 'highly experienced designer' was Kas, a fellow student from Leicester. At college he had relied on me at the end of each class to go over with him the points he had missed, and I knew he had no interest in fashion or design, but was merely doing the course in preparation for taking over a family business in South Africa. Kas's assistant, Heidi, had no design experience at all. Once more it was all down to me.

But I learned: from the production managers, the supervisors, the costings manager and, mostly, from Stanley Leffman, my boss, who knew more about fitting, pattern cutting and make up than the rest of us put together. There was plenty of time to learn. As I soon found out, the proposed move to Savile Row was just a figment of Mr Leffman's imagination.

A lovely man, he ran the factory perfectly, cared for his staff,

17

and provided excellent facilities and working conditions. The London design room idea was dangled as bait before prospective employees, for both Mr Leffman and his son Bertie were convinced that, once in Bridgwater, who could resist falling in love with the place. Who, once they had seen Bridgwater, would want Savile Row? Me, for a start. *I* wanted Savile Row. I tried to explain. It was different for Bertie. He could take off for the bright lights at weekends in his Sunbeam Triumph. On wages of £6 a week, train fares to London were more than I could manage.

The work was enjoyable. The factory fascinated me, the huge blade of the band knife slicing through seventy-two layers of cloth like butter, the machinists zooming through the garments with hardly a glance. I was able to study the disciplines and frustrations of mass production. To buy at the right price, cloth must be purchased in bulk. Designs had to suit the machinery available; every mitred corner would slow down the production line.

My first Bridgwater landlady wore her hair in greasy grey braids coiled around her head, and her opening question was would I be washing morning or evening so that she could prepare the hot water. When I requested morning *and* evening, please, and preferably with access to a bath, she was aghast. Washing destroyed the skin's natural oils, she claimed; a bath once a month and hair wash twice a year were more than adequate.

My second landlady refused my father access to the house. (He was carrying my suitcases.) 'No men allowed,' she said.

'But he's my father.'

'He's a man and he can't come in.'

My third landlady (the factory's personnel department took a hand in this one) kept a clean comfortable home and had a pleasant family, but ham salad for supper every night of the week was certainly monotonous.

During the six months, spring and summer, that I lived in Somerset I certainly explored every bus route of that beautiful countryside and I could see its appeal. But I was far too young for rural obscurity, and when the chance came to work in London I gratefully took it.

Miss Richardson was the chief designer for Slix swimsuits, an interesting, beautiful lady who took me on as her assistant and actually allowed me to design, a far cry from being answerable to a production manager who thought changing a shoulder strap was more than the factory floor could manage. Up on the top floor of No. 47 Maddox Street I was at the hub of everything, and I was happy. I was prepared to stay for ever.

Life was good: I loved my job, I was earning a princely £8 a week, I no longer had spots, I had lost weight and, despite a little plumpness on the thighs, could look at myself in the mirror without qualms. And I was in love.

His name was Alan, and our romance lasted for eighteen months. Remembering the moral climate of the fifties is like harking back to Victorian times. A boyfriend was someone who took you to the cinema and was rewarded with the occasional chaste kiss; he might hold your hand on the first date. After you had been out with him two or three times, depending on the boy, how experienced he was (what an aura that word 'experienced' conjured up), you might exchange a goodnight kiss at the front door. Courtship took a long time, and involved the girl being collected from her home, taken to a series of films and dances, and deposited at her front door again at the end of the evening.

It was the beginning of the fashion for coffee bars. There was no decent coffee in England before espresso arrived. The Palomino in Reading was the peak of sophistication and, like all coffee bars, it had a juke-box. We used to sit there for hours listening to Johnnie Ray and Nat 'King' Cole. About once a week we would splash out and have spaghetti bolognese and, on rare occasions (depending on finance), a piece of strawberry shortcake.

To begin with, Alan was just one of the Reading crowd I went around with. When I began working in London and he was studying at the Royal Academy of Music we were both commuters, and our friendship developed. He played the clarinet and piano but his real interest was in composing. He used to walk me home from the station and after a while we began going out together. Before I moved to London we were inseparable.

He earned money playing jazz at inauspicious venues and I went too. Our physical closeness developed from holding hands to kissing and quite a lot of humid fumbling. He was far too nice to push his amorous advances to the limit; if boys of his type and age had sex it was with girls they picked up at dance halls, with that express purpose in mind, and never with the daughters of people their parents might know. It was all depressingly frustrating, and when Alan and I weren't passionately loving we bickered, a state no doubt induced by sexual tension. When our relationship fizzled out, I was very unhappy.

'I'm not right for you anyway,' he said with all the bitterness of the very young, in our final quarrel. 'You ought to marry a rich businessman. I'm only interested in music. I'm going to be famous when I'm thirty and rich when I'm forty.'

His words lodged in my memory and in later years bobbed up like a line from a song you just can't forget. When I was thirty I was richer than either of us would have dreamed possible. And at forty I was famous enough that when I introduced myself it seemed like name-dropping!

I heard Alan once on Radio 4, a serious musician talking about jazz as he used to talk to me; he taught me quite a lot about music. Twenty years after our relationship had ended, one of those quirky coincidences in life found me interviewing Alan's wife. (I was looking for artists to paint on silk.) It was interesting to ponder what similarities existed between us. Did we look alike? Hardly. Did we have much in common? We were both artistic. If she knew of the connection, she showed no curiosity. For my part I suggested she visit my new showroom to examine the current collection. Her art was essentially geometric, the fashion in the seventies was flowery, and I wondered if she could adapt. She never pursued the work opening but sent a message to say it was not her style.

Back in the fifties life was opening up. Aunt Becky and Uncle Alf invited me along as company for their daughter Joan on a two-week Mediterranean cruise. Despite the advanced age of most passengers, the smallness of the cabins and the bouts of seasickness around me, this was an exciting experience. Flirting with the crew (the only young men on board) shopping in the markets, touring the vineyards and antiquities were all part of this adult, sophisticated world. Only the poverty of children begging in the ports broke the spell, and was to remain the most enduring image of that trip.

Barbara and I even took ourselves off to Paris, which was quite enterprising in 1955. The night flight from Heathrow cost £20 return. We wore out our shoes seeing everything there was to see, and every man we spoke to was a film producer or a famous actor . . . or so they said.

Out of the blue came a call from Mrs Redlich, my college tutor, with the offer of a job with Daintyfit, a bra manufacturer. It offered £10 a week, more money than I was earning, and good career prospects, so I accepted.

My first task was to design a copy of a black lace bra for Marks and Spencer. The bra had been brought back from New York by my new boss, Mr Horvath, and was quite basic, apart from a distinguishing bow design beautifully worked in the centre. Marks and Spencer wanted the bra, I was told, without the bow. This summed up the pattern for my two years at Daintyfit.

In addition, I had inadvertently fallen foul of company politics. Miss Butcher, the head designer, quite understandably did not care to have foisted on her the protegées of Mrs Redlich (I was not the first). My very existence in the design department represented to Miss Butcher a threat to her authority, and I bore the brunt of this in numerous petty ways known to heads of department, the most heinous of which was 'batch samples duty'. Each week a random selection was made from garments produced in the company's various Northern Ireland factories, and it was the task of the young designers to check these several hundred items, measuring every seam to check that each one exactly tallied with the original specification. Should a discrepancy be discovered, there followed an investigation worthy of the CIA, involving the entire management hierarchy of the offending factory and its London offices.

My salvation from the batch samples came in the form of a suspender belt, required by Marks and Spencer to replace an existing model fast losing sales. It had to be longer, but cheaper: a dilemma which I met so successfully that I became known as Suspender Belt Queen and was rewarded with a salary rise and removed from Miss Butcher's jurisdiction.

Mrs Redlich remained in my life for a long time. She and Mr Horvath had known each other for many years. Mr Redlich had died when I was at college, and later Mrs Redlich used to come in to Daintyfit once a week to help on design. She and our boss always behaved with perfect decorum and addressed each other formally, but we all suspected a relationship and eventually they married and enjoyed many years together. They retired to Wimbledon when they sold the business and pursued their great love, travel. Mr Horvath lived to a ripe old age and, nearly twenty years after I worked for them, Mrs Horvath came to my opening party at Bond Street.

I left home to live in London and be near my work. My best friend Marlene and I shared sitting-room, kitchenette (meaning cubby hole with Baby Belling) and bedroom curtained off. There was a communal bathroom and, unless you didn't mind being seen by all the other occupants of the house in dressing-gown and clutching your towel and sponge bag, you had to wait until the coast was clear before making a lightning dash along the corridor.

We were quite proud of our London flat, as we called this glorified bed-sit in Holland Road when we invited friends back for a coffee, although we knew it to be a bit of a dump in reality. It cost us £3 a week, split between us. Marlene, whom I had known since we were five, was always a mad spender, and frequently blew the bulk of her week's wages of clothes, leaving her, after the rent, with nothing to live on.

We were masters of economical cuisine and shopped systematically on Saturday mornings (late-night shopping didn't exist) from the same grocery chains our mothers patronised in Reading: Tesco, Sainsbury's, Home & Colonial. In these shops the walls were tiled, the floors were of polished wood, there was always the smell of freshly ground coffee from the machine in the corner, and shoppers were tempted by open bins of biscuits from which they made their selections and took to one of the counter staff to weigh.

I was better off than Marlene, not just because I earned more than she did, but because I also made most of my own clothes. As each new fashion craze hit the high street, I made an instant copy. Material was ridiculously cheap, even by the standards of the day, and markets offered a vast selection of fabrics. For ten shillings (fifty pence) I could buy my material on Saturday morning and wear the garment that same night. The places to go were Humphrey Lyttelton's jazz club in Oxford Street and a ghastly coffee bar in Soho, The Macabre, decorated with skulls.

Friends from Reading – some had moved to London, others came up to London for a night out – formed the nucleus of my widening social circle. I still saw my cousins frequently, and I made new friends from work; some are still with me. Around the time I left college, two friends from Leicester, Thelma and Jackie, moved to London and their social scene and mine overlapped; at a party at my place, one of their friends met one of my Reading friends; they fell in love and married.

I never stayed at home in the evenings. There was always something to do, someone to meet. I enjoyed going to the cinema and went to the theatre once a week. Thelma was my theatre friend, and Monday night was theatre night. You could always get a seat up in the gods.

Marlene, eventually defeated by economics, returned to live with her parents, and because I couldn't afford to stay in the Holland Road room on my own and was loath to share with a stranger, I moved into a small bed-sit in Abbey Road.

By the time I was earning £10 a week (in 1957 people were bringing up families on that), I was so affluent that I could afford to get my hair done at Raymond of Mayfair, the first of the hairdresser celebrities and known to the media as Mr Teasy Weazy.

None of my friends had cars; in fact nobody I knew could even drive except my father, who attempted to teach me and gave up in exasperation. My husband Peter, many years later, also tried with the same result. I needed countless lessons and failed seven tests before I could take off the L plates.

My mother had no fears about my living in London at that time. Her attitude then was that she had brought up her girls to know how to behave and they were quite safe. It was a case of ignorance is bliss for we did not share confidences in the way that I do with my daughter Aliza – and always have done.

I discovered sex in London. I had already known the pangs of first love, as I thought of my devotion to Alan, and we had actually shared a bed, all night, under the blankets but positively no impropriety! Then I met The First. It was at a party. He took me out a few times and was aged about twenty-five, a man of the world compared with the boys I knew. Each time he took me home there were the usual kisses, but he was the perfect seducer; our lovemaking went a little further every time and gradually reached the point of no return.

It was the classic seduction. How dated that sounds, but these were pre-Pill days and sex created so much anxiety with the fear of an unwanted pregnancy. He used contraceptives when he remembered, and pessaries could be bought as an additional precaution. Abortion was illegal. The shame of becoming an unmarried mother could blight your life. Your parents would be devastated. That sort of thing didn't happen in nice Jewish circles – or non-Jewish ones come to that. Every month there was mounting panic as the time for your period approached. You watched anxiously, counting the days, the hours. If you were a day late, you felt suicidal. And the relief when it arrived was almost better than sex! But even if you'd got away with it this time, there was always the example of some girl you knew or a friend of a friend who, poor thing, was right now 'in trouble'. There but for the grace of God . . .

My first lover was one of those men who lavishes attention on a girl until he gets her into bed, and then thinks he is so great he owns her. Being young and inexperienced I found this out too late, and spent nights crying into my pillow over his crass offhandedness. I thought I was a little in love with him at first. Then I felt I ought to be in love with him because if I wasn't then it was quite disgraceful to be having sex with him. I felt used and humiliated most of the time. I talked about this to the only girlfriend I knew who was an experienced woman of the world. She heard me out, and then said: 'So why do you put up with him if he's so awful to you?'

The next time I met him, he was his usual boorish self, and her words came back to me. Well, why was I putting up with him? I don't need this, I thought to myself. He isn't making me happy.

'Goodbye,' I told him at the door. 'Don't bother to phone.'

I was restless. Daintyfit frustrated me. I had realised from my student days that I worked, and still do, faster than others. There was always time to spare, and I would fill this by experimenting with offcuts of material from my ever-growing sketchpad of ideas, knowing all the while that none of these would ever be produced. It was disheartening, although the pay and the Marble Arch location provided some compensation.

And there was something else. I had lost my sister Barbara to her childhood sweetheart Johnny Stern. She had been in love with him since she was ten years old. Seven years her senior, he used to tease even then, saying every time he saw her, 'I'm still waiting for you.' When anyone asked her: 'What are you going to do when you grow up?' she always replied: 'I'm going to marry Johnny Stern.'

And so she did. She was seventeen, and my parents did everything they could to make her postpone marriage, but she was determined. They married in March 1957; to my knowledge with never a moment's regret.

I missed having her around. Married life had claimed her and for a while I felt excluded. I compensated by growing closer to my college friend Jackie. She too was bored, longing for excitement, worried that life was passing her by – we were all of twenty-one! We spent hours discussing the meaning of life and how to change the course of ours and made a plan to hitch-hike across Europe.

I gave in my notice at Daintyfit and joined the Youth Hostel Association. It wouldn't be glamorous but it was better than wasting my life deciding which bias binding to use and whether moving a shoulder strap half an inch constituted a new design! However, a few days before I was due to leave work, Jackie dropped her bombshell. She was in love. This man was The One. I wouldn't expect her to leave England for six months at the start of such an important relationship, would I?

My mother, secretly relieved, I suspect, said I should go on bended knee to Mr Horvath and withdraw my notice. I agreed I couldn't hitch-hike through Europe alone, but neither could I endure another two years at Daintyfit. No, Mother; the notice had to stand.

I moved out of Abbey Road and back to Reading to consider my next move. Cousin Julian solved the problem. He was heavily into the Youth for Israel movement and told me that groups of young people went regularly to Israel to live on a kibbutz, learn Hebrew and work in exchange for their keep. It was something to do. I wasn't wild about the idea, but I decided I had nothing to lose. And off I went.

3

With a suitcase of clothes for a hot climate, £100 emergency money and the address of a cousin – the sole survivor of Grandmother Levene's Polish family – in Ramat Gan, a suburb of Tel Aviv, I met up with my travelling companions at Victoria station.

It was May 1958. General de Gaulle had just come to power in France and the entire country was on strike. The boys in my group were convinced this was the start of the second French Revolution and that our chances of making it to Marseilles were slim. Blood would be flowing in the gutters of Paris. In the event the only drama was our arrival *sans baggage*. One of the coaches had been uncoupled and vanished en route.

So I set sail for Haifa on the *Theodore Hertzl* with just the jeans and shirt I stood up in. I improvised a top out of my scarf and wore that while I washed and dried the shirt in the evenings. By the time we reached port I had very dirty jeans, I had been to bed with one of the officers, and had two other men dancing attendance.

One boy, Jonathan, had travelled in the same party from England. He was easy to talk to and we shared an immediate rapport. I didn't consider flirting with him. He wasn't tall enough; at that age, looks are all important. And he didn't stand a chance once we boarded the ship and there were so many gorgeous, handsome, suntanned, exciting young Israeli naval officers to flirt with, and I was probably the youngest female on board. Nevertheless, when we arrived in Israel I was happy to find that Jonathan and I were allocated to the same kibbutz, Ma'agan Michael on the Carmel shore.

We drove south for an hour, along the coast. I sat mesmerised by the beauty of the landscape, the Carmel Mountains on one side, golden sand dunes seeping down to a brilliant azure blue sea

26

on the other. It was also a little daunting. This was so remote, so foreign. Supposing I hated it, how would I ever escape? Then, over a bumpy grit road, we reached the kibbutz and the jeep unloaded us in front of the dining-room, the hub of kibbutz life.

Despite a traditional, in most senses Jewish, upbringing I was ignorant about Israel. I suppose I expected Golders Green but sunnier. The food destroyed any illusions on that score. At home good food was taken for granted. Jewish cooking has always been tasty; most Jewish families have a love of food – too much sometimes. In my entire year in Israel, I probably had only half a dozen palatable meals. The staple diet was dark bread, rubbery American cheese from a tin, stumpy cucumbers, tomatoes, olives, hard-boiled eggs. Sometimes oranges and bananas were available. Towards the end of my stay, butter appeared, a gift to Israel from America. As it contained salt, the people in the towns wouldn't buy it, so it was donated to the kibbutz. Worst of all was the fish. The kibbutzniks were inordinately proud of their manmade carp ponds. Why they should prefer to eat these muddy-tasting fish daily when the Mediterranean was just across the beach was a mystery.

We were to join the *ulpan* – which means school – where new and prospective immigrants studied Hebrew half the day and worked for their keep the other half. We were given a share of a wooden hut (there were four girls in mine), with a cupboard and a bed. Communal showers and loos were contained in a block a short walk away. After the six-month *ulpan* course, there was the chance to become a full kibbutz member. Either way, if you stayed you were expected to do a full day's work like everybody else. There was no pressure; at the same time people who freeloaded were not tolerated.

It was a disciplined, full life, and a wonderful community that lived and worked for one another. If you were ill, you were looked after. If you couldn't work, you were provided for. When you grew old, you were supported. They brought up your children, and in the case of the exceptionally bright or gifted, the whole community made sacrifices to give that child special education.

There were no drugs at that time, and on the kibbutz no alcohol. The social mix provided good conversation, good music and homemade entertainment. Sex was high on the list of things to do: for us *ulpan* kids, a great deal of sex. Miles of golden sand along the pine-scented Carmel coast, balmy moon-drenched nights, the magic of being in a foreign place at such a historic time in the world's fortunes and being part of this brave, new, idealistic scheme all added up to pretty heady stuff.

We soon settled in and jobs were allocated. Seeing 'designer' on my arrival form, they put me in the clothing store, mending and ironing clothes as they came back from the laundry. Ironing was uncomfortable in the heat, but the supervisor had a friend in the kitchen, which meant extra coffee and even coffee breaks, rare in kibbutz life, for all of us in the clothing store. As a habitual coffee drinker, I loathed the milky, sugary stuff they produced once a week for Sabbath breakfast. On weekdays it was black tea with lemon and sugar pre-added.

Over the months I shared most duties. The worst was working in the laundry. Two hundred adults invariably employed in dirty jobs, and two hundred children playing outside all day, produced a mountain of washing to be trundled in trolleyloads to the washing line, hung up and brought in. Nobody who hasn't stood lifting and pegging for four hours at a time can possibly know just how much wet clothes weigh.

I harvested fragrant melons and pungent onions and screamed when they asked me to clean and pluck a chicken. Best of all was when I worked in the children's houses. They had better food than the rest of us.

At the end of my first week, as I was walking towards the dining-room with my friends, two boys from our group were standing in conversation with a stranger. He was very young, very thin and wiry, and had a golden tan. His well-cut shorts and plaid shirt looked chic compared with our kibbutz romper shorts and rough working shirts. (We were still waiting for our luggage to arrive.) As we went to meet him I felt a tremendous physical attraction and put out my hand to shake his. I wanted to touch his smooth skin.

'This is Peter Reger; he's from Germany,' said one of the boys.

I was determined to attract his attention. 'What part of Germany?'

'The West, of course, or I wouldn't be here,' he replied curtly, and rather arrogantly. He turned away to take his bag into the hut he was to share, and the rest of us went in to lunch.

That evening we had a party on the beach. Sofia, a voluptuous Polish girl, was homesick and weeping and Jonathan and Peter were among the group gathered around trying to console her, Peter using a smattering of Polish. I was disappointed that I couldn't get his attention, but as the party broke up I saw him leave the group and start to walk alone along the beach and ran to catch up with him.

Rather formally he told me how he had come from Munich and had been in Israel for two months. But the heat of the Negev made him ill, and when he saw the chance of moving to Ma'agan with the bonus of fresh sea breezes and the *ulpan* facility he had decided to apply. We were at once comfortable with each other. He escorted me to my door as politely as if we had been out on a date in Reading, and I felt good when I went to bed, elated by the knowledge that I had managed to attract this beautiful, special boy. He told me he was twenty, but I later found out he was only seventeen.

From the moment I met him until he died, Peter always looked the same age to me: permanently twenty-five. At the end he had a few lines, but even when he was a young man these would appear on really bad days, and he would look desperately weary. When he felt good he looked like a boy, even in his forties. He had a boyish figure and a mischievous expression when he was feeling pleased with himself. Everybody used to say to him, 'Don't you ever get any older?' He was Peter Pan; he never reached old age.

I didn't see Peter the day after that first evening on the beach because I had to go to Haifa to collect the luggage. So on the following day, when I saw him lying on the grass after school and lunch, I made a point of walking close by on the way to my hut.

He looked up. 'Hi. What are you doing?'

'Swimming,' I said.

'Then I'll skip class and join you,' he replied.

After a long walk through the dunes, there was a completely deserted beach of white and gold, and the brilliant blue, warm, sea. Safe enough for the least able swimmer, surf enough to be fun for the adventurous with steep waves that rolled in, roughly.

At once Peter became the little boy, playing, teasing, splashing, grabbing my legs and ducking me. We swam, sunbathed, slept, swam, talked. We stayed until dusk, leaving only because I was on kitchen duty. We walked back towards the settlement, holding hands and stopping frequently to kiss. When I finished work that night, he was there, outside the kitchen door, waiting to walk me to my hut.

For the rest of the week this became the pattern. He was there every lunchtime waiting for me; every evening when I finished work he was standing on the doorstep. Every hour we could co-ordinate skipped classes, we found the time to be together.

That weekend I had a pre-arranged date with Teddy, a beau from the *Theodore Hertzl*. Even had I wanted to, I had no way of contacting him to break the date. Peter was upset, and I felt a twinge of guilt. Teddy was waiting for me at the bus station in Haifa and we travelled by cheroot (the communal taxi, unique to Israel) to Tiberias where we spent the weekend at his sister's house.

We swam in the Lake of Galilee; explored the town; climbed to the chapel on the site where Jesus delivered his Sermon on the Mount; dined under the stars overlooking the lake as I ate my first delicious Arab food. Teddy was in his thirties, good looking, well off, cultured, widely travelled. He had fought in the Israeli War of Independence and bore a bullet scar in his left cheek. He was obviously looking for someone to marry and to have children with, and I knew he was attracted to me. What a pity I couldn't respond.

By then I was obsessed with Peter. He was sitting by the roadside as the bus arrived back at Ma'agan Michael, smoking a cigarette, his eyes on the dusty track.

'I've had a rotten Sabbath,' he said, and I fell into his arms, saying sorry, sorry, sorry.

We went back to his hut – his room-mates were away – and made love all night long. I knew I was involving myself in an impossible situation. Peter was far too young, too mother-dominated, too dictatorial and arrogant. But alone with me, he was also gentle, loving and affectionate. I wanted to look at him, touch him. When we couldn't find anywhere else to be alone, we would take a blanket and sleep on the beach. I would wake at dawn feeling his smooth skin against mine.

30

The sex was wonderful. Despite being very young, Peter was the perfect lover. I was his first serious love, as he was mine. He had experienced sex with someone who worked for the family, a much older woman; and a friend had once taken him to 'enjoy' the services of a prostitute, which he hadn't enjoyed at all. But although we were rapturously involved with each other I held back from committing myself totally. I was just starting out; and so much of life lay before me: work, travel, adventure. I wasn't ready to meet the man with whom I would spend my life. It was all too soon. I wanted to be free, if I wished, to see other men. And the age difference worried me. But all the time I was telling myself to keep my options open, not to capitulate entirely, Peter was persuading, demanding, insisting; and I was so attracted I couldn't keep away.

Within weeks I accepted that Peter was the one . . . and only. When I was with other men, I just wanted to be back with him. Twenty-seven years later, when he was seeking yet another reconciliation after our relationship had reached the all-time depths, he used exactly the same words: 'Don't you see, I just like being with you.' There were many traumas, and these were to make up the pattern of our life together. We fought continuously and yet, however bitter or hateful the rows, at the end of the day we would forgive and forget instantly . . . in those early years.

The kibbutz worked like any village anywhere, and soon everybody knew why Peter was missing classes. The fact that he was way ahead of the rest with his Hebrew – he was remarkably gifted at languages – was irrelevant. He was not fulfilling his part of the *ulpan* bargain, to study four hours a day. The disapproval had nothing to do with our frantic sex life. People weren't prudish. Where there was subterfuge in England, on a kibbutz the atmosphere was relaxed. Men and women went to bed with each other, married or not. Two people would move in together, and when a rabbi was visiting couples would line up and get married, if they felt like it.

But Peter had broken the rules, and the kibbutz committee informed him that they saw no point in his staying. He should take himself off for the remainder of his time in Israel to a nearby kibbutz where they had a more advanced class, which would tax him to such an extent that he couldn't afford to skip lessons.

Our remaining time together at Ma'agan Michael became even more precious, but the new kibbutz was a mere three miles away. We continued to see each other on most days. He would walk me back along the road through the banana plantations, full of the night sounds of hyenas, crickets and night birds. It was always warm; the clear sky always filled with stars. Sometimes Peter stayed with me for the night and walked back in time for his class.

Our allowance was ten Israeli pounds a month, equivalent to £4 in English money. When we were paid we went to the local restaurant-bar and for the price of an orange juice we could dance the night away to Paul Anka singing 'Diana' and to Peter's favourite, 'Quando Quando Quando'. Extra money from home would buy a sweet pancake with sugar and lemon or a plate of stringy beef goulash, a wonderful change from fishpond stew.

We had frequent rows, and one was especially heated because I had spent an evening in the company of a former boyfriend. Peter refused to believe that the relationship was entirely innocent. I stormed off. He said he never wanted to see me again.

The following day the postman delivered a letter, every inch of the envelope covered in stamps and in between the word 'urgent' in three different languages. Inside Peter had written that if I ever wanted to see him again, I must promise to be exclusively and permanently his. He could never want anyone else in life. If I didn't return his love, he would not contact me again. This was typical of Peter: dramatic, ridiculous. I made myself pretty, skipped class, hitched a lift to the top of the hill which was our meeting place, and we walked to where we could sit overlooking the sea and talked until dusk. We swore we couldn't live without each other, and as soon as possible, we would marry.

Since Peter's mother was insisting he return home at the end of November, as already agreed, and he felt that his prospects would be better if he had a good education behind him, he decided he would study in Germany for two years before returning to Israel where we wanted to spend our lives. I agreed I might even join him in Germany while he studied. We'd work and save, then live on one of the communal farms in Israel; he rather fancied chicken farming. I could think of no better future than to spend my life with Peter, here in the sunshine.

*

32

I became pregnant in Israel, and had an abortion. It was easy there, for Israel was one of the earliest countries to adopt a liberated attitude towards abortion. I was afraid to tell the kibbutz authorities and went to Haifa, found a doctor and arranged it myself with the help of some friends. It was a common dilemma. The doctor performed the operation there and then, under local anaesthetic, and sent me home on the bus. It was painless, inexpensive, terrifying. I felt I had done something very, very wicked, and expected to fall seriously ill by way of retribution.

Back at the kibbutz I reported sick, as advised by the doctor, but found myself confessing to the nurse exactly what was wrong with me. 'Why didn't you come to me in the first place? I could have arranged it for you,' she said, as if I had been really rather silly. My attitude that nice girls don't get pregnant reflected my upbringing, whereas she was a tough old kibbutznik who had seen much worse things in life and took it in her stride.

Afterwards I discovered this was quite common practice in the kibbutz, though not particularly approved of when the kibbutz needed more children. Ma'agan Michael had quite enough children anyway. It was seen as a matter of expedience rather than a moral issue, although I am sure on a religious kibbutz it would have been quite different. Children were no problem; they lived communally, visiting their parents after school and work, or during the mother's work if they felt the need. Parents separating did not affect the day-to-day routine of the kibbutz. Everyone took care of all the children. The children were their future.

Peter left Israel in November. I travelled with him to Haifa before he sailed to Naples to catch the train for Munich. I was unbearably sad and sent a postcard airmail to Naples to await his arrival.

My own six months on the kibbutz were up and a group of us celebrated with a grand tour of Israel, travelling by truck and staying at kibbutzim in Jerusalem, Galilee and Beersheba. Sometimes, travelling at night we sang stirring pioneer songs and I felt totally at home in this land bought with the blood and tears of generations. In the far north, in a small town on the Lebanese border, we came across the only café in the entire country selling Coca-Cola and went crazy ordering Cokes.

It was time to make decisions. Jonathan was among a few of

33

our group who elected to remain on the kibbutz. Some returned home; some like me dithered, unsure what to do, working for our keep while we considered our plans.

Peter's letters arrived daily. I missed him desperately and wrote often but he never received any of my early letters and was always convinced (wrongly, in my opinion) that they had been destroyed by his mother's friend, Lisl. When he began his studies at the university and moved away from home, disappearing mail was no longer an issue.

My affairs were in a mess. I was short of money and reluctant to write home for help; since my father had left the family business things had not been easy for my mother. My trip to Jerusalem had unsettled me, reawakened old ambitions. I didn't want to sleep in a field and walk about the city like a tramp. I wanted to be one of the well-dressed, freshly groomed women I had seen coming out of the King David Hotel. Supposing I remained waiting in Israel and Peter never came back? A period of eighteen months was long enough for him to meet and fall in love with somebody else.

The rainy season arrived and Ma'agan Michael became a cold, wet hell. Sandy paths turned to thick mud. It rained without remission for two weeks. I forgot what it was like to sit down for a meal dry and clean.

I began to spend more time with Jonathan. He and Peter had been such good friends and had so much in common. They were both intellectuals and would discuss philosophical issues for hours. I began to go to Jonathan's room when the other boys weren't there; he would come to mine when the girls were out. It was winter, there was no heating and we would snuggle up in bed together to keep warm. Just lie there and talk. Gradually, our affection for each other progressed into something more and we had a funny little affair. I was lonely. Peter and Munich seemed so far away. The sex was a comfort; it wasn't like being with Peter. Nothing ever was.

Jonathan had made a commitment to stay on the kibbutz and become a teacher. As a full kibbutz member he was entitled to a house, and when he suggested I move in with him I was tempted. It was a sweet house, and I coveted his bathroom; it was luxury beyond wildest dreams to have a private shower. But he was

34

casual. He asked me to move in – as good as asking me to marry him by kibbutz customs – without any real conviction. We got on well; he was such a good friend, I thought I could have a nice life with this man. Had he insisted, pleaded, cajoled, my life might have taken a different path. I could so easily have persuaded myself at that point to stay with him. On the other hand, I was receiving Peter's passionate love letters almost daily from Munich. I made my decision and moved to Tel Aviv. Jonathan and I continued to see each other occasionally.

The fashion industry, now such a vital part of Israel's economy, was non-existent at that time. There were few jobs and a glut of skilled labour. The rent on my inexpensive room was subsidised by a charity helping young people to set up, and I managed to feed myself by babysitting and giving English lessons and by dipping into my dwindling nest-egg. It was a miserable existence. I wanted to go home; I wanted to be near Peter. By the end of March I was ready to abandon my plight and wrote to Barbara telling her of my financial straits.

Ten days later a letter arrived with my ticket home, compliments of Grandfather. I was on my way.

4

My parents were waiting for me at Victoria station with Gloria and Sandra, shockingly white-skinned in contrast to the leathery suntans I'd grown used to. To be at home in my own room, to turn on the heater when I wanted to, and to eat my mother's delicious food was perfect heaven.

Peter phoned to say he would visit London as soon as term ended. It was the big talking-point in the family; everybody had something to say about my romance. Uncle Nat, my father's youngest brother, was most practical. 'You go to Germany. See what he's like in his own home, see what sort of family he comes from,' he said and gave me the money to do so. Economy travel, of course.

Peter had told me about his background, that his family life was in no way like mine. His parents fled Germany before the war, went first to Poland and then to Czechoslovakia where he was born and where they spent the war years. His mother, who could pass as non-Jewish, crocheted baby clothes which she sold on the streets; his father, who could not, stayed hidden at home. Eventually the Germans came for him and he was interned in a concentration camp.

As the Russian army moved in, Peter's parents fled with him on the first available train which happened to stop in Munich. The remnants of the Jewish community there provided temporary shelter in a school. After a while Peter's father took his son from the shelter, left his wife, and set up home with a new girlfriend. Peter could not recall how long this period lasted but always said it was the happiest of his young life.

Meanwhile, his mother met Lisl, at that time twenty-two years old, formed an attachment and set up home with her. Eventually his mother decided to reclaim Peter, which proved a violent episode. The little boy didn't want to leave his home. She insisted she was taking him to the zoo, but he resisted and she had to drag him along the street until he fell and cut his chin.

Piecing together the events of their day-to-day existence as he described it, I saw his mother, Josepha, as a joyless person, cold and critical, who had brought up her son to believe that childhood is a time to learn and study in preparation for an adulthood of duty. Her own life had been wretched. Her father by all accounts was a dictatorial man who prevented her from studying and deprived her of the education she rightfully deserved. She escaped into a loveless marriage. She had grown up through the poverty of the Great Depression, devaluation and then the war. She later saw her family perish in a concentration camp – she never spoke of this.

Her sayings were: life is a struggle; we are here to suffer, anybody who expects more is an idiot; what is there to laugh at? only fools walk around smiling. She had fearful bouts of rage which would flare up without warning. She and Lisl were constantly in noisy conflict. Peter's home life as a boy, with two neurotic women and not even the relief of visitors, had caused him deep anguish. It was not the most welcoming image of family life. Nevertheless, I set off for Munich, exhilarated at the thought of seeing Peter again, and eternally grateful to Uncle Nat for making it possible.

The view from the window as the train cut through the Rhine valley showed a vista as lovely as anything I had seen at home or in Israel. I was still acutely uncomfortable about the Germans and, when I thought about it, amazed that someone like Peter's mother who had endured so much at their hands could want to make her home among them. It was a subject I hoped to discuss with her when we got to know each other. In the event, during twenty-five years of knowing her, with a few rare exceptions, I was never to establish a rapport beyond the most basic common politeness of strangers, and often not even that.

I had forgotten how thin Peter was. The formal suit he was wearing quite threw me, but only for a second, and then Peter and I were in each other's arms and walking away from the train and out into the streets of Munich, talking all the time, pausing sometimes just to gaze at each other. We walked slowly, both reluctant to arrive at his home, for there was so much to catch up on. I was also nervous of meeting Mama. I was determined to make a good impression and had dressed carefully, befitting a future fiancée, in my very best navy blue two-piece with pencil skirt and a crisp white blouse that I'd changed into shortly before the train reached Munich.

We were there, and I just had time to take in the spacious, spartan apartment and then Mama and Lisl arrived. Mama, a gaunt woman of about fifty with dark bobbed hair, was wearing a severe forties-style costume; Lisl was plumper, with hair cropped like a man and dressed in a masculine shirt and trousers. As Peter made the introductions, his mother scrutinised me. Her first words were: 'People with dark hairs shouldn't wear blue. It doesn't suit them.'

Such was the stuff that passed for conversation in that household. Whether Peter should buy a blue suit or a grey one was discussed for a month, and the final decision was always Mama's. When he had the tailor taper his trousers she was hysterical. Once, after we were married, Peter bought a sports jacket which she didn't like and she refused to speak to him for months.

During my first few days in Munich, Mama took charge of us, telling us where to go, what to eat, who to see. We were not permitted to remain in the flat when she and Lisl were out, in case Peter forgot to lock the door after us, or damaged the record-player or forgot to turn off a switch. This was just absurd to me, who had been in possession of a front door key since the age of twelve, had been allowed total freedom to come and go, and had in my parents' absence been responsible for the house and three younger sisters.

Mama didn't approve of my wardrobe; she didn't approve of our choice of engagement ring (although she instructed us where it should be bought); she didn't approve of my antecedents when she learned that my father had married the daughter of a shoe-maker. Surely they had known it was against the rules for the son of a businessman to marry the daughter of one so humble? I pointed out that, as they had both been born in England, they weren't governed by the rules that she lived by. Her response was to give me a look of pity that I should be so uneducated.

The arguments, from which in the main I managed to remain

38

aloof, raged around me and I made excuses for her, believing that suffering had made her bitter and irritable. However, I could not avoid being affected by the stress. Even long after I had married Peter, both he and I had only to hear his mother's voice on the telephone to feel apprehensive.

Lisl was sweet to me, proffering the few international words she knew. Our relationship improved as I learned German and has indeed endured over the years, having developed into a mutual love.

The sparsely furnished apartment was as cold and unrelaxed as Mama herself. There was no single comfortable chair. ('Comfort? Bourgeois!') Most rooms were used as offices. Meals were eaten in the square entrance hall. At the far end of the reception room was a curtained-off alcove which enclosed the bed Mama and Lisl shared. Peter's room was Mama's office during the day.

Mama had already decided I needed a dress for our engagement party, and summoned Lola, her dressmaker. I loved the full-skirted silk print dress she made for me; dressmakers were a new experience. At home Mother made our clothes or we bought ready-made. Mama despised ready-to-wear which was inferior. I suspected she enjoyed the power of employing a dressmaker; the business of tinkering with alterations, two millimetres off the collar, three off the sleeve.

When I announced my plans to find a job so that I could be near Peter for the duration of his studies, she wanted to know all about my career and was most put out to learn that a designer's job was done mainly in a factory. She decreed that this was not suitable for the future wife of her son, and that I should train to become a dental nurse or a beautician.

I was becoming swamped by her determination to reshape me, and my natural ebullience was taking a sound knocking. There was a brief respite when, inventing an excuse connected with his college at Augsburg, Peter and I managed to escape for a weekend. My head cleared in the fresh air, and I was able to work out a plan of action. I would go to London and take a temporary job, and Peter would join me there in July. Meanwhile, I would start looking for a job in Germany.

Mama was in exceptionally good humour during our engagement party, but the following afternoon, over the ritual coffee and

39

cake, she began to scream hysterically, her face contorted with rage. I could not understand the torrent of abuse, except for the phrase she kept repeating in German: 'I don't want it, I don't want it.'

I sat in silence. Peter answered back. Lisl tried to pacify. Mama was eventually led away to her bed. Peter and I went out alone that evening, and he explained that the reason Mama had been so angry was that she was against our marriage. I was socially unsuitable. She had always told him a man had two choices where money was concerned: to be born with it or to marry into it. I was a poor catch. What's more, I was too old for him. I was utterly depressed and apprehensive at having to face her in the morning, but nothing more was said. She was her usual self, and there was no sign of the previous afternoon's hysteria.

Soon afterwards the visit came to an end. I had mixed feelings; I was of course sad to be leaving Peter albeit for only a short time, yet relieved that I would soon be in the bosom of my nice, normal family once more. The next time I saw Peter, it was on home ground. His holiday with us was in complete contrast to my German visit. He loved my family, was enchanted by my sisters, and everyone loved him.

By a stroke of luck, I was offered a job with Janet Dickinson, a highly reputable swimsuit company. Their designer had been rushed into hospital midway through designing the collection. They were delighted to have somebody as experienced as me to take over temporarily, and as I was only interested in staying until I could organise moving to Germany it was the ideal arrangement.

After my undemanding time at Daintyfit and the long break in Israel, it was wonderful to be designing again, sorting through half-finished garments, abandoned patterns, items awaiting alteration. The look was less sporty than Slix, but the quality and all that went into it was comparable. What's more, I was earning £15 a week. When my six-month temporary employment was over, my boss Mr Gold paid me the compliment of asking me to stay.

Peter and I spent Christmas together in Germany. After a day with Mama and Lisl, we took the train into the Bavarian Alps and stayed in a quaint wooden pension. Pretty and cosy, it looked like fairyland nestling in the snow. We stayed in bed so late each morning that we never saw another guest. The landlady served our coffee and rolls wearing traditional Bavarian costume, and we would spend the best part of the day walking through the crisp snow in the sunshine.

On New Year's Eve we rocked and rolled into 1960 with a roomful of strangers acting like old friends, linking arms and singing to greet the New Year. There has never been a better New Year's celebration, although Peter and I were to have many more luxurious ones.

Before Peter and I parted in Munich, I inserted an advertisement in several trade papers, stating that I was looking for work in southern Germany as a swimsuit or lingerie designer. By March, I had received one reply, from a Swiss company based in Zurich which, as they pointed out in their charming letter, was not too far from southern Germany. I checked the atlas. True, Zurich was reasonably close to Munich. I sent off my *curriculum vitae* requesting a salary of one thousand Swiss francs a month (worth about £90 in 1960) and wrote to tell Peter the impending good news.

Instantly an express letter arrived from Mama. Nobody earns that sort of money, she said. Contact them at once and say you'll take half. As I'd already checked Swiss salaries with the consulate in London, I ignored her advice. A week later a letter from Zurich came, asking when I could start.

Zurich on a balmy April day in 1960 evoked love at first sight. The more I settled in, the more fond I became of the lake, elegant shops, old houses, wonderful food in excellent restaurants, well-fed, well-paid people living in comfortable homes, lakeside beaches and ski slopes just a few kilometres away. I found a brightly furnished, scrupulously clean studio apartment ten minutes' walk across the river from my workshop.

My boss, Herr Biedermann, made anything and everything he could hope to sell. In a tiny factory employing fifteen machinists, he had a collection of nearly a thousand items and was constantly adding more, from corsets with steel supports to flimsy lace underwear. When I had been working there a while, he asked me to suggest how we might cut down the collection. I drew his attention to some obscure garment, saying, 'This hasn't been made since I was here.' He replied: 'We must keep that. I have a customer in Einsiedeln [a small village in the canton of Zurich] who orders one every year!'

I designed bikinis and swimsuits, lacy half-cup bras with heavy padding underneath which made the wearer spill out over the top, heavy longline bras and cheap stretch nylon panties of tubular material, which apparently sold well but were so ugly I couldn't imagine who would buy such things. A year later I had my answer: the panties were perfect for pregnancy; the fabric grew with the baby.

The two cutters, total age one hundred and forty years, were suspicious of foreign designers and kept me under close surveillance, reporting back to Herr Biedermann my every misdemeanour, such as coming in to work five minutes late and, much worse, being on first-name terms with the manageress, Romy.

In August Peter joined me. He, too, thought Zurich a delightful place and, with his college education at an end, he found a job in a private laboratory developing hormone face cream. He was assistant to the owner, Mr Moldevani, a colourful Hungarian entrepreneur; and he earned a salary far higher than he could expect in Germany. Under Swiss law it was illegal for an unmarried couple to share accommodation and a landlord seen to be conniving at this could be fined heavily for running a disorderly house. For this reason Peter rented a room at the YMCA.

We were blissfully happy and decided to get married on 1 January 1961. My parents were to arrange the festivities and Mama began sending me swatches of material and advice on my wedding dress. On this I stood firm; as far as dress fabrics went, I couldn't have been in a better place.

Peter and I went to England three weeks before the wedding to establish residence and Peter insisted on visiting the register office. They told him to come back two days before the wedding for a special licence. 'But don't you want my signature to prove I am here?'

Not necessary, they said. 'Just sign when you come for the licence, to the effect that you have been here for three weeks.'

Peter was amazed at such trust. 'In Germany this couldn't happen. You would have to sign a document, witnessed and dated.

42

They would require proof, otherwise why should they believe you?'

Mama arrived on Christmas Eve. Lisl sent her love and regrets; she didn't like flying. I was disappointed. Mother had made the full Jewish welcoming meal, with at least eight courses, and the table was set with the best china and silver. But Mama and Peter had been arguing during the drive from the airport, and the row continued through the introductions. My father, for once lost for words, tried unsuccessfully to lighten the mood.

When we went into the dining-room, Mama lifted her plate to inspect its pedigree, and then repeated the performance with the candlesticks. She wanted to know what we had planned and when we explained that we thought we would spend a relaxed family day, with a birthday party for Peter on Boxing Day, she was adamant that she could not possibly spend two days in Reading of all places and would like to be taken to Harrods tomorrow. Not a good idea, said my father; the shops are closed on Christmas Day.

The following morning, without a word to her hosts Barbara and Johnny, she left, stopping on the way to tell Peter and my parents that she couldn't stand 'a puritan English Christmas' – as if a German town on a bank holiday is *not* the most quiet place in the world – and joined Lisl in Austria.

And so Peter was married without a single relative present. I wore the dress of ivory satin embroidered with silver thread that Lola had made for me. The sun shone, of course. After the service in the Reading synagogue we had a reception in the adjoining hall. My father drove us to Heathrow and we flew to Paris. Mama had said her wedding gift would be the honeymoon, but now we weren't sure whether the offer would still stand. In any case, it rained every day and we hurried back to our little studio in Zurich.

Mama sent flowers as a gesture of conciliation, and summoned us to visit. The next weekend I stood quaking on her doorstep. Peter kissed me. 'I'm still happily married to you,' he said.

'And I'm happily married to you . . . but not so happily married to your mother,' I replied.

First came the recriminations. Hers. My family had not taken trouble planning her entertainment; they had neglected her. She became heated and had to lie down to calm herself. Lisl and I prepared coffee and cakes, and Mama began on the next issue. The honeymoon; what had we spent? We itemised the modest pension, the simple restaurants, the inexpensive bottle of wine to celebrate, the single bottle of champagne when we visited a nightclub.

Restaurants? Couldn't we have bought food and eaten it in our room? Why champagne, what's wrong with Coca-Cola? I suggested she might make the contribution she thought fit and leave it at that. Not the point, said Mama, we must learn the folly of being extravagant and ungrateful.

She asked about our other wedding presents, and Peter told her how generous my family had been, particularly my grandparents, with gifts of cash. She wanted details. 'In Deutschmarks,' she said, 'not pounds!'

I counted the minutes until we could get away. The nicest thing that weekend was spending nearly all our wedding present money on an ancient Volkswagen, with two little windows like eyes in the back of its head. We drove it home, and thereafter used it at weekends, exploring every inch of Switzerland, while in Zurich we got on with our beautiful, happy life.

Mr Moldevani was a man dedicated to the pleasures of life. He structured his and Peter's day around the enjoyment of a lavish breakfast and a gourmet lunch. In between he made a few phone calls and worked in the laboratory. It was a delightful routine, but unfortunately there was a fly in the face cream . . . money. Wages were never paid on time, and the intervals between pay days increased each month.

The situation could have continued indefinitely, but in April we had a nasty shock when I found I was pregnant. There were no plans for a baby; we had one room, no furniture and, although we lived well, our lifestyle was based on two excellent salaries, one of which – the one paid regularly – was now in jeopardy.

We were totally unaware that Zurich was probably the easiest place in Europe in which to obtain an abortion, and felt too shy to discuss our problem with other people. So we tried several remedies based on tales I recalled from my college days. One weekend we drove to the mountains, and found a rock for me to jump off. Violently. Peter did it too, holding my hand because I felt nervous. We spent most of the afternoon in this activity, and then collapsed laughing on the grass. Still pregnant in my case.

Equally futile was the method that involved swallowing quinine tablets with half a bottle of gin while sitting in a hot bath. I have never experienced such appalling sickness; nor have I been able to look at let alone smell or drink gin to this day, or swallow a sugar-coated pill of any sort.

'We can always kill ourselves', said Peter, 'if things get too tough.' And then, completely seriously, he swore that he would kill himself if I should die or leave him. He wouldn't want to live without me. After that day this was something he repeated occasionally. I realised then that he saw the birth of our baby as the end of our life as we knew it. But I, with my experience of a happy family life, knew it was a beginning.

Come what may, the pregnancy still intact, we had to make plans. We would need more living space, which meant moving out of the town centre into the suburbs. If I was to continue working I would need to employ someone to look after the baby. If I stopped working we wouldn't be able to afford a bigger flat, and Peter's wages were so erratic that he felt insecure about money and his future.

After the gin treatment, the sickness became permanent and it was impossible for me to get to work on time, so in order to keep on schedule I began taking work home in the evenings. It was the first time Peter had seen my professional work, and he was impressed. 'I didn't know you made such pretty things,' he said.

A few days later he told me he had been thinking about my work. 'If you are worth a thousand francs a month to Herr Bieder-mann, you must be worth three thousand to yourself. I think you should stay at home with the baby, and freelance.' In my experience, freelance designers were designers looking for a full-time job. But Peter had enough confidence for both of us. And thus was set in motion the plan that determined my future life.

When we eventually broke the news of the baby to our mothers, mine said: 'If everybody waited till they could afford a baby there wouldn't be any children in the world.' Mama was excited too, and advised that I should take the baby to live with my mother, and that Peter should return to Munich until he had enough money to provide a home for us – suggestions we disregarded. Mama got busy crocheting all-in-one baby suits to fit a six-foot child with a five-inch waist – and generously arranged regular financial payments to tide us over the next few months.

We found a flat, bought a bed, a cupboard, two Buffet bull-fighter prints and moved into our new home in Zurich. It was September. I was to leave Herr Biedermann in November, but by utilising my summer holiday I had already completed my first freelance assignment, with a swimwear company in Bavaria, which earned me a handsome fee. I continued to work for that company, as a freelance, for many years.

The baby was due to arrive on 26 December, Peter's birthday. I flew to London in mid-December, and Peter followed by car, arriving on Christmas Eve. On the morning of the 27th he ignored my strange little cramps, expecting much stronger stuff to announce the debut of his child, and went as planned to Harrods with my sister Gloria, to decimate the baby department. When they reached London, Peter decided to phone just to check, and, discovering that I was in labour and had left for the maternity hospital, he did a U-turn in the Brompton Road and raced back. Aliza was born that evening. 'Not even pretty,' said Peter, who had been hoping for a boy. He soon changed his mind and continued to boast about his beautiful daughter for years to come.

He visited me in the nursing home, and along with the roses was a copy of Mrs Beeton's cookery book. 'While you're lying here with nothing to do, how about reading this? You might as well learn to cook. You're going to be at home a lot in the future.'

It is said that a baby brings good luck, and it certainly worked that way for us. Having lurched through my pregnancy in a state of terror about our financial burdens, and how we would manage with one more dependant and one less salary, to our amazement once Aliza was born and I began working from home we were better off than ever. Peter advertised my services in every European trade paper, and answered every advertisement he read. Almost at once I had all the work I could handle and was earning four times my previous salary.

He also had a new job, as sales executive with a company producing scientific equipment, earning an excellent salary and working so close to home that he could slip back for an hour during the day if my business required his attention. The first thing we did once we felt assured of our newfound financial security was to move back into the heart of the city, to a much larger flat with a balcony and set in gardens with play areas for children.

Peter typed all my letters, met all the clients, negotiated fees, made my travel arrangements, and booked my hotels. I designed the garments and visited the factories to oversee any production problems. My ambition to travel was now reality. Six weeks spread throughout the year were spent with the swimsuit company at the village of Benediktbeuren in Bavaria. There were also at least four trips to Paris, plus meetings in Amsterdam, Oslo, Bologna, Vienna, Tel Aviv, Copenhagen, Cologne, Cannes, Nice. I was travelling so much I began to look forward to being at home. The hard work, the long hours, the effort put into running the home were stimulating to me. I thrived on it and my work benefited. I had all the design freedom I wanted, the only proviso being to make the garments desirable and saleable.

Communication was no problem, for dressmaking has its own international language. I had only to hand my cut-out pieces to the machinist, point to the seam and indicate in sign language the particular finish I wanted and she would know at once what was required. Cutters recognised pattern pieces without my knowing the words for them in their language.

If it was frustrating sometimes to see a sample I had been so pleased with changed beyond recognition, that was part of the deal. Once at a trade fair in Dusseldorf I looked in vain for my designs among a client's display. One of the directors greeted us. 'How nice to see you. How do you like your garment? It's our best seller.'

It was *my* bra top, with *their* V-neckline. Often I suspected that clients paid me a great deal of money for my most original creations only to prevent others buying them. They then worked on them to suit their own production line, in effect producing a variation on what they were already making. I could afford to be pragmatic, I was doing so well.

Our food came from the best shops. We bought a big new Ford Taunus, and began spending weekends at places like Davos instead of the tucked-away resorts we had visited when money was tight and the cheapest pension was all we could afford. We no longer looked at the prices on the menu before we ordered. Peter, on

Mama's advice, bought three diamonds as an investment and had one made into a ring for me.

We dressed expensively. I bought an original Courrèges coat in white to wear with the fashionable new mini-skirts, and shopped for shoes at Charles Jourdan, the very latest in shoes. Aliza's wardrobe grew even faster than mine; with clothing bought by Mama and us, she was probably one of the world's best-dressed toddlers.

It would have been churlish, with so much of everything to be thankful for, to feel less than wonderfully blessed, but what was lacking in those years was friendship and companionship. All my life I had made friends, and needed them. Since our marriage it had become obvious that Peter did not want the company of other people. His naturally loving manner became tense, moody and possessive as soon as I showed signs of developing an acquaintanceship with somebody else. Few people broke through the barrier.

I managed to make friends with an English neighbour whose child played with Aliza, and later we got to know her husband. Another neighbour with a Hungarian lover became friends with us, and to her I owe my foolproof, much-appreciated recipe for goulash. Not many friends in six years. When my sisters or my mother came to stay, Peter would demonstrate cold moodiness and his least lovable qualities. He made us all feel tense. I tried not to dwell on these disadvantages. His occasional unreasonable behaviour seemed a small price to pay for all the positive things we enjoyed: a happy marriage, a generally good life and a lovely daughter. We even had money in the bank – £8,000 by the time we left (I had been earning more than 100,000 SF a year – around £10,000).

We were forced to leave Switzerland for reasons totally beyond our control. In 1965 the company Peter worked for was taken over. The new public company closed the Zurich office and transferred the entire operation to their head office close to the Liechtenstein border, inviting the staff to relocate, all expenses paid. Not only did we not want to move to this remote spot, but from the point of view of my business it was totally impractical. It brought to the fore our realisation that Peter's contribution was an intrinsic part of my business, and that he was far more gainfully employed chasing work for me than in his present full-time occupation. So he declined his company's offer of relocation. However, we hit a snag. During the fifties and sixties, the Swiss authorities had granted large numbers of work permits to foreigners. Now, amid growing complaints that the national character was becoming 'diluted', a law was passed requiring companies to cut down their foreign workforce. To avoid massive sackings, obviously inhumane, a plan was devised whereby when a foreigner left a job he or she could be replaced only by a Swiss citizen.

As a British citizen resident in Switzerland for five years, I had been granted a full residence permit, but a German could apply for this only after ten. The only way Peter could remain in the country was by obtaining a work permit, for which he was eligible to apply. But a prospective employer could employ him only if the company had already achieved its requisite foreigner reduction percentage. Inadvertently we had burned our boats.

The wrangling went on for a year. *I* could employ him. No, they said, that was evading the law; a foreigner was not permitted to start an independent business. We altered our approach. We asked permission for him to stay, supported by me; I earned enough for both of us. They refused. It was immoral for a man to live off his wife's earnings. We thought of every way possible that would allow us to stay in Zurich but in the end we were forced to admit defeat. Where would we go next?

We needed a large city, accessible to an international airport, with a fashion-conscious population and where we would be permitted to live and work. It had to be London.

5

We awoke on our first morning in our new home in London: December 1966, grey and cold, bare windows, a large scruffy dilapidated room. We had left behind a beautiful, warm apartment with polished wood floors, high-tec American-style kitchen, and a bathroom with plumbing tuned to an efficiency undreamed of in dear old England. Our depression matched the drizzle outside. Peter and I cried in each other's arms. 'The lorry is still parked in the street,' said Peter. 'Let's load up and drive back!'

Instead we dressed and went out into Westbourne Terrace to find a café open for breakfast. Not easy. That was the most miserable day of our married life, so far.

'Children, do you realise what you have taken on?' my mother had said when she called to collect Aliza who was to stay with her while we sorted ourselves out. She had taken in at a glance the broken floorboards, the sagging, doorless kitchen cupboards, shabby 1925 bathroom, and the absence of fridge and oven. It certainly hadn't looked this bad, just challenging, when we had viewed in August.

For the next two months we papered and painted, sanded and hammered, aided by Ursula, the German mother's help who had been part of our life in Switzerland and had come along to find out about London and the whole swinging Carnaby Street scene, news of which had percolated through to Zurich. Somehow, I always felt, the sixties happened without me. We came back to London from time to time but our home was Zurich, and the Swiss took a censorious view of what they read was happening in Swinging London. I remember my friend Joy's mother-in-law clucking disapprovingly over her two-year-old grandson. 'Get his hair cut. What does he look like, a Beatle!' Certainly in Switzerland the skirts were creeping up, but creeping up more in the style of Courrèges or Ungaro than that of Carnaby Street and Mary Quant.

It was exciting to see our London flat transformed from miserable tip to elegant home, but frightening to watch our money disappear. One of my clients wrote from Germany to say the contract would have to be cancelled now that I was in England, as we were too far away. We decided enough was enough, put away the pots of paint, sent for Aliza, found an excellent machinist, Mrs Hayes, and got down to the serious business of earning money.

Peter, working along the lines he had first followed in Zurich, had begun looking for clients, and was finding it very difficult to convince the British lingerie industry that they needed me. He contacted Bertie, the son of my old boss Mr Leffman, now running the firm, and was invited to meet him in the showroom in Savile Row. The design room was *still* in Bridgwater! Bertie was impressed by the samples but said it was impossible to get this type of work done in England. If, however, we could manufacture, then he would undertake to sell for us. Fenwick's and Selfridges were always on the lookout for pretty underwear.

We left his showroom somewhat dejected, and wandered through into Bond Street and Fenwick's underwear department. Clearly they needed some of our pretty styles. 'If we could get them made', said Peter, 'I wouldn't need Bertie to sell them for us. I could do that myself.'

We went home and Peter sat down with notebook and telephone to make appointments. Next day, shoving a few of my current styles into my small sample case, he left the flat. I sat at home and waited.

At last he returned, with a long, sad face. My heart sank. 'What happened?'

He tried hard to maintain his gloomy expression but had to burst out laughing. 'I've got my first order.'

'How? You don't even know the prices. We don't have a workroom. How can you have an order?'

It seemed Peter had said all that to Miss Taylor of Fenwick's and she had replied: 'I'll place the order. Go away and make it up. Let me know the price when you've worked it out. Deliver in the autumn.' So Peter had taken his first order for three dozen bra and brief sets, price and delivery date unknown.

At Miss Selfridge he received a similar enthusiastic response. As he produced his samples from the case, the buyer exclaimed: 'At last. Something pretty coming in!' She said that, as soon as he was organised and could offer delivery dates, he should let her know so that she could order at once.

By happy coincidence, dining with my cousin Jean Olman and her husband Stanley, we learned that his father's factory in Walthamstow was looking for work. Their mainstay was suspender belts for Dorothy Perkins, but the mini-skirt had been the death of the suspender belt. Stockings were out, tights in.

We agreed with the Olmans, father and son, that Peter would sell, we would purchase the cloth, and they would handle the production. The company was born and a few months later, in June 1967, Janet Reger Creations Ltd was registered.

We expected to begin in a quiet way. But Peter, let loose with the order book, overloaded production immediately. I found problems at the factory, which I visited every day, dropping Aliza off on the school bus and taking the Tube from Paddington to Walthamstow. The workforce was accustomed to handling rigid fabrics and producing cheap, basic suspender belts. My designs called for soft, flimsy laces. Delivery dates were threatening to swamp us, and as fast as the girls were sewing, we were unpicking their mistakes. We'd invested our last penny in the cloth, and now it was do or die.

Finally the garments were deemed as near perfect as possible, with the help of strategically placed rosebuds to conceal the awkward mitres. Peter loaded the boxes into his car and we cracked a bottle of champagne to celebrate.

It was August 1967, and we made our first delivery.

Nothing could stop Peter as he rushed round England taking orders. By Christmas he had sold ten times the production facility of the factory. To make matters worse, old Mr Olman received a nice safe order for his good old suspender belts and, understandably, put the girls on to them.

I extended my cutting table at home, bought a small electric rotary cutter and inserted an advertisement for homeworkers in the London *Evening Standard*.

Finding the right workers, like finding the right mother's help, is like the old joke . . . you have to kiss a lot of frogs before you find the prince. There was the elderly Indian lady who accused me of being cruel when I said I had no more work for her. She was incapable of sewing a straight line. 'It's not my fault I have bad eyesight,' she said, aggrieved. 'I do my best.'

Sometimes the clothes would come back smelling of curry and paraffin stoves, a heady mixture which penetrated every fibre. We stretched a line outside in the yard and pegged the garments in the fresh air until every whiff had disappeared.

Most of the women were supervised by their husbands who negotiated rates. One continually argued about the price for bras, insisting that we should pay double for bras with two cups! One Pakistani family consisted of a mother and her eldest daughter who worked full time, plus the younger children helping after school with menial tasks such as trimming off cotton threads and sewing bows and rosebuds into place. The woman's husband attended to the business side, ensuring that his wife and daughter never left the house and earned a small fortune. One day he confided how sorry he felt for 'the women in this country'. Oh really, we asked, why was that? 'Their husbands don't take care of them. They let them work behind counters, or sit in an office all day typing, with nobody to protect them.'

I cut and bundled the pieces. Peter delivered to the outworkers, collecting last week's work at the same time, and Mrs Hayes finished off each bra personally; she had the magic touch. Bras are the most difficult piece of clothing there is to sew. Our dining-room was the packing station. Peter, Ursula and I inspected every garment before it was packed. Ursula, despite constant pressure from her family, was continually postponing her return to Germany.

We worked day and night; the flat was a mess but the rewards were satisfying. The landlord who lived below began to complain about the volume of packages going up and down in the lift, and at the same time we decided it would be nice not to have our carpet covered with threads, so we looked around for a workroom close by. It had to be cheap, because although the business was growing fast, somehow we were always looking for money. Payments were slow coming in.

53

'Try sending statements,' said Stanley, during one of our money moans.

'What's a statement?' asked Peter.

Stanley explained. We rushed out to buy a duplicate book. Peter sent out statements, and the money came in. Thereafter, whenever we were short of cash, Peter would say: 'Come on, Ursula, statements!'

Peter found a large room above a garage in Southwick Mews, Paddington, just a few minutes' walk from home. The rent was £7 a week. We painted it throughout, installed a toilet and moved in.

Our timing couldn't have been better. Soon afterwards, old Mr Olman retired and sold his factory and we would have been left with only our outworkers. We employed a trainee machinist and Mrs Hayes agreed to come in full time. By now I had given up my freelance design work. I had all I could handle with my own label, and it seemed unfair to offer my old clients, and friends as they seemed, second best.

Our first big thrill came with a royal request. Princess Anne had rushed into Way In on the eve of a foreign tour and seen our garments. We received a frantic call from the buyer. 'Princess Anne needs a C cup, we don't have it in stock.' Neither did we, we didn't even make a C cup at that time. Sadly, we had to disappoint her; there was no way we could help.

One day we opened a glossy supplement and saw one of our garments, beautifully photographed and with the credit 'Neat-awear', the name of a small chain of boutiques.

'Why shouldn't we have our name in the paper beside the picture?' Peter wanted to know. As with statements, he learned fast and began a campaign to familiarise himself with the fashion press, and inviting them to see our collection.

By this time we had taken on a secretary-cum-bookkeeper, Stella Stilwell, who eventually became sales director and remained with us to the end. Meanwhile, Peter needed an assistant, someone who could help generally with office administration, and Brenda came into our lives, selected from the applicants for her glowing references. When her P45 arrived it showed that she had taken a large drop in salary to join us. I wondered why. She wanted less responsibility, said Peter; this had been explained at the interview.

This surprised me, and later even more in view of her formidable efficiency. We all felt we had found a treasure in Brenda.

By the time Brenda and I met, she had been working in the office for a week. Peter, uncharacteristically, seemed intimidated by this woman who struck me as unprepossessing and somewhat dowdy, with a hearty, jolly-hockeysticks voice. Her conversation all sounded like something from a book, both the dialogue and the subject matter. Her life, it seemed, had been full of drama, tragedy and romance. She talked a lot about herself and about Eric, her devoted, kind, rich husband.

Before long she confided the story of her one great love. He was Greek. They had fallen in love and she had gone to live in Greece with his family. On the eve of their wedding, she told me, he had been killed in a motor accident. Returning home to her village in the home counties she had been ostracised because she had been engaged to a foreigner. Only Eric had shown friendship, and she had subsequently married him. This story reached me via Aliza, and I was amazed that Brenda had discussed this with a seven-year-old child. I was married to a foreigner, and nobody ostracised me. I couldn't understand anyone being so reactionary in twentieth-century commuterland.

Apart from the occasional slip I tried to keep my scepticism about Brenda's stories to myself. It was bitchy of me to be so critical, and I was concerned not to interfere with her work, which she did well. To Peter, Brenda was the paragon of virtue. She also took it upon herself to educate him, ironing out his accent, correcting his vocabulary and putting him right on what she saw as his grave errors in the way staff and customers should be treated. Peter was sometimes discourteous, he offended often because he didn't stop to consider. Our customers, however, accepted his little foibles. The buyers were all women, and Peter was very good-looking and loved to flatter and flirt, so many were a little in love with him. He was an excellent salesman; the most we ever sold was when Peter was handling sales. But Brenda intimidated him and made him feel inadequate, always organising him and telling him what he was doing wrong, so Peter gradually let Brenda take over office administration.

Once Aliza, who had become very fond of Brenda, asked why she had no children, and was told there had been a child, a little boy, who had been killed in a car crash. She was travelling in the same car, pregnant with another child at the time, and the shock killed her unborn child too. Now she could never have a baby.

Aliza was distraught. We all felt very sorry for Brenda. At times the office was shrouded in melancholy, and people tiptoed about, speaking in hushed tones out of consideration for Brenda because this was the anniversary of Brenda's fiancé's accident or of Brenda's baby's death. But she was excellent at her work, did all the jobs Peter hated, dealt with the customers Peter couldn't handle and became indispensable.

Although Brenda occasionally dined with us at the flat, surprisingly she never reciprocated. We had seen pictures of her lovely farmhouse and been told about the lifestyle she and Eric enjoyed. Peter sometimes used to say, 'They're richer than we are, I don't know why she bothers to work.' Because of this implied wealth, and because he was a little in awe of her Englishness, Peter felt embarrassed about giving her a Christmas cash bonus like the rest of the staff and used to buy her a present instead.

Hints of a mysterious illness in her past reared up from time to time, and she was frequently absent. I noted to Peter as our staff expanded, that Brenda took more time off than anyone else. If she caught a cold or got stung by a bee, that meant at least a week in bed! But as he was quick to point out, her work never suffered. She was super-efficient.

It seemed that everything we did worked, thanks to my charmed life. One of our best customers, Neatawear, went into liquidation and even as we mourned the passing of our customer there came a call from a lady who introduced herself as Sheila Gore, public relations person to the late Neatawear. Having just lost her job, she was about to go freelance and was offering us the opportunity to become her client. She knew our work, liked it, had seen Peter's efforts at publicity and felt she could do better for us. Peter told her we couldn't afford her services. But Sheila, true to form as we realised when we got to know her better, did not take no for an answer and insisted on a meeting.

She breezed into the flat (it contained our office and the sitting-room was still a workroom then), short, busty, vivacious, garrulous. When she proposed to work for next to nothing initially, because she was convinced we would be able to pay her a realistic fee by the second year, we said yes. We had little to lose and we liked her.

So began a working relationship and friendship that was to last fifteen years to our mutual benefit and enjoyment. Her input was the turning point in those early years. Sheila pushed, wangled, organised, and originated more editorial column inches than were received by any other designer (with the possible exception of Mary Quant) in England at that time. The name Janet Reger became synonymous with beautiful, sexy underwear.

Sheila became an integral part of our daily life and work, and one day Peter, thinking far ahead, raised the spectre: 'What will happen when Sheila is too old for us?' As she was close to forty at the time, and as ours was essentially a sexy, youthful image and the fashion press girls were getting younger all the time, it was evident that in twenty years Sheila would be out of step. We agreed between ourselves that when the time came we would suggest she employ a young assistant, and felt very relieved. We weren't to know the need would never arise.

Soon business was expanding so dramatically that we were out-growing our production capabilities. I did everything except sew the garments myself; Peter did the selling, all the office work and deliveries to outworkers. My sister Sandra came in occasionally to help with the filing, and Ursula handled all the packing.

By the time Stanley came to help with the cutting and out-workers and Peter took on a junior to assist in the office – my old workroom at the flat – we were groaning at the seams. So we spread along Southwick Mews, into another building and then, a little later, to the house next door. By 1970 we had a staff of twenty.

My colourful lace designs continued to sell, and I discovered a source of hand-blocked printed chiffon from France which, trimmed with lace and printed ribbons, inspired a whole new collection. Orders kept rolling in. We had also started making pure silk underwear and this created a stir. Each time a garment appeared in a newspaper or magazine we would be inundated with enquiries, and sometimes cheques. Often the nearest stockist to the correspondent was miles out of the way, and gradually from this consumer interest, and the fact that my young assistant Julia was an exceptionally good fashion artist, we hit on the idea of direct selling.

We produced a catalogue on pink paper with pretty sketches and launched our mail-order business. Not wishing to offend our wholesale customers, we decided to remain anonymous, and called the mail-order collection Bottom Drawer. But the hand-writing was unmistakably mine so the nom de plume fooled no one. Bottom Drawer turned out to be a little goldmine.

We moved out of the draughty, leaky, inconvenient flat which sucked up any amount of money we chose to pour into it without our ever feeling we had got it right. But once again we needed more work space. There was no room for an office in our new flat just across the road. We solved the problem, gained further much-needed work space and also achieved a split between work and home, by renting a rather shabby disused shop and basement just around the corner from Southwick Mews in Southwick Street.

This became the territory for me, Mrs Hayes and Julia, with our design-room and premises for new machines, and, completely by accident, it started a whole new development. The shop became our cutting-room, and we set up a showroom in the base-ment with a rail of garments, a small table and a couple of chairs. One day a woman arrived. She had tracked us down from a newspaper credit which gave our address and was surprised to discover a rather poky little cutting-room instead of a luxurious shop. She looked around. 'My God, what a dump.'

'This isn't a shop, we're manufacturers,' I replied.

'Never mind, can I buy something? I've been to Harrods and they haven't got my size.'

We didn't keep very much stock, as we made to order for our retail customers, but we showed her what we had. She took a selection into the loo to try on, and bought the lot. Before long there was an endless stream of customers and we rearranged the cutting-room with a partition, and made the front into a pretty but extremely small public shop.

Southwick Street and that area of Paddington were scruffy in 1966 when we moved to England. By the time we had made the shop presentable, the surrounding area had improved too, though it was still a far cry from the upper reaches of Bond Street and

Knightsbridge which were the hunting grounds of the sort of clientele which was now beginning to tread the path to our door. The advance party were the fashion journalists, and then came the wives of pop stars and the junior league blue-bloods.

As Peter said, we had nothing to lose. It was a good way of selling the over-cuts, and since the bell rang every time someone came through the door, Julia or I would simply leave the work-room to attend to the customer. It was a shop without any sales staff as such.

Like everything else we touched, the success was phenomenal. Bianca Jagger was among the first customers. She spent lavishly but we didn't have a bra small enough for her boyish figure. You couldn't avoid seeing the customers naked. Angie Bowie's was the perfect body; she moved around the shop completely naked and was a fantastic customer, fantastic as in big spender, but so were they all. It was as if our customers had alighted on a cornu-copia of pretty feminine lingerie and just couldn't believe their luck. Neither could we. The self-launched retail operation exceeded anything we would have expected had we set about it deliberately. In the first month it was taking at least five times what we might have estimated.

The size of our mews factory was insufficient, and I tried various sources of production but the intricate nature of my designs was beyond the scope of most machinists. Eventually I managed to locate a tiny Derbyshire factory run by a husband and wife, who were prepared to take on anything to keep their girls busy, and were capable of working to my specifications. I was delighted with the results. Then one day, telephoning them with a new order and instructions, I was shattered to be told they were about to close down. Lee and Val Parks were such good people, and I was sad for them. I was also worried on my own behalf. How would I replace their input?

A week later Lee Parks telephoned. He'd been thinking, he said. 'You seem to have permanent production shortage. I have thirty experienced girls about to lose their jobs at the end of the month. Why don't you buy the factory from me? I'll make it financially easy for you, because I'd really like to see the girls kept in employ-ment. They're about to get the sack.'

6

We had expected Wirksworth to be a grey, industrial place with factory chimneys belching smoke; neither Peter nor I had ever been to Derbyshire and we were at once pleasantly surprised and delighted with the splendour of the hills and dales, the soft grey-stone buildings and villages of miniature houses clinging in terraces to the steep sloping streets.

We made our way through the sleepy village to the factory, St Mary's Gate, formerly the church hall. Too expensive for the church to keep up, it had been let for a nominal rent on the condition that it was maintained in good order and repair. We liked what we saw. Big double doors led on to the factory floor which housed forty-five machines, cutting and examining tables. There was a small canteen upstairs and overall plenty of unrenovated space which could be put to use.

We did the deal with the Parks. Both sides wanted to move quickly; we needed the production, they planned to move on to other things. We agreed that it was most important to inform the staff before the rumours began to circulate.

Until now I had little experience of 'labour'. In London we employed a good-natured mix of West Indians and Asians who, as long as the money came in at the end of the week, didn't mind what they were asked to do, including answering the telephone and making the tea.

Wirksworth was a whole new territory. As soon as Lee Parks informed the workforce that Janet Reger would be taking over the factory, there would be no redundancies, and that I would be talking to them myself at the earliest opportunity, a few girls gave notice immediately. Maybe they were not prepared to work for strangers from London.

The day we arrived we were introduced to the key people –

Mrs Brindley, in charge of production, and her sister Tessa, part-time office helper – and liked them both. We reserved judgement on the third essential employee, the cutter, and went on to meet the girls assembled in the canteen. I showed them some of our samples, and Peter once more assured them their jobs were safe.

There was silence. Then one voice piped up: would the present piecework system continue? I explained that our small-quantity, high-quality production didn't lend itself to piecework rates. Instead we proposed to raise the present basic wage to an hourly rate which would increase everybody's wages. There were no further questions.

Next day Mrs Brindley told me that four girls had given notice as a result of my remarks about wages. I was astonished that they should leave without at least waiting to see how the new regime and wage structure worked. What I was offering could only be to their advantage. After studying the payroll I had been shocked at the small pay packets many were taking home. Work at the factory had been slack, so not only had it been impossible for the girls to make up their wages on piecework, it had been equally hard for the Parks to pay them.

We raised the weekly wage from an average £8 to £12, more than many local factories were paying their most skilled workers at maximum productivity. I mistakenly thought this would make everybody very happy, but some girls still muttered that on the piecework system they could earn double. This was nonsense and I had the old wage records to prove it.

Laboriously we eased our way into full production at Wirksworth and gradually phased out the London operation, retaining a few of the better girls to work exclusively in our Bottom Drawer section at Southwick Street. In theory Wirksworth should have been ideal. Even allowing for constant travelling expenses and overnight accommodation for myself and usually Julia too, it made economic sense. But we reckoned without the difficulty of teaching the girls new methods, and the painful slowness of a factory not motivated by piecework, which pushed up labour costs out of all proportion.

In London we used rough justice to sort out the good from the bad. Fair work and speed were rewarded. Poor quality, after allowing time for learning, ended in the sack. We rarely lost the better workers. When I suggested this method to Mrs Brindley and Tessa they were horrified. There would be a total walkout if it was discovered some earned more than others. I bowed to their judgement but have often wished I had insisted on introducing my tried and tested methods from day one.

In London we took our lunchbreak relaxing with a sandwich in the workroom. In Wirksworth I was told it would be unpopular for me or members of the staff to use the works canteen at the same time as the workers.

Although teething troubles had eased by the end of the first year and the work was improving, we still lost money remaking poor-quality work and on general slowness. I discovered a practice which absolutely infuriated me. In the past each girl had been allocated a certain job, and if her particular station ran out of work, she went home. I required versatility from the girls and began to train them to do various tasks. To counteract this, when the work on their machines was dwindling, some would start to unpick it in order to do it all over again, rather than switch to another job or machine where they could be more useful. At times I felt I was banging my head against a brick wall.

When I introduced a bonus scheme it stirred up jealousy and bad feeling. When production was good and the bonus was high, everybody said how fair it was. If we had a bad week, there were delegations to the office complaining that the scheme was unfair. When I awarded Mrs Brindley a salary increase – well deserved; she was a treasure – the cutter refused to work in a place where a woman earned more than he did and walked out.

When I took over the factory there was union representation and the girls paid ten pence a week subscription. In our first year Mrs Brindley went away on holiday and delegated certain responsibilities to her young assistant, who showed promise and was being trained. For obvious reasons, it is absolutely forbidden to eat or drink at the machines or at the packing tables in the factory, so when the acting supervisor found chocolate and cakes in the packing-room, she admonished the staff about it, and Lily, a packer who had been recently appointed shop steward (it amounted to collecting the dues), turned the issue into an argument.

A few days later the dispute erupted afresh when a camiknicker was discovered bearing the stains of orange squash from waist to crutch. Lily the packer blamed the production girls downstairs. The checker said that there was no way a damaged item could get past her; it must have happened in the packing-room. A search revealed a bottle of orange squash hidden behind a curtain in the packing-room. The acting supervisor had the job of telephoning me to warn of the delay in dispatching the order. 'And if I find food in the packing-room again, I'll tell Mrs Reger the reason why,' she had said.

'Right,' said Lily, reaching for her coat and handbag, 'I'm not being spoken to like that. We're on strike. One out, everybody out!' And she marched from the factory, alone. Nobody else could be bothered to get involved, especially as in this instance the packing department was at fault. Lily wrote to say she would come back if and when she received a written apology, and I replied that if she didn't feel like coming back to work that was her choice. As nobody volunteered to take over collecting the union subscriptions, it was the end of the union.

The rumour went around Wirksworth that Mrs Reger had thrown the union out of the factory. When I heard this, I asked the girls: 'What do you actually want a union for? We are a small business. I'm here every week. If you've got a problem, something you're not happy with, it isn't as if you are working for a remote unavailable owner miles away, you can talk to me about it.'

We formed a committee made up of representatives of the different work categories: nightwear workers, underwear workers, examiners, supervisors and office girls, adding more sections as we expanded, and held monthly meetings at which aspects of the work could be discussed and suggestions made. But all anyone wanted to talk about was when they were going to get another rise – even if they had just had one – and whether the tea was hot enough. I had hoped for a dynamic situation, and was disappointed. I wanted them to be involved, to understand the economics of the business, to realise that if everybody worked together, we would improve efficiency and they would benefit.

There was a deep-rooted misunderstanding which I never successfully overcame. The girls would take the retail price of a Janet Reger piece – £30 or £500 – and compare it with what they calculated they earned for making it – £5 or £8–9 depending on the number of hours – and assume the difference was all profit. They neither understood nor wanted to understand that a pair of knickers is made up of more than just the cost of labour.

I tried worker participation, as preached by politicians, but there wasn't any. The average worker didn't want to participate and still doesn't today. I have seen no improvement of any kind in this attitude since I first took over the factory.

Some of the girls' husbands were fiercely pro-union. Each time you sacked somebody – a rare event – the husband would turn up to sort it out. Then there were the arguments about the last week's wages when a girl left. We used a system called 'week in hand'. This meant that when somebody left, they received wages for the week they had worked plus holiday pay and any other entitlements. The following week, they would be paid for the week they hadn't worked (the week management had held in hand). 'But what about that first week when I didn't get paid?' they would say.

'That's why we paid you for the last week you didn't work.'

'But when I started I was told that when I left I would be paid a week in hand.'

'But this is it. We didn't pay you for the first week you worked; we are paying you for the last week when you didn't work.'

More than half the girls who left didn't understand the principle and were convinced they were being done out of a week's money. The wages clerk used to have to sit down, go through the calendar counting the number of weeks worked and showing that this tallied with the number paid for.

Sometimes it went on for hours. Sometimes husbands came round arguing. I always took the same attitude. 'It's your wife who worked for us, not you. If she's got any queries, she should come and talk to us. And if she still isn't satisfied she should go up to Matlock and speak to the employment office and I'm sure they will convince her she hasn't been done out of anything.'

A few of the girls joined the Transport and General Workers' Union. One day I received a call from my personnel manageress, who was most distressed because, she said, 'Somebody is standing outside the factory distributing offensive leaflets.'

The literature came from the TGWU, exhorting those girls who were not union members to join at once. They were being exploited, it claimed; paid a pittance. The pamphlet printed company earnings for our best year (no mention of the lean years) and compared this with the take-home pay of the lowest-paid worker. To underline the point, they noted details of directors' remuneration, gross, pre-tax, and asked: 'Why should they earn so much and you earn so little?' Then, for good measure: '*And they're married* . . .' as if Peter and I, being married, should each draw half a wage. It was ludicrous. It was, after all, our business: built by us, our hard work, our investment, our risk-taking.

I complained in writing to the TGWU but no more was heard from them. I got the girls together and went through the letter with them. I was loath to dignify the libellous remarks with explanations, but felt compelled to contest the leaflet's general tone, which made us out to be running some sort of Victorian sweatshop. They must make up their own minds whether or not they joined the TGWU. For my part I disagreed with what the union was doing in trying to cause trouble, and made it clear I would not allow meetings in work hours.

'If you want to have a meeting, have it in your own time,' was my message. Some joined, some didn't, and there existed a division between members and non-members, but the fuss died down and there was no further hint of union militancy. I kept aloof.

We had moved our production from London, taking over a small factory and twenty-four semi- or unskilled workers and three low-paid staff. In ten years the factory grew to a payroll of one hundred and twenty, mostly trained by us to a high level of skill, and well paid. We expanded, renovated and improved using local labour. We established a home there above the second factory, supported local trade and brought business into the area. Sadly, that counted for nothing when disaster struck.

Around this time I acquired my dragonfly trademark. During our era of the painted look, we employed artists to paint on silk. One, Veronica Holden, always included a dragonfly somewhere in her design; often so inconspicuously we had to search it out, which we always did. When we came to create our own logo, the dragonfly was essential. At first it was a highly stylised creature, half-woman, half-insect. It has remained, through various metamorphoses, ever since.

*

For some time Sheila Gore had been urging us to find a more prestigious London address than Southwick Street. We were making more money there than seemed possible. Customers (you could call them that in Southwick Street, later they were clients) almost relished the expedition into deepest Paddington. There must have been great satisfaction in discovering our treasure trove where least expected, the gem in the bran tub. But it didn't fit the Janet Reger image, said Sheila, and we agreed. I don't recall the expression existed then, but it was time to go upmarket.

Peter, never as happy as when he was setting up a 'great new concept' (his favourite expression), went in search of new premises and, after we had been gazumped on a few properties, he was offered what had been his first choice – at No. 2 Beauchamp Place, a house on three floors plus basement.

I made a special collection for the opening launch. Peter, who had started buying and selling pictures, came across a collection of Edwardian lingerie at auction. It had belonged to Heather Firbank, an eminent socialite of her day. He reported back in great excitement and rushed me to Sotheby's to inspect it for myself. I had to have it: the nightgowns and drawers, fine long camisoles and pintucked petticoats trimmed with handmade lace and embroidery, all of them in first-class condition.

I put in an open offer, and bought the lot. I told one of my lace suppliers what I had bought, and a few weeks later he came back to me with the most wonderful old Nottingham lace which had been in his stock-room since before the war. The combination of Firbank originals and old lace inspired me, although I substituted silk for cotton and linen. Personally I love cotton, but it never sold as well as silk. The window looked stunning.

We were so afraid nobody would turn up for our opening party that we invited twice as many as we had room for, and three times as many came. Champagne flowed and the party spread from basement to attic.

I now operated from the elegant environs of Knightsbridge, which befitted a designer of international calibre, as Sheila was always reminding me. I kept my workroom, but the little shop in Southwick Street died.

We now included among our regular customers those who came to steal my ideas. The rag trade discovered us at Beauchamp Place.

One American lady who visits once or twice a year blatantly questions the assistant as to which style and colour is selling best. It's cheeky but I'll start worrying when they find someone else to rip off; it will mean I've lost my touch. From the first day of being copied, I've been spurred on to keep a few steps ahead. Ideas are not my problem. I have more than I can ever use.

Beauchamp Place also put us on the map for the legitimate trade. For every buyer taking home garments to copy, there were many genuine customers on the lookout for something good, rare and essentially English. And when these asked the girl in the shop: 'Where do you buy these beautiful garments?' she was able to say: 'Mrs Reger makes them,' and direct them to my showroom which was also Peter's office.

We were learning about retail first hand. At Southwick Street the shop had been a very amateurish mopping-up operation where we sold extra cuts to round up figures for a wholesale order. Now with the wholesale business expanding, our Bottom Drawer booming and Beauchamp Place pulling in the rich, the smart and the trendy, we had to be professional and disciplined. I devised a primitive book-keeping system to monitor sales, production and orders.

Through this I learned the first rule of retail: you can't get it right. This is how it works. Every day people come into the shop, love the goods, ask for bigger sizes. You stock bigger sizes. No sooner are the bigger sizes in stock than the only customers to come in are emaciated midgets. Similarly, we make floor-length nightdresses; everyone asks for short ones. We make short nightdresses; the customers say long ones are prettier. They ask for plain untrimmed designs. I make them. They want more lace. And so I continued, and have done, to make the clothes I want to make, to the highest possible standard of quality. If a customer wants something special, is prepared to pay the extra cost and be patient, then I'll provide that service.

Within only a year of opening Beauchamp Place we were ready to expand further, and targeted Bond Street as the catchment area for big-spending tourists and the super-rich Arabs buying homes in Mayfair. Peter did a frantic forage into the estate agents' registers and came up with Brook Street, right on the junction with South Molton Street. Its spacious ground floor enabled us to display nightwear and underwear on the same level. The lower ground floor was even bigger, and Julia, Mrs Hayes, the pattern cutter and I, moved our design department there with barely a backward glance at shabby little Southwick Street. The best was yet to come; these were the good years when everything we touched turned to gold.

As the business grew, Brenda built up a close-knit group of staff reporting to her rather than to Peter or me. We were stupid to let that happen. While she was undoubtedly able, Brenda's conviction that she knew better than anyone how things should be done was occasionally irritating, such as the time she decided to take over the staff party. She booked the venue for the Christmas lunch and insisted on keeping it a secret. Peter was quite agitated, and almost begged to be told. But she refused: it was her big surprise. But Peter wasn't a big surprise person, I explained, trying to be tactful. He might hate the place she had chosen. She dug in her heels and, in the event, Peter did hate the place. We had been there before. It was a touristy nightclub of the worst sort, where they pour you a glass of wine and upturn the bottle in the bucket and say it's empty, and then add the date on to the bill. And who books a nightclub for lunch? Peter sulked all through the party.

When Peter said he wanted to make Brenda a director of the company I did not object, although Sheila Gore said it was a mistake. There had been a few run-ins between Sheila and Brenda, mainly over Brenda's obvious attempts to muscle in on Sheila's domain. 'Will you please keep that woman away from the press!' Sheila said to Peter one day. 'She doesn't know how to handle them.' Peter could see it was true, and also that Brenda didn't project the Janet Reger fashion image.

Some time after Brenda's elevation to directorship, she lobbied to be included on a sales trip to America. Peter insisted on buying her a whole new wardrobe of clothes, but Brenda ignored the expert advice of Shirley at Leonard and (to me, inappropriately) selected the slinky crochet clothing popular at that time. She had supreme faith in her own taste, even to the extent of criticising the Janet Reger collection and suggesting she could do better. However, her superb ability as an administrator explained why I turned a blind eye so often and so readily.

★

Around the time we opened the Beauchamp Place shop, Peter, who was working very hard and under pressure, developed serious stomach pains and thought he had an ulcer. After extensive tests, his doctor diagnosed the cause as nervous tension, and referred him to a psychotherapist.

The sessions continued for some months. He came home one day and said he had something to tell me; something he had not told his psychotherapist. No doubt it would have been a useful piece of information for her. He had a series of therapists over the years but never opened up to any of them. He was very secretive with people he didn't know, including those who were supposed to be helping him, and then wondered why they couldn't.

I sensed Peter was about to tell me something extremely important, but what he had to say came as a shock. He had suddenly realised, he said, the reason for his tension. It was a result of guilt about the other women in his life, and the lying and deception. Now he wanted to confess.

That was when he told me that it had begun in Zurich. I had suspected nothing in Switzerland. When we came to England I began to have my doubts, but would at once tell myself it was only my imagination. By that time we had been married nearly seven years. Since life was much more free and liberated in London, it was easier for him to become involved with other women. As he became more blatant, I became more suspicious and even more convinced that my misgivings about his fidelity were based on fact. But I could not have known for certain, had he not told me, and even though I had had my suspicions I was totally unprepared for what he told me that day.

I listened as Peter went through his score, a mere half-dozen at that stage. The jealousy was sheer pain. He had offloaded his suffering and passed it on to me. It drove me mad, and that was when I began the shouting and screaming that became part and parcel of our marriage until the end. He wasn't confessing in order to begin again, faithful and true. He was confessing in order to rid himself of the uncomfortable guilt so that he might enjoy his next encounter the better for being untrammelled by complex emotions.

I learned after that to spot the clues. He always 'happened to bump into' these rather attractive girls, and he would try somehow to work them into our life. A model, a buyer. (She has an important job now. I still see her but she doesn't know that I know about her and Peter.) Later there was the girl we employed as manageress at the Bond Street shop.

I stopped counting, there were so many. Peter could fancy almost any interesting woman, just for a fuck. But not long term. He would have to be pretty smitten before it would last longer than to jump into bed a couple of times. He swore he never wanted to live with anyone else, be with anyone other than me. The rest were just for fun and excitement.

During these amours, our own love life was uninterrupted. I could not rely on any clues in that direction. There were other signs, just giving so-and-so a lift home, just dropping so-and-so off at her mother's or her friend's – and taking a long time about it. 'What took you so long?' I'd ask when my suspicions were aroused. Or, 'How come you don't want her husband to know you've seen her if it's so innocent?' And 'Why are we inviting her? I don't see why she has to come.' He always had an answer.

As Peter grew older, his need to screw around increased. It became an obsession. So long as the woman was presentable, he didn't resist. If he had to hunt, he preferred to hunt somebody special. He would go out and I would know he was seeing another woman. Sometimes he didn't even bother to deny it.

From time to time he would coerce me into what he called 'an agreement' that I would accept what he was doing, and not make a fuss. And I would hang on to my feelings as long as possible, and then the jealousy and anguish would well up and explode in a great, hysterical row that would make him angry, and achieve nothing except a passionate reconciliation at the end of the storm.

Peter was a person of extremes. In Israel he had been excessively moralistic. His puritan ideas probably made him feel that much worse about his lapses. I think he began to wonder what he had missed, by meeting me so young. He had to prove to himself that he could attract other women. Any man can attract one woman. What about the others out there?

Sex was a sport for him. He enjoyed it. In his view, somebody new was more exciting: like finding a new golf partner. You don't know how they're going to play; how they're going to react; what they're going to talk about. One or two of the women fell in love with him, and sometimes he wanted me to help shake them off: take his phone calls, or pretend he wasn't there. It was tawdry at times. He was by nature honest. He didn't lie and disapproved of those who did, and that made his infidelities so unbearable for me. He had to tell me the truth.

Sexually, Peter was superb, and it upset me that, however satisfying our love life, he still needed other women. We had something special. He always said that if I should leave him, he would take his own life. The happier he was with me, the more he wanted other women. When life was wonderful he lusted after every woman in sight for the sheer joy of it. When he was miserable, his libido failed.

His affairs – who, when, why, how – came to dominate my life. However marvellous things were: business, lifestyle, Aliza, the perfect moments Peter and I had, there was always the nagging ache that wouldn't go away. I couldn't blot it out. But several years after that first confession I retaliated.

As the rows became increasingly bitter, when the marriage hit the squalls, I used to say: 'If you can do it, so can I.' Peter always replied: 'It's different for a man.' But after one particularly acrimonious dispute he said: 'From now on I'll do what I want, and you can feel free to do the same.'

But you don't just jump into bed with another man because your husband says you may. More than a year passed.

His name was John, and we met through friends. He was very attractive, and lingered over my hand when we parted; the flirtation gave me a pleasant buzz.

He and his girlfriend Sally came to dinner, although they were on the verge of separating. When I went into the kitchen to make coffee John followed and tried to kiss me. It was rather flattering, especially as Peter was flirting outrageously with Sally in the dining-room.

Next day John phoned and we arranged to meet. I told him how angry Peter had been. 'How can he object, when he makes no secret of the fact that he's seeing other women?' John said.

Apathetically I drifted into an affair with John, meeting him at his flat. Initially I was nervous about going to bed with him and, once I had overcome that, there was the guilt to deal with. Peter guessed, and was very upset.

Peter and I went on holiday and while we were away he made me promise not to see John again. 'The same applies to you, Peter,' I said. 'I'm not the one who wants to run around, but I'm not sitting alone at home waiting. Those days are over.' He promised, but nothing changed. I picked up the threads of my unexciting affair with John, who already bored me to tears. When we didn't make love there wasn't anything to talk about. And in the end I didn't want to see him anyway.

John and Sally parted and he then married someone else. Peter forgave John now that he did not represent a threat and we remained on friendly terms, two couples meeting occasionally. John's new wife never knew that we had once been more than friends.

I had boyfriends I thought I was in love with before I met Peter, but that's the nature of youth. He was intensely jealous of the men, boys really, who had been part of my life before I knew him. Yet I've never fallen in love with anyone else, only Peter.

7

The seventies were our golden years, no doubt about it. Aliza was growing into a lovely, intelligent girl. Our business was booming and we had more than enough money to do anything we had ever dreamed.

The rich and the royal, the glitzy and the glamorous bought my garments. My designs appeared in television productions (*Bouquet of Barbed Wire*); on the stage: Petula Clark wore the most expensive nightdress ever for a dramatically short run of *The Sound of Music*; and even on film: a bevy of lovelies clad in nothing but Janet Reger romped with Terry Thomas in a totally improbable comedy called *Spanish Fly*. I knew I had become a household word when a character in a Tom Stoppard play said: 'Don't get your Janet Regers in a twist.'

In Beauchamp Place, where it sometimes seems that every other face is famous, the whole street turned out the day Britt Ekland came to the shop – just to see her 'chauffeur'. Rod Stewart and his sleek yellow Lamborghini parked outside created more of a stir than any royal customers have ever done. Royalty, to this day, wander in to only the slightest ripple.

We worked hard, and played hard. In between the spectacular holidays, there were visits abroad to trade fairs and weekends away to relax. Peter was the ideal travelling companion. But increasing success did not make our day-to-day life any easier or alleviate his moodiness and bad temper. In the early days he had been mostly reasonable and occasionally irritable. Later this was reversed, and the fights became more devastating. Although we always made it up again, each row became increasingly exhausting.

As the company and the payroll grew, the staff divided: design and production on one side, sales and finance on the other. Each waged war on the other, fuelled by jealousies and internal politics. For the first time in our lives, Peter and I began to quarrel over business. It was almost a joke, but I could see that office friction was eroding the fantastic working relationship that had been the cornerstone of our business. Others resented the closeness between Peter and me, resented my personal publicity; even the fact that Aliza was mentioned in articles about me caused certain lips to curl.

As fast as wedges were driven between us, Peter and I would draw close again. Even in the hateful times, we could communicate: especially in business meetings, where we knew what the other was thinking without having to go outside to confer in private. We said many terrible things to each other at that time, and I often threatened to leave him. In twenty-seven years, he never considered it an option. Once when I yelled at him to go, he packed a case, made a dramatic farewell to Aliza and his fish, and walked towards the door. Something attracted his attention on the television. He stopped, perched on the arm of a chair, and then slid into the chair and settled comfortably. When he took his shoes off, I realised he was staying after all. I could only laugh.

The business kept us together, acting as an intermediary in our reconciliations. Something would happen at work, and we would forget our private quarrel and get on with the job in hand. When the marriage was good, Peter was stimulating, interesting, loving and tender, kind and generous. I stayed with him because I loved him.

When I saw one of his black clouds approaching, I would some-times suggest he went into therapy again. Invariably a depression coincided with a business worry and, apart from not wanting to waste money on a psychiatrist, he'd say: 'There's nothing wrong with me that a hundred thousand pounds won't put right.'

Summer was a bad time for Peter. At the beginning of each year we were buoyant after the Christmas trade. By March spring had arrived in the shops, and I was busy with orders. In June I would begin the autumn production and the shop would become quiet for the long dry season when very little happened. Wholesale customers had paid for their spring orders; there were no more cheques to look forward to. From June until September Peter

74

would sit adding up figures on scraps of paper, estimating how long it would be before we were broke. A few months earlier, those same figures would have convinced him, and us, that he was about to become a millionaire. In millionaire mood he became overly extravagant, forgetting the bills that were due. His black moods were deadly, but once they had passed he could get on with the next project.

Since the advent of Stella, who took over the selling, Peter had been somewhat under-employed and bored. Boredom was tackled by thinking up great new concepts. (As a joke Stella had book matches printed with 'Peter Reger, a Great New Concept' on the cover.) New concepts or projects meant investment, sometimes our profits, sometimes loans, usually a mixture of both. He would leap in with great enthusiasm – then the bills would start to arrive and he would go into reverse. Paintings were taken from the walls and sold, and there would be no meals in restaurants or new clothes. Once during an economy campaign (we were practically millionaires at the time) I needed to replace a broken flan dish and spotted one reduced to fifty pence in the sale window of Jackson's, Piccadilly. He adamantly refused to let me buy it. We stood on the pavement arguing. He won. (Later I went back and bought it.)

Peter was never mean, just illogical. He was always first to put his hand in his pocket and pick up the bill in a restaurant. In the early Southwick Street days, when he noticed one of the girls collecting money before she went out for the sandwiches, he decreed that in future the company would pay for the staff's sandwich lunch. He gave cash bonuses and underwear to staff at Christmas. When we bought new curtains he would never sell the old ones; they were given to anyone who wanted them. His philosophy was: 'If we're doing well, the money should be spread around.' He drove a hard bargain in business, but spent freely and tipped generously – unless it happened to be one of his black moods when he was about to go broke.

New staff were nervous of him because he shouted so much, but the established staff were used to his ways. They knew he was all bark and no bite. He frequently threatened to sack staff but never did so (that was left to me): not even the typist who posted out the file copies with the letters. When we shopped for clothes

Peter always pushed me into buying the most expensive dress. At the age of seven, Aliza wore Pierre Cardin.

Spending money was one of his greatest pleasures. Household linen was a passion with him, and he could get as much fun out of choosing pots and pans as a new car when he was in the mood. Like most rich youngish men he indulged himself with cars. He had a grey Rolls-Royce *and* a purple Bentley but went back to the Daimler, his favourite. It was always his ambition to have a sports car but it was never practical. The ring I wear all the time was a typical Peter purchase. A new jeweller had just opened in Bond Street near the shop. We were looking in the window one day and I said how nice the ring was, whereupon Peter walked in and bought it.

Saks, Fifth Avenue had been taking small quantities from us for several years. The buyer, Mrs Wasserman, didn't visit Europe but worked through a proxy buyer, and this lady tried for years to persuade Peter that we should visit New York to sell our collection in person.

Neither of us was attracted to America, which we imagined to be an overpriced cultural desert, and believed New York was populated by rich ladies in Crimplene who ate too much. It was hardly our idea of a pleasure trip; nor did we wish to risk money with no guarantee of an order. But eventually we were convinced by the American buyer and I was delegated by Peter to visit Mrs Wasserman. Peter hated to travel alone; I loved it as I always expect to find adventure around the next foreign corner. I still feel that, even when visiting a provincial town in England for the first time.

October 1976 was my first experience of America. The yellow cabs at Kennedy airport were more decrepit than I could have imagined, and I felt at once that I had stepped into a scene from a movie. Driving into the city along the highway, recognising familiar names, crossing the river and coming face to face with Manhattan, I found everything to be dirtier, older and more fabulous than I had ever visualised; and by the time I reached the Plaza Hotel I wished Peter could be here, too, in this heart-stopping place.

My film star sensation continued: the bustling lobby, the Palm

76

Court coffee lounge where an orchestra played, my suite as big as a ballroom. Exhilarated, I unpacked and set off to walk the streets. There was not a shred of Crimplene to be seen, but instead elegant clothes, sharp accessories, and everyone looking bandbox smart. My eyes ached from the dazzle of the shop windows. When I stopped for coffee it was freshly made. The waiter wished me a nice day. I telephoned my sister Gloria from my bedroom. I'd left her number at home and anticipated complicated investigations to find it. 'Somewhere near Kingston, Ontario,' I told the hotel switchboard operator, and within seconds Gloria was on the line. By the time I fell into the triple-sized bed, having dined with some distant relatives who drove in from Long Island, I was aglow with pleasure.

At three in the morning the pleasure had turned to panic. I had an appointment at 10 a.m. with one of the most prestigious and influential fashion buyers in America, and I had never sold a thing in my life before. What on earth gave me the idea I knew the first thing about business in this tough business town? Unless I sold at least five thousand pounds' worth of lingerie, I couldn't even cover the cost of the trip. And, apart from that, if I failed there would be no return trip to America, and I knew I wanted to come back. I lay awake the rest of the night torturing myself with anxiety, trying to read, tidying my samples case and rereading my price list.

My first-ever breakfast on American soil was wasted. I drank so much coffee I felt nauseous by the time I reached Saks; then I sat in a café nearby and drank more coffee until the store opened.

Mrs Wasserman, seventyish, was plump and jolly, warm and enthusiastic, and told me at once how much she loved my things, and had loved them from the beginning despite their being a little 'homemade' (this accompanied by a cheeky grin). She said how pleased she was to have noted lately certain improvements in the manufacture, and now that I had come to New York she could place a proper order. She introduced me to the store's president. We lunched in style and, having walked into the store a trembling jelly, I left feeling like a star! And I had taken a huge order. After that we couldn't go wrong.

When Peter and I returned to America the following May it was with a group of British designers, surrounded by all the razzmatazz the Americans love and enter into with such endearing delight. The climax of the trip was a glittering fashion show at Bullocks Wilshire, the Los Angeles store, where I finally understood the meaning of the expression 'to be fêted by'. The only thing Americans love more than success is celebrity. Flaunt your celebrity status, show you have the energy to stay the pace and they'll interview you for every newspaper in town, invite you on to every chat show and give countless lunches, cocktails, dinners and breakfasts in your honour. Anyone who's important enough to appear on *Good Morning America* is just about as VIP as you can get . . . which I did, and I was.

I caught up, after all those years, with my old flat-mate Marlene, working in the film industry in Los Angeles. We giggled like teenagers about those days in Holland Road, and said weren't we lucky we had done so incredibly well for ourselves.

I produced a new collection of hand-painted garments for the launch of the Brook Street shop and threw a party for the press, at which their applause confirmed that once again we had backed a winner. We now had two busy retail outlets as well as the mail-order catalogue, and our high profile had increased interest in the wholesale market. Wirksworth was stretched. We took on new girls and no sooner had we trained them than we were ready to employ a new batch of unskilled workers. My determination to introduce new and different garments – and thus beat the copyists – meant that the trained machinists continually needed to learn new techniques. By a stroke of luck we found an excellent sewing teacher who had been training girls in a high-quality knitwear factory. She joined us and set up a small training section, from which moment standards at Wirksworth improved, and we avoided the costly repairs and remakes.

Around this time, Brenda's illness returned. It accounted for her dragging herself into work late and taking days off. When asked how she was, she said she didn't want to talk about it, and we respected her request that we should say nothing about her poor health. She began attending hospital as an outpatient, and to help, we issued an open invitation for her to stay with us on the nights preceding morning appointments to save her the journey from rural Kent. When the hospital appointments became more frequent, and she expressed the wish for a place of her own in town, we rented a flat for her exclusive use. We still did not know the nature of her illness, or the treatment, but she told us she was undergoing tests for an accurate diagnosis.

Peter still kept track of the accounts with notes in his Financial Times Diary and a Kalamazoo cheque book. I am blessed with a good memory and always knew what stock we had and the state of production. We scribbled notes regarding cashflow forecasts and new projects along the margins of *The Times* or on scraps of paper, and formulated expansion plans while I cooked dinner or, late at night, in bed. Thus we had built up a turnover of nearly £1 million a year. Erratic though our business systems may have seemed, they did work. Until the day we decided to get organised.

By 1977 not only were the factory, and the Beauchamp Place and Brook Street shops bursting at the seams, but we desperately needed more office staff to handle the proliferating workload and a book-keeper to control the paperwork created by ever-increasing sales worldwide. Peter set out to find office space. He found a suite above an empty shop at No. 12 New Bond Street, just opposite Asprey's. When he learned that the shop too was about to go on the market he couldn't contain his excitement. I was dragged from Brook Street and taken to view at once, but Peter had already convinced himself we must take both.

For the first time we had a project that needed more money to finance than we could provide on sales projection and short-term overdraft facilities. But we were apparently riding the crest of a wave; we couldn't go wrong. We were blind to both the enormity of the commitment, and the impossibility of making such a commitment with short-term finance. We took little account of the fact that more sales involve more production and the ever-increasing costs of servicing more production. Instead, we rushed in. We bought No. 12 New Bond Street in the autumn of 1977 and, after gutting and refurbishing the premises to the very apogee of luxury and chic, the new shop opened in February 1978.

I wore a St Laurent satin skirt and blouse for the opening party which surpassed all our previous parties for lavishness and crush. The entire fashion press and most people in the London fashion business, as well as friends, relatives and rent-a-crowd drank to our success until the early hours.

For the first time I had a private office. Peter had found a magnificent studio at No. 103 New Bond Street: a bright sunny top floor with plenty of floor space, two offices and roof terrace. We moved in my cutting tables and machines and I took on extra machinists to work on samples and couture orders.

Julia was now responsible for the extra staff we had to employ, and could no longer perform all the myriad duties she had assumed over the ten years of working so closely with me. I had never had a secretary; Julia and I thought as one. Suddenly all the staff seemed new: new typists, new people answering the telephone, new girls sewing, a new pattern cutter for underwear. I was drowning in paperwork, and Wirksworth was in such chaos that I needed to spend at least two days a week there.

We employed a new factory manager, of whom I had great hopes. He created a bonus scheme, and then disappeared without trace while he planned the next move in his strategy. His greatest fear was running out of components, and he addressed this problem by ordering in vast quantities. As deliveries arrived, it was clear we had enough bias binding, hooks and buttons to last ten years – the complete opposite to my policy of never having money tied up in materials. Fortunately Joy, my wages clerk and a treasure (later to become buyer), spotted the problem and was able to halt the mighty flow, or some of it. I still have stocks of bone casing surplus from that time; it's quite obsolete, we never use it.

The Bond Street shop soon proved to be a remarkable money-spinner, but before we felt the benefit of this Peter had begun to work himself into a state of abject depression and anxiety over the ever-increasing costs. The new manager had been an expensive mistake; I had a new secretary and new sewing staff had been added to the payroll.

By this time Brenda was in charge of hiring and firing office and shop staff, and for the first time Peter had occasion to criticise. We had always chosen girls who looked good and dressed well, and this had nothing to do with money. A girl who has a feeling for clothes can make the most of herself on tuppence-ha'penny. Julia spent little and always looked stunning. Now it seemed that Peter was for ever asking why we had such unattractive girls in the shop. Even our bank manager said: 'You need girls who look more like Bond Street.' So Peter took over and employed a high-salaried girl to manage the shops. He also took on Minoosh, who remained with me until 1989 when she left to have a baby.

Our friendly bank manager agreed to finance a second factory in Wirksworth, and we took over premises in West End, the centre of the tiny town, just yards from St Mary's Gate and built on the hillside with wonderful views over open countryside. As I organised the relocation of part of the factory into the new premises and installed additional machines, Peter at once had another new concept: relandscaping the gardens. Before long we had converted the top floors into a flat and talked of one day making that beautiful part of England our home.

On the advice of our bank manager, we employed a management consultancy to help reorganise the ever-growing buying, production and distribution problem. In other words, to tell us how to run our business.

Meanwhile, in Bond Street the Arabs were spending money. A few wealthy Americans and some Arabs had found us in Beauchamp Place, but Bond Street was their village. It was the custom for some families to send an agent who would request goods to be sent home or to their hotel for a private view. Others would stand in front of the racks of nightwear, pull out three or four garments, put these to one side, and say: 'I'll take the rest.' Payment was by wads of notes. After such a swoop, we would be left with empty rails and the problem of how to find more stock instantly.

8

Peter and I quarrelled about the manageress. I discovered that he had been taking her to bed. That evening we attended a farewell party for Julia at Brown's Hotel. She was leaving to get married. The row continued as we made our way home. Stella was spending the night in London with us. Peter went sullenly to bed and Stella and I ate dinner together. When we had finished our meal, Peter was asleep. I crept into bed without turning on the light so as not to disturb him.

I was woken in the early hours by the loud, laboured gasps of Peter's breathing. I tried to wake him, first gently and then, as he didn't respond, by pummelling him and forcing him awake. His face had turned grey.

I leaped out of bed, noticing as I switched on the bedside lamp the glass of water and his empty bottle of sleeping pills. I rushed downstairs and phoned the doctor's emergency number. The girl on his answering service told me she would try to reach the doctor. Meanwhile: 'Dial 999 at once. Right now, don't wait.'

Stella had come downstairs by this time, realised what was happening and gone to Peter, trying to revive him. It seemed for ever before the ambulance came. Stella was calm. 'I presume you'll want to go with him in the ambulance,' she said. 'So I suggest you put on some clothes.' I looked down. I was naked. I opened a cupboard and grabbed a most unsuitable light cotton dress. I remember I froze all day.

Peter was taken to St Stephen's Hospital and Stella and I waited while his stomach was pumped. The doctor came back. 'He's going to be all right. Obviously he's still dazed and a bit vague, but he'll live.' Stella went back to the office to maintain an appearance of normal business procedure. It wouldn't look good for business if word got out that Peter had attempted suicide.

I sat with him all that day, with Peter berating me for 'interfering'. The social worker looked in. 'It's strange,' she said. 'Your husband is the one who has attempted to take his own life; he is angry, and you are the one who is weeping.'

When Stella returned, she brought a letter Peter had written the previous day, addressed to me and left in the office for me to find, presumably after his death, although it didn't actually say that he intended suicide or that this was goodbye. It was a rambling complaint, blaming me for not allowing him to lead a free life and enjoy himself in his own way. His depression was all my fault.

I was at a loss to know what to do. The doctors advised that he should certainly remain where he was for a few days, to regain his strength and to consult with the psychiatrist, because he was going to need long-term psychiatric treatment. He refused to agree to this and demanded I bring in his clothes. The next day he discharged himself from hospital.

Gradually he calmed down and became more coherent, and we were able to talk things over. His first requirement, he said, was to go away for a long holiday, 'to think', and he intended to ask our friend Virginia Royston in Mustique, where we holidayed every winter, if he might stay with her for a month or two. Meanwhile he grudgingly consented to consult the hospital psychiatrist as an outpatient and both the psychiatrist and Peter's doctor advised against the holiday plan. To sit alone on an island would do him no good in his present state of mind. A rest was certainly a good idea, but in a place where he could also receive psychiatric help and the therapy of country walks and gardening. It would be too expensive, he said, and would not be persuaded otherwise.

He began to confide his business and money worries, first to the psychiatrist and then to me. The steps we took to address these problems were sadly to prove disastrous, pitching us on the slippery slope that would eventually lead to liquidation.

This was the time of the oil crisis and strikes. American customers had been wiped out for us overnight by the high pound. Although our own shops were still doing as well as ever, our account customers (Beaty's group, Jolly's of Bath, Rackhams, Kendal Milne, Scofields) were cutting orders drastically or in some cases dropping out completely. As Peter kept saying, we were committed to maintaining turnover; we had a large staff to keep busy, but sales were falling.

Another problem was that for years we had had the market to ourselves. Only Janet Reger made the Janet Reger class of underwear: expensive silks, which were beautifully made, hand finished, and decorated with lace and appliqué. They were luxury items, and the look was exclusively ours. But we were being copied. Manufacturers were coming into the market with Janet Reger-inspired garments, which were mass produced cheaply using inexpensive fabrics, entirely machine-made and selling at a fraction of the price. We asked ourselves why we couldn't join the competition. Why not produce our own budget collection, copy our own underwear inexpensively, and sell it ourselves?

We took a nightdress that was selling very well, made it in a cheaper silk material, trimmed it with inexpensive lace and two rows of ribbons instead of four as in the original. It involved less work time but still had the same look, the same cut and was very pretty. We placed an advertisement in a daily paper. Beryl Hartland did the sketch. We advertised it as a design by Bottom Drawer, the name we had registered years before when we began retailing.

The response was good. We covered the cost of the advertisement and made a reasonable profit. We tried again, with another design. Also good. And again. We sat down to analyse the results. These were not bad, but we knew damn well if we had written Janet Reger on the ad we would have done a great deal better. We made the decision to start advertising the garments as being by Janet Reger but on a scale worthy of the Janet Reger name. Simultaneously we became involved with Scotcade, an aspiring mail-order company which was pioneering high-class direct sales through advertisements in the quality Sunday papers.

We ran the risk of offending our wholesale customers, who saw us selling a cheaper garment not offered to them. To them our reply would be: order in the same quantities, and the garment is available wholesale. What we strived to do was to compensate for our falling order book, and keep the existing workforce at the factory in full employment and the cashflow in accordance with forecast.

Scotcade ran a spring offer, and planned to follow this in the autumn. The results were good. We were satisfied, but Scotcade were not. If they put a clock or a set of saucepans on the page, they ensured a better response. A Janet Reger nightgown looked prettier than a set of saucepans, but they were in mail order, not fashion.

We did our sums. We knew what they had bought from us, what the margin had been between the wholesale and the retail price, and figured we would do well to concentrate on this lucrative market. Calculating a break-even figure of £40,000 per advertisement placed in an important Sunday supplement (photography, artwork, advertising space) we could expect to take £55,000. We decided to go it alone.

The first day the advertisement appeared in *The Sunday Times* we held our breath. It always amazed me that the response to a Sunday paper advertisement could arrive on Monday, but it did because people with advance access to the publication write in before the paper or magazine has officially hit the news-stand. The Monday response is a barometer of things to come.

Peter had been taken ill and was in hospital. He made me promise to telephone him first thing on Monday as soon as the post came in. When I arrived at Bond Street and ran upstairs to the office, the girls were virtually knee-deep in envelopes, coupons and cheques. They hadn't finished counting, but the response was in thousands. I asked if Peter had been told. No, said one of the secretaries, Brenda thought we should keep him in suspense a bit longer. I bounded up the stairs to Brenda's office and berated her. How would she feel if she were paying all these costs and taking the risks? The response to the advertisement would be a great weight off Peter's mind. I pictured him waiting anxiously in his hospital bed and was furious. But she loved playing power games.

By the second day we had received twenty thousand orders, and altogether took £100,000 on that first advertisement. We thought we had found the solution to our problems. It was big money and provides instant cash: it is banked before the garments are delivered. Post came in to the upstairs room at Bond Street. The girl in charge, who had been on the brink of redundancy before the mail-order operation began, worked out her own system of coding and stamping each order as it arrived and entered it in a book. Then three times a week batches of coupons were sent to the factory where goods were packed and dispatched. Stock control was a series of boards, written in colour, giving an instant picture of availability and, more importantly, what was likely to be the best seller. We kept supply level-pegging with demand. The whole operation ran like clockwork and we provided a very efficient service for our customers. We had no computer and still don't.

We took on more staff. At the time of Peter's attempted suicide we had been laying off machinists. Within weeks we were taking on more, increasing our payroll during the two years of mail-order success from seventy-five factory workers to one hundred and twenty-five: cutters, machinists, hand finishers, packaging and office personnel.

Costs – wages, postage and advertising – rose steeply over that period; nevertheless, we were making money although nothing quite matched the phenomenal success of the first offer. Perhaps people thought it was now or never, so that we mopped up the market of customers who thought it a once in a lifetime chance to buy Janet Reger.

In one year we had mail-order sales in excess of £300,000. We had discovered a new way to make money: a way that not only replaced what we were doing on the wholesale side but brought in the money fast (wholesale customers rarely pay within thirty days), involved no chasing cash and was, at that point, more lucrative than any other sales method. We had found a way of beating the slump and keeping the business going; indeed, we were forging ahead. It was harder work, because of the volume of paperwork, production supervision, photography. But it was exciting too. Once more we were on the crest of a wave.

By now our catalogue bore the Janet Reger name; sketches were out, expensive photographs were in. I suspect that just as there are bedrooms where Janet Reger bras and knickers are folded away in tissue paper and lavender for posterity or special occasions, so there are coffee tables where the first Janet Reger catalogue featuring languid girls in elegant silk will still be found. There was even a glossy hardback book about us, *Chastity in Focus*. It sold out. I guard my one and only copy carefully. So much was happening . . . too much. It was the beginning of the end; the business was dying.

*

One evening Peter telephoned me in Wirksworth. 'It's terrible news, I'm afraid. Poor Brenda has leukaemia. There is no hope. She's asked us to say nothing to anyone else. She wants us to keep it secret for as long as possible.'

I felt dreadful. Peter was devastated. I sat down at my desk, shattered by what I had just heard. As soon as I could collect myself, I called her.

'Brenda,' I said, 'this is awful. I don't know what to say . . .'

She explained that the leukaemia was deep rooted, that there had been a remission but now it was active. She would be undergoing treatment for a long time, and was dreading it. Please would I not say anything to a soul. She must face this alone; it would be our secret.

I returned to London, and we met. She spelt out the hard facts. Without treatment, she had six months to live. Even with treatment, they could offer no more than eighteen months. We were both crying in the restaurant.

Long after I left her, I lay awake, worrying. Yet one small remark jarred. In the midst of tears, in the course of conversation, Brenda had said: 'I don't suppose I'll live to see forty, now.' But she *had* seen forty. She was over forty, as I was.

A few days later Aliza phoned me in Wirksworth, sobbing. She had just heard the news. Who told her? Brenda did. Brenda bravely attending hospital every day for injections, earning the admiration of all for her determination to battle on. We could only whisper about her illness because she had begged each and every one of us to respect her desire for secrecy, but by then it was an open secret. Contacts who knew us only by telephone would enquire: 'And how is Brenda?' Our Hong Kong customer phoned through to say she had located a clinic in China where leukaemia was treated, with excellent results. Should he make arrangements?

Brenda insisted that she wanted to continue working as long as possible; she would just go back to the company flat and lie down when she felt ill. Would Peter understand if she sometimes left early? Of course Peter understood, and after that she left early every day for her injections.

Despite her illness, Brenda continued to wield power in the office. All the post was seen first by her, and she inserted herself into every aspect of the business, to the extent that she took over much of Peter's role. Only Sheila's press and publicity domain remained inviolate.

Brenda happened to meet a man who had connections with a mail-order company which serviced some of the *News of the World*'s reader's offers. Excitedly she reported back. It was a good introduction but not earth-shattering. We were already doing mail order, and could easily have approached the *News of the World* on our own account. Peter told her to put Sheila in touch with the contact.

Brenda protested. 'This one is mine,' she said.

Now Sheila went into battle. 'I don't interfere with your work. Please leave the newspapers to me. If you want to come along to the meeting, that's fine, but I'm in charge.' Peter agreed, and Brenda had to comply. Sheila was upset by Brenda's subsequent handling of the meeting, and said that if Brenda was to remain, then she was leaving. Brenda stayed and Sheila bowed out.

When an offer is placed in the editorial section of a newspaper, as opposed to running an advertisement, it carries with it valuable inbuilt editorial authority. But the publication makes no financial commitment. The manufacturer must service the offer. He doesn't make thousands of garments on the off-chance, but at the same time sufficient stock must be carried to satisfy reader demand. If delivery is delayed while the manufacturer scurries around getting it together, the result is disgruntled readers and an angry editor. The skill lies in balancing all the options: make a small amount to hold ready and waiting, have cloth under the table to make more as soon as the initial response can be gauged, and ideally choose a fabric that is easily available should the garment prove a runaway success. We knew that outrageous items never sell in quantity in a reader's offer, so avoid anything too extreme.

I provided Brenda with appropriate garments in suitable colours. She had one foot out of the door when she turned back and asked: 'Can I show them the red striped sample?'

'No, Brenda. I need a commitment on the red stripe because we won't be able to buy the fabric again.' If I bought a hundred metres and it wasn't enough, I'd be in trouble. If I bought more to put under the table and we didn't use it, I'd be stuck with it and never able to use it again. It was far too distinctive.

Pale pink, peach, blue . . . people always expect these colours in an underwear collection. You can use the same fabric in a variety of styles so the fabric is never wasted. But red stripes are another matter.

'But I don't want to give them the red stripe as a reader's offer. I just want to show it to the fashion editor as an idea for a separate feature,' she persisted.

'Brenda, no. That's for Sheila to do another time. You just stick to the *offer*.' I couldn't have been more precise.

Ignoring my instructions, she took the red stripe basque and frilly petticoat from the sample collection. Of course the *News of the World*'s fashion team loved it. It made a great colour spread. And that was the garment they decided to run in consultation with Brenda.

We had in stock fifty metres of red and white striped Swiss cotton and the manufacturing company had none. I began a frantic search, culminating in Frankfurt at the Interstoft cloth fair, seeking out any spinners who might be able to match it. It wasn't *just* a red and white stripe. It was a particular red, a particular white and a particular stripe: two little stripes, a space, then two little stripes. There was no way you could get away with any old stripes, as the offer was already photographed in colour.

Frantic with anxiety – we couldn't afford to lose face with the *News of the World* – and after scouring the length and breadth of Interstoft, I finally found what I was looking for. I had to buy huge stocks, because it was an import and I couldn't risk not being able to get more once the offer was up and running.

Despite being beautifully presented in the *News of the World*'s colour supplement, the offer didn't sell. I still have red striped material to this day. This was Brenda's first major mistake and it cost the company serious money.

Our catalogue had always been produced on a very tight budget. It could have been more beautifully done, but not without being more expensive. Julia and I did it between us, using photographers and models prepared to work to our budget. The catalogue operation made a profit, until Brenda turned her attention to catalogues. First she criticised; then she directed the items to be included; then she took over the photography. Her initial project was excellent: a combination of an inexpensive but talented photographer and experienced, highly paid models and, most importantly, she kept out of the way.

Next time, having redesignated herself 'catalogue producer', she took detailed charge at every stage. It was a disaster, referred to ever after as our Hearts and Flowers catalogue for its elaborate decoration, and it marked the beginning of the end for all our catalogues.

Why did we put up with it? With hindsight, it is clear that this flaw in management should have been addressed smartly, brutally if necessary. I was aware. I was irritated. Yet I was concentrating on design and production at the time. Given the warning signs, we should have kept a tighter rein, but Brenda always managed to convince Peter, who was supposedly in charge of the office, that her way was right. It was not until the evidence was too alarming to ignore that he finally stepped in and took over the catalogue publication himself. Thus Aliza came to learn about fashion photography, by assisting Peter on the sessions, attending to props and other details, and developing an eye for a picture.

9

That summer a particular Arab family spent over fifty thousand pounds with us in the shop. Aliza, who was dealing with them, developed a friendship with one of the daughters, occasionally spending the day at the household's huge estate in Buckinghamshire, partly because such a good customer warranted a great deal of attention; more because the two girls were about the same age, got on well together, and the young *sheikha* was desperately bored and allowed out only in the company of her brother. Her days confined to the house seemed endless, a broken fingernail on one of Aliza's visits creating a welcome drama. Aliza knew that her friend Lyndsey had a beautician friend, Pamela, and after a few phone calls, Pamela arrived to do the young Arab *sheikha*'s manicure. Both were grateful for the introduction.

We met Pamela briefly when we put in an appearance at Aliza's farewell party on the eve of her departure to run our Munich shop. I noticed her, and she noticed Peter. A lot of eyelash-fluttering and teasing went on. Peter was always interested in women, and always responded to their charms. She was making up to him, and I thought it unseemly behaviour to chat up your friend's father in his house! It never dawned on me that he would take her up on what she was fairly blatantly offering. She was too smart, too quick with her comments – on past form he was more attracted to quieter, softer women.

The following week Peter had business to attend to in Munich, but cried off because he had so much to do in London. He asked me to go in his place, and I did, spending the week in Munich helping Aliza settle into the shop and flat. Pamela phoned Aliza every evening, which Aliza, feeling somewhat cut off from her friends, found touching. She did wonder at the expense involved. Don't give it a thought, said Pamela; she had a rich boyfriend who didn't mind her using his telephone. As it turned out, she was in my flat using my telephone!

Arriving at the very last minute for the opening party, Peter announced he must leave first thing the following morning. I recognised at once the signs that Peter was becoming preoccupied with somebody else: always in a hurry, no time to talk, leaving me to attend to aspects of the business he usually regarded as his exclusive territory. I was also aware that I had been removed from the scene most effectively.

We had taken a house in Mustique for Christmas, and Aliza's friend Lyndsey had been invited. She was dithering about whether to join us or her brother in South Africa and, unknown to me, Peter intervened, suggesting to Aliza that she invite someone else instead. Perhaps 'that very pleasant girl who came to your farewell party'.

Had I heard him, it would have rung warning bells. Peter was the last person to invite an outsider on a family holiday. He was painfully possessive of Aliza and had ruined numerous holidays by sulking over time she spent with friends. So the first hint came when Aliza told me she had decided to invite Pamela as our guest.

The snow started early that December in Derbyshire. I had been staying there all week, and when the Friday weather forecast was bad I was nervous about driving home. I phoned Peter. He was a brilliantly competent driver, used to driving in snow and ice, on mountains; he drove anywhere, any time, for hours on end and never got tired. I fully expected him to say he would drive up and we would spend the weekend together. I was surprised that he didn't. Apart from the fact that we had been getting on badly and a quiet weekend together was what we needed, Peter hated being alone. Instead, his advice was to stay put and not attempt to drive in those conditions.

A week later, on the eve of our departure for Mustique, came another warning signal, and this time I picked it up, considered it and decided to ignore it. I was packing and mentioned to Peter that I needed some cosmetic and toiletry items. There was no time to shop now, but if I couldn't buy them at the airport, I'd telephone Aliza in Munich and ask her to bring them when she joined us on Christmas Day.

Peter suggested I phone Pamela and ask her to bring them. She was after all a beautician, and would know exactly what I wanted. I pointed out I could hardly phone a mere acquaintance to ask a favour at this late hour – it was nearly midnight.

Nonsense, he said. These young girls always stayed up late. Pamela wouldn't mind at all. He picked up the telephone and dialled her number. And I felt a sharp tingle of apprehension. How did he know her number by heart? He'd only spoken to her once or twice. I didn't challenge him. It was an easy number; he had an excellent memory. I put it out of my mind.

The few days Peter and I had to ourselves before the rest of the party arrived were the best we had had for months. We weren't quarrelling; there was no stress or tension. We swam, walked, ate by candlelight under the stars. The arrival of Julia's husband John from New York, the first of the rest of the crowd, did nothing to impair our honeymoon togetherness. He and Peter got on well, and Julia and I had a sisterly closeness. Her marriage was going through a bad patch. She had parted from John and returned to London, and the holiday in Mustique was intended as a trial reunion.

Christmas Day came and Aliza telephoned from St Vincent. Peter took the call. Her flight was late. She and Pamela had missed the connection (at the best of times you have about three seconds to do this), and even with private charter it was now too late to fly to Mustique, where there are no facilities after dark.

I wasn't worried about Aliza. We had been visiting Mustique since she was fourteen years old, and she knew her way around the islands. It was at that time such a small, safe community. She and Pamela would spend the night in the hotel on St Vincent and take the first flight out in the morning.

Peter's disappointment at the delay was so evident that John commented on it. Peter must be unusually attached to his daughter, he said, that a few hours' separation could matter so much. But Peter's heightened excitement and restlessness made me uneasy.

'Let me speak to Pamela,' he said, and Pamela came on the line complaining about the tiring flight and now this frustrating delay. He reassured her. 'When you arrive tomorrow, it will all be worthwhile. You'll see.'

I had never heard him express such warmth towards one of Aliza's friends. I felt excluded from something. Peter came off the line and telephoned Air Mustique at once to charter a plane to collect the girls at seven the following morning. He was up with the sun, saying he might as well fly over to St Vincent, meet them and bring them back.

My idyll was over when I watched Peter and Pamela together. There were too many exchanged looks, and I realised that they knew each other better than the initial brief contact at Aliza's farewell party could have allowed. There was a familiarity which I recognised instantly.

We ate breakfast and drove to the beach in the Moke. Pamela fluttered and sparkled far too much to ignore as she continually made contact with Peter, and he with her. 'Come on, Pamela, I'll show you our favourite cove . . .' and off they went.

All that day I watched and felt sick with apprehension and humiliation. When she got up from sunbathing and went in to swim, he followed soon afterwards. When he took a stroll, she followed. They didn't take their eyes off each other, and I couldn't take my eyes off them. I could read the signs. They wanted to be alone together, but I wasn't having it. I certainly wasn't going to make it easy for them. I made it clear that I was around too, and that I was not going to disappear into the background.

Possibly Pamela picked up my signals, for on that first day she showered attentions on the handsome, charming John (to Peter's obvious chagrin). Aliza had told Pamela that John was having marital problems. Pamela oozed warmth and sympathy and insisted on tending the wound when he slipped and cut his ear on a rock. John was not responsive. He could deal with his injury himself – he was, after all, a doctor – and said to me later: 'Women like Pamela terrify me.'

That evening we went for drinks at the Cotton House. 'Pamela, I must show you the pool,' said Peter, leading her away from the terrace. When we were alone later, I tackled him. Why should he keep taking Pamela off to show her things? She was Aliza's friend.

He was angry. I was doing one of my jealous acts again!

'I never do a jealous act unless I have very good cause,' I replied. 'But I do know the signs when I see them after all these years.'

Aliza was embarrassed by Pamela's blatant flirting with John, but it was a day or so before she picked up on the liaison between her friend and her father. That seemed too bizarre to consider, although she had realised from day one that her holiday 'friend' was someone she barely knew. Aliza was just twenty, Pamela nearer thirty; they were years and worlds apart.

Julia arrived, and after she had been on the island for a few hours, took me to one side. 'What's that supposed to be?'

She was referring to Pamela. 'I don't want to talk about her,' I replied.

'I'm not surprised,' said Julia, intercepting one of Pamela's meaningful glances but unaware that Peter was already in the thick of the affair.

On Mustique everyone travels in a Moke, usually overloaded with people hanging over the sides. Now, for the first time, Peter became concerned about the suspension. We were too many for one Moke, he decided, and began to manipulate the ferrying backwards and forwards so that he was left on his own with Pamela; or Pamela was not ready when we were leaving and he had to go back for her.

'You're having an affair with that girl, aren't you?' I demanded after one of his convoluted excursions in the Moke.

'No.' He was at his most incredulous. 'You're crazy to think that.'

'Peter, I know you very well, and I know you are.'

'No I'm not. I'm not.'

'I don't feel good with her here, I want her to go,' I said.

'Stop being so silly, I don't know how you got this into your head.'

After Pamela's arrival, Peter's loving attentions to me stopped. He contrived ludicrous excuses to quarrel. One evening I tried on a pure silk wrap I had made for myself in Wirksworth. It was black and white with a huge crimson flower on the front – the sort of outfit you could wear only to a party in Mustique!

'Do keep it on,' said Peter. 'It's beautiful.'

I was just about to begin cooking supper, and there was no way I intended my beautiful dress should make its début in the kitchen. I took it off and stepped into a robe.

He began shouting angrily that I was happy to 'dress up for somebody else' but not for him, deliberately winding himself into a rage. It would have been funny if he wasn't so serious. I couldn't chop and fry onions dressed like that; there wasn't even a dry-cleaning shop on the island. I tried to placate him. I'd wear it for dinner, I said. But it wasn't enough to fend off his fit of sulks, which persisted throughout the evening.

Pamela went to bed early with a headache. The rest of us went for after-dinner drinks with friends. No sooner had we settled down, glasses in our hands, than Peter announced he, too, had a headache and would be returning home. It was a transparent ploy. He was not cut out to be the great deceiver, was no good at lying or covering his tracks.

We did not stay long with our friends. When we returned, Peter would have heard the Moke coming up the track. He was asleep in our room, the door closed. Pamela was asleep in her room, the door closed. The house was wide, with the bedrooms opening off a central living-room. On the table in the living area, a lighted cigarette still burned in an ashtray on the table. In their haste to avoid detection, Peter had forgotten to stub it out.

One morning I came down to the pool and found Pamela and Peter there, lying close together. She was caressing his leg with her toes, rubbing her arched foot up and down, up and down. When she saw me, she continued. I don't know why I didn't push her in and hold her under.

She played games with us. Talking one day to Julia about the rich boyfriend she had in London, she listed the things he had bought her: ear-rings, dresses, this outfit and that. I lay there fuming. She wore a swimsuit with matching skirt in a very delicate fabric, appliquéd with flowers. I recognised the ensemble as being by Armonia, an exclusive Italian label. I had seen it in Harrods and wanted it, but reasoned that to risk wearing something so costly on a tarry beach was silly. Besides, we had spent a great deal of money that year opening two new shops and Peter had advised me 'to go a bit easy' when shopping. And she was flaunting it. Her married boyfriend had bought it for her, she boasted, and I knew to which married boyfriend she referred.

Every year in Mustique, between Christmas and New Year, Kai and Christina, our holiday friends for many years, threw a party. Kai was one of those men often described as living life to the full . . . an incorrigible womaniser and usually, from the moment he arrived on the island, a little drunk – unashamedly so, we *were* all on holiday! His excesses were part of his considerable charm. He was warm, amusing, hospitable, and everyone was always pleased to see him. Events were to show that he and Christina had reached an impasse in their marriage. They were on the brink of separating, but I was too wrapped up in my own problems to notice.

That year the party was particularly lavish. Kai chartered an old ferry boat, hired a steel band, and flew in special delicacies from Caracas and Martinique. The day offered everything. Sea and sun, clear blue skies; the band playing; waiters circulating with trays of champagne, rum punch and *pina coladas*, as guests boarded in a mood of frivolity and *bonhomie*, greeted by Kai. Four of us went aboard. I looked around for Peter and saw him and Pamela standing on the shore, deep in discussion. It became clear to anyone watching, and many were, that they were talking about whether or not to board the boat.

There had been an argument at breakfast. Peter had said he didn't think he wanted to go to Kai's party. He would be bored sitting on a boat all day. Don't be ridiculous, we chorused. Kai's parties were always fabulous. Everyone would be there. Mustique was like a village to the regulars, and even a stranger couldn't fail to be warmed by the fun and hospitality.

Obviously Peter and Pamela planned to have the day to themselves. Now, confronted by our combined disapproval, he'd lost his nerve and allowed himself to be persuaded to come along. Until they reached the jetty. I watched Aliza walk down the gangplank and speak to them. She was not enjoying the holiday and was uneasy about little things she had noticed. She had said nothing to me, although she had challenged Pamela over what she saw as Pamela's making a play for her father, which Pamela had categorically denied.

Whatever Aliza said, it had the desired effect and Peter and Pamela came aboard. Most people were on the main deck. Peter climbed up the stairs to the upper deck 'to sunbathe' and Pamela followed. John, Julia and Aliza all trotted upstairs and came down to say it was far too hot and sticky up there. They were telling me not to go. But I did. Pamela lay on her back. Peter lay at right angles, his head on her stomach, stroking her hand. There was no pretence; everybody on the boat – which was the same as saying everybody we knew on the island – could see what was happening.

Smiling and chatting, mixing and mingling, somehow I got through the day, my heart like lead. Then in the privacy of our bedroom we quarrelled bitterly. 'I know what you're doing, it's got to stop,' I screamed, fuelled by jealousy and hurt pride. By the next day I had calmed down and contrived to get some time alone with Peter on the beach.

'This holiday is absolute torture for me,' I told him. 'I hate it. You are making a fool of me. You are having an affair with that girl. I can see it, everyone can see it. I know you well enough to know exactly what is going on and I can't stand it.

'I've got two suggestions to make. Either I leave today or you tell her to go. Please stop lying to me and making a fool of me because it just makes it worse.'

He was quiet. Then he said, 'It's true. What do you want me to do?'

'Tell her to go.'

'All right.' I had a sneaking suspicion that by now he was getting a tiny bit bored with Pamela. 'What shall I say to her?'

'I don't give a fuck what you say to her. Tell her to go. You deal with it.'

'I'll get Aliza to tell her. She can say she wants her to leave.'

'Don't be ridiculous, Peter. Don't involve Aliza. Either you tell her, at once, or I'm leaving. It's as simple as that.'

'All right,' he said. 'I'll tell her to go. And Janet . . . I'm really sorry.'

It was as if he were apologising for forgetting to put the milk bottles out. Nevertheless, I felt better.

But next day he had still done nothing. Better, he thought, to book her flight to London, and then break the news. The only problem was that there were no seats on the London flights. So far as I was concerned she could sit on Barbados for a week. I just wanted her off the island and out of my house.

New Year's Eve dawned. Pamela didn't come down to the beach. I watched Peter as he drove back to the house on some errand. Was he going to the house to break the news, or to make love to her? My anger built up. During the day Peter said there was probably a seat on the next day's flight.

New Year's Eve was always a big night at the beach bar. Pamela was all dressed up in a gorgeous outfit, another gift, she boasted, from her boyfriend. There was an elaborate buffet but because Pamela and I were both vegetarian (a state I return to intermittently), we were served first and found ourselves sitting alone at our table.

'Isn't this beautiful,' she said. It was beautiful: fragrant, romantic, a heavenly place. She leaned across the table and patted my hand. 'I'm so glad you're having such a wonderful time, Janet. You deserve it, you work so hard.'

I pulled my hand away. 'I *was* having a wonderful time until you arrived, and I shall have a wonderful time when you leave.'

She was stunned. 'What do you mean?'

'I mean I shall have a wonderful time when you leave, and it had better be soon otherwise I'm afraid I might do something very unpleasant.'

She was aghast. 'What are you talking about? What have I done?'

'Pamela, I won't tolerate your staying in my house and screwing my husband, so please get out.'

'You must be crazy,' she said. 'I don't understand you.'

It was a convincing performance, if you hadn't been involved in all that had gone before. 'Pamela, don't go through all that. Peter's already told me it's true.'

'I don't believe you,' she said.

'Whether you do or not, it's the truth. He would have told you to get out, but he hasn't got the nerve. I suggest you get yourself back to the house; one of the beach bar boys will give you a lift. Pack your bags. Your plane goes in the morning. I don't ever want to see you talking to my husband again.

'Don't try to talk your way out of it. I am feeling very violent and if it weren't for all these people I'd probably be scratching your eyes out right now.'

I said all this in a calm voice. The rest of the party came back to the table. She was silent, picking at her food. After a short interval she got up and began to walk up the beach, possibly in the direction of the loo. She looked at Peter; it was their signal and he got up to follow her, unaware of our conversation.

People were dancing and partying. I sat and waited, and then stood up and followed them along the road at the side of the beach. I saw that she was talking with great animation, waving her hands. I supposed she was telling him what had passed between us.

They didn't see me coming. It was dark on the beach but people were about, walking along the sand, going to their cars. She had her back to me, her short blond hair shining and swinging in the light breeze. I grabbed her hair and yanked it. 'I told you I didn't want to see you talking to my husband.'

She was shocked. Taken by surprise she could not defend herself and I smacked her across the face, several times. 'I told you never to talk to him again. I told you to pack and get out of my life. You weren't listening. I meant it.'

I turned to Peter. 'And as for you, you can go with her as far as I'm concerned. I'm not leaving.'

I saw her hand go up as she realised she had lost an ear-ring (never to be found again – I didn't know that until much later). She stood crying. Peter got into the Moke, telling me to go back to the beach bar and stop making such an exhibition of myself. He would take Pamela to the house and come straight back.

He did, his face like thunder for the rest of the evening. I just felt numb. Pamela packed her bags and moved into the spare room by the pool so that our paths would not cross. Peter reported that she was 'desperately sorry' and wanted to talk to me. I refused.

They left before everyone was up. Because, he said, he couldn't get her on a morning flight, and wasn't prepared to leave her sitting alone until the early evening flight, it was only fair that he should spend the day with her. He would come back after he had put her on the plane. He refused to discuss it further.

It was our twenty-first wedding anniversary.

Peter expected that, whatever he did, I would forgive him. His view was that we were a unit. We were married. We had a life together, a child, a business. Whatever happened we had to forgive each other. Therefore he could afford to hurt me for the day, because I would still be there. Pamela was different; he could not take that gamble with her. He didn't want her to walk out and the door to be closed completely.

At breakfast I told John, Julia and Aliza that Pamela had left and that we had quarrelled. They made no comment, just accepted what I said. We went to Colin Tennant's party without Peter. Pamela, I said, had been called back urgently to London. (Everyone would know this to be untrue as telephone calls from overseas were common knowledge.) And Peter was ill with an upset stomach.

Colin's New Year's Day lunch parties were becoming something of a tradition. Credited with having put Mustique on the map, he owns most of it and it was his gift of land to Princess Margaret which enabled her to build a house there although she never uses it at Christmas. His hospitality is legendary, as is his courtesy to everyone. The household is rarely less than ten, plus innumerable houseguests. One of the Tennant children told me, 'Daddy says it's cheaper flying us all out to Mustique than opening up the house in Scotland for Christmas.'

It was a lovely party. I didn't enjoy myself but it was preferable to sitting at home alone. Afterwards we went back to the house and sat on the terrace, from which we could see the airstrip. We could see Peter and Pamela; they walked out to the plane and stood waiting for the luggage to be loaded. I could tell from his posture that he was angry and unhappy.

In Mustique people always wave goodbye when you leave. To my horror there was Colin Tennant, with wife, children, his whole household, all lined up on the runway for a Mustique send-off. He had an ever-changing supply of houseguests, and this was a farewell to one of them. I saw Peter and Colin talking together. Well, that was his alibi blown. Not that it mattered; my excuse would have been recognised for what it was. Our marital skirmishing was all round the island by then.

With Pamela gone, Peter settled into a serious sulk, and his mood affected us all, with the long silences and brusque monosyllabic questions and answers. 'Don't worry, Mummy, he'll start talking when we're on the plane home,' said Aliza, referring to Peter's travel nerves and his need to take his mind off being thirty thousand feet above land.

For two days I endured his behaviour. Then at Peter's request we went to Pasture Bay, not a favourite with us because it is difficult for swimming. We parked our belongings and he walked off, to sit on a tree stump gazing into the distance. I joined him there and, very quietly, without anger or recrimination, I spelled it out.

'Peter, I'm leaving you. I've decided I just don't want to go on living with you. I can't take it any more. I would like to have the rest of this holiday in peace. I want to lie in the sun, go to bed early, relax. We're going back to a tough year ahead, and I want to feel ready for work when I get back to London. Please, I want you to stop behaving as if I have done you some terrible injury and just allow us all to enjoy what is left of our time here.'

I felt strongly that, having made the decision, this time I would stick to it.

10

My first move was to the flat in Wirksworth, and then to a hotel, followed by a miserable little studio flat, and then a larger flat, painted bright pink throughout, in Hyde Park Street. I needed a base in London. I needed to make a new start and to get my life together.

Peter watched me pack my things in total disbelief, followed by rage, followed by his being frightfully sophisticated and helping to carry my bags downstairs. When I told my mother I had left Peter, she said she understood why, but had thought I would never do it. My family had to know, and so did my personal assistant. Peter was so anxious not to publicise our estrangement that he volunteered to come to a family wedding sooner than have me announce the real reason for his absence. These weddings and barmitzvahs had been a bone of contention for years. Peter hated them and in the past I had gone so far as to arrange a holiday so that I could genuinely plead being out of the country as an excuse to decline an invitation and thus avoid a row with Peter.

There was no sign that anything had changed, although Peter was continually asking me to go back: 'You know you want to come back. Just come. Don't be stupid.'

Or: 'Come and we'll talk.'

'We're talking now. What are you offering?' Nothing, of course. Deep down I was hoping that something would make things different and we would get together again. I missed him so much. But I kept my distance, and he used business matters as an excuse to keep telephoning me.

I was constantly busy, chasing production, following up orders for the spring collection and working on the autumn collection which had to be ready to show in February. I was always under pressure; the fashion business *is* pressure, a treadmill that you never get off. Peter turned up in Wirksworth one day to the consternation of the staff. He rarely visited the factory at that time. I heard his loud voice in the vestibule. He was slightly deaf and as his hearing deteriorated, his voice got louder.

'We've got to talk. You won't come to me, so I've come to you,' he said. He wanted a fresh start. 'Do you realise,' he said, 'you're pushing me towards that girl. I am so desperately lonely.'

I'd assumed Pamela had moved in by now. 'Well, she hasn't,' he said. 'It's our flat, and I don't want her there. But you are pushing me; you're making me dependent on her. I'm asking you to come back, so let's talk about it.'

We spent the whole weekend talking, but not getting anywhere. Sometimes it was pleasant talk, sometimes it wasn't. Sometimes we made love, sometimes we fought. His mother and Lisl were on the phone almost daily. Mama said women didn't walk out on their husbands. If a man runs around a bit, that's the nature of men; what was I making such a fuss about? 'Don't you see he needs you?' she asked.

Every now and then she said the right thing: 'Stay away a bit. It won't do him any harm. He'll come running.' In her way, she knew him.

And so the weeks passed. It was a spring Monday morning when Aliza telephoned from Munich. I could tell at once she was very upset. 'It's Daddy. He'll be angry if he knows I've called you.' She was still smarting from the way her father had used her in his ploy to bring Pamela to Mustique and relations were strained. 'He has just been speaking to me. He sounded drunk.' We both knew Peter never touched alcohol. 'He's just come out of hospital. He's taken an overdose. He said he has nothing to live for. Nobody cares whether he lives or dies.'

She was frightened and panicky. I phoned him. 'What do you want?' he demanded. It was the slurred speech I recognised. I had never told Aliza about the first suicide attempt. 'I don't want to talk to you,' he said.

'Peter, you don't sound well. Would you like me to come over?'

'Keep out of my life. You've done enough damage to me. I'm quite all right.'

'If you're all right, why aren't you in your office?' I wanted to keep him talking.

'That bloody Aliza's been talking to you . . .'

'Peter, you tell your twenty-year-old daughter that you've taken an overdose, and expect her not to tell her mother? I want to see you and talk to you.' He hung up.

I went to his office in Bond Street. It was the first time I had set foot in it since we had split up. Brenda was with him. She was very much Peter's friend: he liked her, and she amused him. He very much enjoyed the cut-and-thrust of their conversational repartee and she was very much in love with him: that was obvious from the beginning. She was extremely shocked by the Pamela affair.

Now she wore a concerned, worried look while Peter was angry that I was there. 'Stop being ridiculous, Peter,' she said, and was organising coffee when Peter stormed out of the office, got into his car and drove off. Brenda told me what had happened. Her part in it began when Pamela telephoned and said, 'I don't know if you know who I am. I found your number in Peter's book.'

It seemed that Pamela, driving past Cadogan Gardens on Sunday morning, decided to call on Peter, having first telephoned and got the answering machine. She rang the front doorbell; no reply. She asked one of the other tenants to let her into the building and rang the bell of the flat. She could see a light and knew he was in. She put her head against the door and heard sounds of someone stumbling. The sounds came closer, reached the stairs and began to move down towards the door. Then came the crash as he fell.

She banged on the door and called his name, but he didn't answer. She ran downstairs to our landlady, Mrs Regal, for the spare key, opened the door and found Peter slumped at the foot of our apartment's stairs, unconscious. Pamela called an ambulance. He was rushed into the Middlesex Hospital where his stomach was pumped out. She had saved his life.

He didn't thank her for it. He discharged himself from hospital on Monday morning, looking deathly, old and weak. He was more than likely to walk under a bus in that state, I said to Brenda, who agreed. She had rushed to his bedside as soon as she knew, to sit with him through alternating moods of belligerence and self-pity. Mostly she had held his hand and comforted him, and begged him to seek psychiatric help. After all, if he felt so strongly about the collapse of his marriage and family life that he sought to end it all, maybe he should do something about making it work. He wouldn't listen and told her not to interfere.

I bumped into him once in Bond Street. He was driving. I was coming out of St Laurent. I was loaded down with Calvin Klein and St Laurent carriers and had just had my hair cut, another sign of my rebellion. Everybody was bobbing their hair then and it was the first time I'd had short hair since Peter and I had first met. He stopped. 'My God, what have you done to your hair?' Then he looked down at my shopping and laughed. 'Getting a new image together, are we?'

He hesitated. 'You're looking very well, apart from the hairstyle.'

I was getting into my car. 'Doesn't matter whether you like my hairstyle or not, does it?' I remarked. 'I've been having a lovely afternoon, spent a fortune.' And I drove off.

I wasn't worried about money, I had reorganised my working routine to give me an office above the shop at Beauchamp Place where I could meet clients, and I had taken on a factory manager because I had no intention of working full time in Wirksworth. Beautiful as Derbyshire is, it did not provide the right environment for a woman alone.

I still did not think there was anything seriously wrong with the business. We were running three spring advertisements which, based on previous performance, seemed bound to bring in between £50,000 and £100,000 each. We had good spring orders at that point – not wonderful, but quite acceptable – and the shops were doing good business.

There was already one lucrative deal on the horizon. One morning I had taken a call at the factory from a gentleman who introduced himself as Jeff Turner representing Vantona. Could I spare him a few minutes that afternoon? He arrived and came straight to the point. They wanted to market a range of bedlinen with a designer name on it. 'We'd like it to be yours. If you don't agree, we'll do the range anyway, and go to another designer. We'd prefer to have Janet Reger, since lingerie and bedlinen provides a neat association.' It was as easy as that.

But far more important was the proposed deal to market a Janet Reger collection with Berlei. It promised to make big money and

106

would play a major part in our business . . . how right we were in that, though not quite in the way we anticipated.

Aware that our 'image' was crucial to Berlei, Peter and I forgot our differences for the afternoon. He picked me up from Hyde Park Street and we went to the meeting together.

Whichever way you looked at it, the Berlei deal had seemed mutually beneficial when, early in 1982, we were approached by Berlei's chief executive, Bryn Harries. Berlei produced bras and corsets, supplying a dying market. Corsets belonged to an older age group, a generation that was in decline. Our generation of customers would not start buying corsets in old age.

Berlei had not ventured into the underwear market before and the deal gave them an exclusive Janet Reger underwear range, designed by me. It didn't prevent us making our own range, or selling licensing rights for other products. But the association provided Bryn Harries with a collection of beautiful lingerie which Berlei needed to counteract its fuddy-duddy image at that time. My fee for designing this collection was £15,000, plus royalties. (That first-and-only collection was successful, but my company was not destined to receive a penny royalty.)

We signed the contract in April. In October Bryn told us that he and Maurice Lucas, the sales director, had just made a management buy-out. What they didn't tell us was that they were on the verge of bankruptcy. When we read this in the newspaper we thought Bryn a very shrewd cookie. The truth was, he was more stupid than shrewd, but that came much later.

Berlei had always had a reputation for being 'difficult'. When in my teens I applied to them for a job, I was turned down on the grounds that I was Jewish. At the interview a comment was made that I have never heard elsewhere, before or since: 'I suppose you're going to want all those dozens of Jewish holidays, and to finish early on Fridays.'

I replied that I was not particularly religious. I'd probably want a couple of days a year for special occasions and I'd be happy to take them as part of my annual holiday. My teacher at college said later: 'I knew you wouldn't get that job.'

Now the change of ownership, to Dunlop, meant a clean slate, and for that reason I was responsive to the deal. Also Bryn Harries, a former Marks and Spencer merchandiser, was an impressive operator – or so I thought at the time. I later believed that the deal with us had helped save Berlei's skin at a time when Dunlop were thinking of putting in a receiver – I had to admire Bryn's panache.

(By a strange coincidence I was already linked with Berlei, but I did not know this at the time. Keith Berlei's ex-assistant Val, married Lee Parks, whose father set up a factory at Winksworth to make components for Berlei. It was because Berlei were in decline that the Parks took on my work, and it was of course their factory which I'd bought. Keith Berlei was in fact killed in a motor accident on his way from Derbyshire to London.)

From a very early stage our solicitor, Ronald Norman, was unhappy about the contract, but we all know how cautious solicitors can be. Nobody realised what was just around the corner, but he always said that we should have made the contract in our personal names and not tied up either Janet Reger Creations Ltd or the trademark.

Berlei drew up the contract and sent it to Ronald Norman for approval. He wanted it rewritten but we were eager to sign. 'We can get them to reassign the deal when it's up and going,' Peter said. 'No point in sending it all back for them to rewrite. We want to get this off the ground. My company's me anyway.'

'It may feel like that now,' Ronald Norman said. 'But if things ever start going wrong, Mr Reger, you'll find it isn't quite the same. Your business and you are two separate entities. It's always good to keep something for yourself and not put everything in your company.'

I had made two important decisions in Mustique: to leave Peter, and to tackle an issue which was becoming a major problem . . . Brenda's illness. We were all affected by it; emotionally it was a considerable concern to us all, and from a practical point of view, Brenda was the last to arrive in the morning, and would leave at four o'clock in order to attend Bart's for her daily injections. We had the expense (a major item in our depleting bank balance) of maintaining the company flat for her to make hospital attendance easier for her, while at the same time I had no idea where the sickness was leading. She continued to give the impression that her illness was terminal, and it was just a matter of time before she lost the fight. And yet she had outlived the original prognosis

. . . did this mean the original prognosis was wrong? In my present state of indecision and insecurity about so much in my life, I needed to know the truth about this. Neither did she look ill; she was no less buxom, and her thick hair gleamed with health.

I had no one in whom I could confide and voice my confused thoughts, without betraying my promise to her not to discuss this with her colleagues. Broaching the subject with Peter was out of the question. In desperation I sought professional advice, choosing at random from the Yellow Pages a name from the list of private investigators. It happened to be a bureau specialising in company investigations.

They reported back that, during the three weeks of their enquiry, Brenda had at no time visited Bart's or any other hospital. This explained nothing; the investigator dealt with facts, not explanations. I did not tell Peter of my discovery immediately. To this day I am not particularly proud of having resorted to checking up on her; it isn't my style, and never was. It served its purpose because I no longer feared for her life, so I did nothing, and said nothing. In the event, Brenda's relationship with us was soon to come to a dramatic conclusion.

It was almost a year since Brenda had supposedly been given eighteen months to live, and her colleagues were in a state of suspended mourning for her. Yet her ability to run the office was undiminished by her attenuated working day. She also acted as intermediary between Peter and me at this time, keeping each of us informed of the doings of the other.

Meanwhile, she had been discussing a licensing deal with a hosiery company. As a perk for the introduction she asked Peter to assign to her a percentage of the takings. I did not agree to this.

One morning Sheila Gore telephoned to ask if I was going to the meeting that afternoon.

'What meeting?'

'Janet, I don't want to cause trouble, but there is a meeting to discuss licensing and I think you ought to be there.'

Peter and I were living apart. I called him. 'What's this about a meeting?'

'It doesn't concern you. Brenda and I can deal with it,' he said, somewhat aggressively.

'If you don't mind, I'd like to attend,' I replied.

In this mood, I went to a meeting in Bond Street at which Brenda and Peter proposed to assign a Janet Reger licence without the permission of Janet Reger. There was more to it than one hosiery licence. Brenda had prepared for insertion in the financial pages of *The Times* and several other publications an announcement (paid for by our company) to the effect that she was our licensing agent and that all enquiries regarding possible Janet Reger licences should be addressed to her.

Correspondingly, we, the company, were drawing up a contract with her to the effect that she would earn commission on the said licences, exactly as a licensing agent does. Except that she was then employed by the company, and would continue to be so, earning a company salary.

Because of my estrangement from Peter, and my desire to break with him completely, I had begun to get legal advice concerning my breaking away from the company and setting up on my own. I later dropped the idea, but along the way I picked up an incidental piece of information: that it was illegal for a director of a company to act as an agent and draw commission, since he must be seen at all times to be acting in the company's best interests. (I've since learned that this is not quite the case, but being thus armed at the time, albeit inaccurately, gave me the confidence to fight.) Quite apart from 'legality', it was ludicrous that we should be expected to finance Brenda in setting up a new business.

I sat quietly through the meeting, listening. Then I said: 'I don't approve of any of this. If Brenda wants to set herself up as a licensing agent, that's fine. Let her resign and start up on her own. When we started in business we didn't have a nice kind employer or previous client that very generously helped us get started. On the contrary, most people were working against our competition. If you want to set up on your own, do so, Brenda; I'd be quite happy to be a client. But I don't think you should expect to start up using our public relations department, our money for advertising, or our advertising agent to write the ads for you.'

Peter was muttering away in the background. But I insisted that before any decision could be made there had to be a formal board meeting, according to the rules. I wanted things done correctly. I pulled rank. Peter had one share more than me, but I knew at the end of the day I was the one with the real power. However much

Brenda and Peter wanted to kid themselves they knew that, without production and without a designer, which were both in my hands, they had nothing to sell and nothing to negotiate with. You can't do business with a non-existent product. I was the product, and Peter was clever enough to recognise that.

Brenda was tight-lipped. 'I fully understand, Janet. You want it to be done legally. You have a point but . . .'

Months later there was one surreal episode. After a day in Wirksworth Julia, Brenda and I were driving to London in order that Brenda could have what she continued to refer to as her vital daily injection at Bart's. There was a serious hold-up on the motorway and we were running at least an hour late, which meant Brenda would miss her appointment. Don't worry, she said, it would be quite all right. They would give her the injection in the casualty department. Everyone there was familiar with her case.

The rain lashed down as we reached Swiss Cottage. I wasn't sure of the way. I told her, 'I'll head towards the City, then you'll have to direct me. I know it's somewhere near Smithfields.'

Brenda protested. She couldn't allow me to drive so far out of my way, and she would take a taxi. But there was no chance of finding a taxi, and I wouldn't hear of dropping her off in such dreadful weather, especially with her being so ill. 'I absolutely insist I'm driving you to the hospital,' I said.

We reached Smithfields; 'You'll have to direct me from here,' I said. Brenda was nonplussed and couldn't find the way. I cruised around looking for the hospital entrance until we saw some parked ambulances.

'There it is,' she cried.

But I had spotted another sign on the opposite side of the square: Casualty and Patients' Entrance. 'Tut tut, Brenda,' I said. 'Considering you're here practically every day you don't know your way around very well, do you?'

She had a ready explanation: the taxis always approached from a different direction, wasn't it confusing? I dropped her off.

11

It was November, freezing cold and pouring with rain. Peter phoned me at Beauchamp Place asking to see me, and I went to the Bond Street office. He began at once by producing facts and figures on his scraps of paper, to show me how bad things were. In retrospect, this was the point of no return: the moment when Peter said: 'This is really terrible. I don't know what I am going to do. I think we are going to go bankrupt.' He didn't use the term 'liquidation' – he wouldn't have known the difference. We knew how to make merchandise. We knew how to sell it. We knew when we were making money because we kept books. And he knew we weren't making money and he was panicking.

I didn't believe it could be so bad. This wasn't the first time Peter had panicked and things had always turned out fine. We weren't living together, so were out of touch on a day-to-day basis. I was accustomed to his mood swings, which were usually connected with money. We both enjoyed spending the money when it was there, and as I have said he used to tighten up when it wasn't to a degree that was laughable. When you have a turnover of more than £1¼ million and start talking about cancelling the papers to save money, the situation is ludicrous. The moment things improved he would do a complete reversal. Life would become exciting: 'What are we going to do with all this money? Let's go shopping.'

So initially I wasn't worried, apart from the fact that I was sorry to see him looking so bad. He used to get a worn, haggard look about him when he was down and I knew this well. I tried to cheer him up. 'Things aren't that bad,' I said. 'We've been through this before.'

Optimistic as I am by nature, I had to agree that the sales figures were depressing, but Christmas was ahead, and we had always done well at Christmas. We might just manage to pull ourselves out of it by then. I agreed with Peter: we really must have a major cut-back, and go into our accounts very thoroughly to see where we could make savings. We were struggling with very high interest rates. Our account customers had not placed the huge orders that usually could be relied upon in November, and Peter's concern was that, without this inflow, we would not be able to cover our outgoings and finance the very quiet New Year period.

We began by discussing the crisis with our accountant. 'With increased overheads caused by high interest charges, inflation and a decrease in turnover, your only answer is to put your prices up,' he said. Hardly practical. Since we were having difficulty selling at our existing prices, how could we expect to sell if we increased them? 'Quite,' he said. 'I can see that. That's everybody's problem in times like these.'

We called a meeting with our senior executives and Sheila Gore to discuss ways of drumming up publicity and sales. These people, too, were used to Peter: one minute he was telling them he was about to become a multi-millionaire; a few months later he was being thrown into debtors' gaol. So nobody was taking it that seriously and I was trying to temper my concern with discretion. It didn't look good to spread the word that Janet Reger was in severe financial difficulties.

On a family recommendation we called in a firm of experts who examined the books and set some targets for sales up to Christmas. We tried to feel optimistic but the senior accountant, dealing in balance sheets not wishes, warned me that we might have to go into liquidation: 'I'm not sure that you are going to come out of this solvent.'

It was beginning to be frightening. Neither Peter nor I was sleeping at night. We were both very nervous. We decided to patch up our marriage at that point, to try living together again because we felt it would be better to stand together to face any problems that were coming. Also, it was insane to have two sets of household expenses. I moved out of the small furnished flat I had taken and back home into our flat in Cadogan Gardens. We had been apart for almost a year.

As Christmas approached we were doing fantastic business in the shops, but had appalling mail-order sales, and I began to channel some of the mail-order stock into the shops. It was too much, too late. The provinces were doing badly. Our own shops in Beauchamp Place and Bond Street were performing well, but they alone could not support the low sales across the country and the world.

We needed an injection of money and sought advice from professionals, not fully understanding that, by the very nature of their role, at the end of the day they seek an advantage. Those in the business of finding finance expect to receive a fee from the investor, and this must influence their choice and what they recommend. We were very naïve.

Melvyn Langley, the accountant we had retained, advised us against asking our bank, the National Westminster, for more money. With our figures, he said, the bank would refuse us anyway. Our only move was to present true figures elsewhere and hope to find a backer. We were vulnerable, and were offered risible sums of money in return for our business. We had always thought business was about producing merchandise. It isn't, of course; it's about financial dealing. I'm still not so brilliant at that but I'm learning.

We were introduced to a potential backer. He had money; we had our backs against the wall. He could see it would be possible to buy us cheaply because we were desperate not to go under. He could sit on the assets until property prices improved. Meanwhile, with my trademark and his own interests in textiles, he could manufacture in the Far East.

Dangling the carrot, he began by offering to invest. We could stay on as directors at wonderful salaries but he would first need to go through our books with his accountants. We made our books available, and his team moved into our book-keepers' offices at Bond Street and at Wirksworth, all at 'his' expense. 'I'm not charging you fees,' he kept repeating. They did a thorough job, working out profit ratio, mark up, what we should be doing, what we had been spending money on that we shouldn't have. He was absolutely horrified when he heard that Peter had bought some pictures, demanding to know how Peter could buy pictures when the company was in trouble. But the company hadn't been in trouble when Peter bought pictures years earlier.

The real reason for these criticisms was that this investor was trying to turn me against Peter. He wanted me but not Peter. He wanted the name, the figurehead, the designer, the person conversant with production. He didn't want a salesman. Neither did he want a managing director. He was a salesman himself, and wanted to install his own finance people. Sales and finance were Peter's departments.

He insisted that he intended, if he bought in, to keep the business going but that was probably not true. More likely this was an exercise in establishing how cheaply he could pick up an ailing big-name business, give it a run for the small amount he was investing in inspecting the books, and decide later what to do.

At the end of the day he came back and offered us a private deal. He would buy the company, with contracts for us. He would go with us to the bank and do a deal with them for a partial repayment of the money we owed. The bank would give him quite a large discount in return for his buying the company and putting his capital and his workforce behind it. In reality, he would have asked for our loans to be transferred to him; it would not have cost him a penny of real cash. We didn't understand the full implications then, that what he was proposing could actually be to the detriment of our creditors. I have learned now to look around the corner a bit. At the time I just thought he was pretty shrewd.

His offer was: £2,000 for the Beauchamp Place premises because the lease had nearly expired; between £8,000 and £10,000 for the Bond Street shop; the factory, with the cottages thrown in, he said was worth £20,000 'because who wants a factory out in the wilds of Derbyshire?' The cars were practically write-offs (two Jaguars). Then, having added all these very low figures together, they were discounted 'because the company wasn't making much money'. Until that year it had been a very profitable company – and had been for fourteen years. At the end of the day the Bond Street shop alone fetched more than he was offering for the lot. Without actually saying no we decided we would look for other finance, and if we couldn't find it we would approach our bank after all.

That investor's offer was an insult financially, but it was his 'conditions' that promptly made me reach a decision. Reading his draft contract I saw that I would be allowed so many days' holiday each year. With that one phrase came the realisation of what it would be like to work for someone else after twenty years of independence. I had a vision of clocking in and clocking out, and

I knew I would rather do anything than ask someone's permission to go on holiday. I'm very conscientious about not walking out when I'm needed. On the other hand, when I need a week's holiday and the time and the money are there that is my choice.

When we eventually told him we were not accepting his offer, he replied: 'In that case you'll be going to the bank soon because there's no way you're going to survive. And I will be there to make my offer anyway, with or without your co-operation.'

By Christmas Eve we knew it was all but hopeless. With hindsight, I believe we should have fought harder, concentrated more on finding finance. But we weren't clever enough. We had signed personal guarantees to the bank when we were borrowing to expand at eight per cent. Within a year the interest rate had risen to twenty per cent. We had shops, factories, property, but almost overnight conditions had changed.

The financial climate was like that of 1990–91. We had borrowed when everything was worth so much, and on paper it still was; but goods weren't selling, nothing was happening, and the property market had slumped. It is one thing to say that one of my shops is worth £100,000, the other £160,000, and my house is worth £200,000. If nobody wants the properties or can afford to buy them, then they are worthless.

We were already borrowing to the hilt. Melvyn Langley's advice was: 'You have such huge debts you couldn't pay them off if you lived to be a hundred. You are insolvent and the only thing you can do is to go into liquidation.'

Today I question that advice. I think very few banks actually make the unpopular move – unless they have to – of driving people into bankruptcy and making them homeless. They do not like bad publicity and, with a company like ours, publicity would be unavoidable. Banks are more inclined to make a deal, and might even be prepared to waive some of the debt temporarily, especially if they feel their customer has an earning potential.

From an accountant's point of view there was a certain rightness about it, to say I'd got my business in a bloody mess and was never going to get it right. The best thing for all concerned would be for me to pack up and do something else. The problem was we loved our business; we'd brought it up; it was our baby. And we didn't know what else to do anyway. We'd been working for so long, it was impossible to conceive that this was really going to happen, that we'd reached the end.

In the middle of our depression and shock, wailing about how we got ourselves into this mess, we temporarily forgot our differences and were even talking to each other. But the atmosphere was strained; Peter was acutely depressed while I was still very angry with him. I would handle it differently now. I can control my anger. Our relationship wasn't good but because we were trying to save the business we were united in our efforts and worked our butts off.

At the end of the day we'd come home together, eat, talk, analyse events, the day's takings and sales, and have really animated discussions; and if something remotely good happened we had a buzz almost of happiness. We even had little celebrations. The shops took money in the build-up to Christmas so there were moments of euphoria.

We continued with our own economies, as we had done since Peter announced his fears to me in November, and clung to the slim hope that this nightmare would end. After all, hadn't we always been so lucky, always fallen on our feet? We'd had problems before and made contingency plans like letting the flat and living in a hovel, or breaking into Asprey's, but we'd never needed to resort to such desperate measures, always managing to pull things around.

I'd had an idea that Peter liked, which was uniting us at that time. An American acquaintance had previously shown interest in investing in the business. If with his help we could buy the freehold property at St Mary's Gate we could produce there, and if we couldn't raise sufficient money for that, we might just buy the lease back in Beauchamp Place and make a tiny workroom upstairs. The rent there was low, and there were only eighteen months left on the lease. We could sew things and do a couture operation from the shop.

In mid-December the accountant who was advising us went on holiday for a month. Our lawyer went away for Christmas, and so did the bank manager. We were left to struggle on our own. Money was coming in, but so were bills from suppliers, interest on our overdraft, and a reminder on our advertising account which stood at £32,000.

When money is tight you still have to pay for essentials; the rest can wait. But sooner or later the people you've kept waiting start getting more and more angry and begin to put on pressure, and then you pay those who are applying most pressure or the people you need for the next lot of supplies. We managed to pay rent and wages, juggling the money until a decision could be made.

Our bank manager knew things were extremely tough. It was a tough year. Laker went under, DeLorean went bust. Unemployment soared to three million. The bank manager said that other customers had told him they were finding things difficult right now. But he had heard Peter say many times that we were having a financial crisis and five minutes later business was wonderful, and I suppose at the end of the day he would have said of Peter: 'This guy seems to know what he's doing. The books looked good at the end of last year.'

When we closed the shop for Christmas, Aliza and I flew to Florida where I hoped to discuss finance with our American entrepreneur. The pound was very strong against the dollar, which gave us a very cheap bucket-shop holiday (ironically, the same reason we weren't selling well in the States), and we were met by our courteous American. Perhaps he would help us rescue part of our operation, or all of it.

He was interested, certainly, but couldn't do anything fast enough for us. He came up with ideas and suggestions but he told us that he had recently become involved in another deal and didn't have the ready cash. Funds wouldn't be available for at least six months, and we could hardly expect our creditors to believe for six months that the cheque was in the post! We parted very good friends.

Peter had spent Christmas at home, consoled by Pamela. He was at his most trying, spending much of his time whingeing. It had the effect of winding me up and making me even more fraught and distressed than I already felt.

He was going through a curious lethargy which began then and continued until he died. He would go downstairs in the morning and sit in the kitchen on a stool, which wasn't his style at all – he expected to eat breakfast at the table with his hot toast and freshly squeezed orange juice. He would take a bite out of a piece of toast and leave the rest, turn on the radio, and toy with a cup of coffee sitting there in his dressing-gown, poring over the newspaper but hardly reading it. Then he'd move into the living-room, still reading the paper, put on a video, and sit around in front of the television all day, not dressed and unshaven, waiting for me to come home so that he could ask what was for dinner.

Then the mood would swing. He'd wake up on a good day, take trouble with his appearance, leave the house early and go out on an expedition looking for pictures, which he was dealing in with his mother and Lisl.

In the early weeks before we separated completely and during the period of our liquidation, he would go out on his energetic days and start negotiating on behalf of our business, or come into the shop and try helping me, which I didn't really want by that time because he was out of touch.

Curiously, news of our financial straits had not yet travelled the grapevine. We'd never been prompt payers. Although we'd always made profits because of our fast growth and lack of outside money, our cashflow was always appalling. We were constantly in arrears, so this year was not in any overt way different from previous years. During those weeks Peter was truthful with our creditors, explaining that money was tight and he would do his best, sending them small instalments to keep them going.

Around Christmas money came in from many of the smaller customers that had been dragging their heels. Once they'd got their Christmas trade behind them most would be able to pay off all their bills, so January was always good for money coming in. This is all standard in the rag trade. The fact that somebody owes money doesn't necessarily mean they are going broke – especially at that time, when business was bad, and the problems were universal.

I returned to work on 1 January 1983 (having stopped off in New York to discuss business with another possible financier, a long shot which didn't succeed) and prepared for the New Year sale to open in mid-January. As always, customers crowded in to our two London shops, the shop in Wirksworth and the one in Munich; money poured in.

Our problem was a long-term one: huge loan repayments, high rent commitments and the fact that wholesale orders were poor. Shop takings had been down all the previous year and there was no sign that they were going to get better, since interest rates were still incredibly high and the retail business was in recession nationwide. We had a large stock mainly of unsold catalogue items and also a couture order made for an old-established customer in Hong Kong, who had failed to pay her last invoice. The goods were half-made and it was more expedient to finish than to abandon or alter them, which meant we possessed a huge quantity of couture lingerie in tiny Chinese sizes.

It was easy, while the January sale was doing such good business, to tell ourselves that things would work out; something would turn up. There were still the promised royalties from Berlei, expected to materialise in the coming year, and we had just signed a contract with Vantona that augured well; the merchandise was already sold wholesale. We were also in the process of signing a deal with a stocking manufacturer which had guaranteed minimums.

The two factories in Derbyshire were officially closed until 6 January and it made sense to leave them closed. We had prepared an excuse, a white lie that this prolonged closure was due to lack of cloth deliveries. In fact, we hadn't called in the cloth because, knowing we were on a knife edge, we didn't want to hurt the suppliers. So long as they could be persuaded to delay their delivery and invoice, the cloth remained their property and would not be swallowed up in any liquidation procedure. That way the suppliers didn't catch too much of a cold.

We owed money to the bank, to the advertising agency, to a model agency, to our insurance company . . . it seemed we owed money to almost everyone, but not so much to our small suppliers. Whatever way we looked at it, the whole pack of cards was collapsing. The Christmas advertising, the huge debt to the bank, the VAT and £100,000 tax were all throttling us.

During the week the factory was closed I called a meeting in Wirksworth of several key people to explain exactly what was going on. I said that I would not be calling the cloth in after the Christmas break as things were very unsettled, and that we were having a meeting with the bank to see whether or not we could proceed in business. There would be no return to work as planned and I would be writing to inform the staff of this. I offered to answer any questions and told them I felt sure we would resolve the situation, which, at that time, I honestly felt to be true. I was

Above: Peter and I, early seventies.

Right: A family occasion, my niece's wedding in 1982: (*left to right*) me, Gloria, Mother, Sandra, Barbara.

Below: Me, Peter and Aliza celebrating the opening of the shop in Munich.

Above left: French lace underwired bra and waist slip from our 1977 collection, available in sage, peach or black.

Above right: Joan Collins dressed (scantily) for *The Stud* (1978).

Far left: This silk princess line nightdress trimmed with large bows appears in our 1990/91 catalogue, the first since the liquidation.

Left: We called this nightdress 'Suzy', 1977 – lightweight silk trimmed with antique lace, masses of ribbons and a hemline of handkerchief points.

Left: Peter and I in the office on the day of the liquidation, 1983.

Below centre: The re-opening of the shop in Beauchamp Place, 6 April 1983.

Below: At work in Beauchamp Place, April 1983.

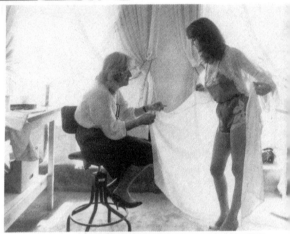

depressed and miserable. I didn't believe this could be happening to me. Peter did. He kept saying: 'We're not getting out of this, you know. This time it isn't going to work.'

The staff meeting wasn't terribly emotional. They were concerned but seemed to have such trust in our ability to solve the problems. They were all senior employees and as such understood a great deal about the business. My personal assistant knew better than anybody that of late I'd been having meetings with accountants and possible investors, which could only mean things were tough. But the staff also knew that things had sometimes been tough before. The general mood was that it would be hard but we'd make a few cut-backs, tread warily, then everything would go on as before. Or nearly as before.

During this time Melvyn, the accountant, returned. The only advice he could give us was to phone our bank manager, make an appointment and tell him that we were insolvent and were going into liquidation. He would come with us, go through the figures and see if we could persuade the bank to allow us to pay our personally guaranteed debt over several years, and keep our trademark. 'You will have something from the Berlei contract,' Melvyn said, 'which guarantees you an income for the next four years.'

Melvyn collected us in a taxi from Bond Street, and together we drove to our bank in Westbourne Grove. As we hurtled towards the deadline, Melvyn said: 'This is the worst bit. Once you've got this over, once it's out in the open and everybody knows what you're doing, the pressure is off. There are going to be a tough few months ahead but this is the thing you're dreading most, and I know it seems as if you're going to die. Right now life stops. The minute you get past that moment and life goes on, everything starts getting better. This is the worst moment you're going to have.'

And in a way he was right. There were worse moments to come, but these had nothing to do with the liquidation so much as with other things that were happening.

In every awful situation there is always humour. Sitting in the taxi, Peter said: 'Do you remember how we came to be with this bank? Westbourne Grove is a funny place to have a bank.' He reminded me that when we arrived from Switzerland he was

121

carrying quite a lot of money for those were the days before everybody flashed credit cards. He didn't want to walk about with so much cash in his pockets so the first job was to get the money banked. The next morning he went out into the street, turned left and went into the first bank he came to and opened an account. If he had turned right that morning we would have banked not with the National Westminster but with the Midland.

'Well, I'm sure Mr Eden will be delighted to know the reason we're all here today and not up the road,' Melvyn said.

It made us laugh, a very short-lived laugh I must say, but I've learned, probably since that moment, that if you can step outside a situation when it is most painful, you are able to depersonalise it and this gives a sense of balance. Even Peter managed to laugh.

Mr Eden had no idea of the bombshell we were about to drop, although he no doubt guessed it was not good news. That is another of the mistakes I can see with hindsight. I now think it would have been cleverer for us to have gone on our own to our bank months before. We should have been really open, and said: 'Look, we're terrified. We don't see how we can make it through next year. We don't know where we're going to get the money to call in our cloth to make our garments and deliver to our shops. We can't go on selling our existing stock because it's either in tiny little sizes or pale blue [the garment we were offering on our Christmas mail order]. We won't survive that way. And we won't survive if we can't guarantee enough orders to pay the rent and cover everything else. We just don't know what to do.'

I think we might at that point have been able to talk to our bank manager about spreading our long-term loan maybe over a longer period, or asking him to allow us to defer repayments until business picked up. I have learned that a bank will consider this, taking interest only and no repayments for six or twelve months. Instead of that, we just went in and said, 'We're not going to survive,' which possibly annoyed him a bit. I wasn't so used to dealing with banks then as I am now. I misjudged the mood and the individual. Perhaps had we involved the bank more, asked advice, then they may have offered help. But we were frightened. We felt we had reached a situation that was beyond our control.

12

We were on a slope, heading downhill fast. Had there been something to break our fall, some slight obstacle to that downward path, we could perhaps have caught hold, regained our balance and clung on.

With hindsight, we should have said to our creditors: 'As things stand, if we go out of business right now you'll lose a lot of money. If you'll bear with us and support us, judge for yourselves if you think the plan works or not, and back us a little longer, we'll pay you something every month out of our takings, but we must keep these very high credits with you.' And we should have said it sooner. By now it was too late.

From an initial capital of £5,000, the business had grown from a turnover of £20,000 in the first year, to £40,000 the next, then £80,000, and so on, doubling year by year. Growth was always big, but we were geared for that. We borrowed for it, bought for it, staffed for it.

Now we were advised that by going to the bank in this way, declaring insolvency and going into voluntary liquidation, we could appoint our own liquidator. On this advice we appointed Melvyn himself. The bank was entitled to appoint a receiver over his head, but he thought this was unlikely, mainly because he did not consider the company's assets of sufficient worth. He seriously misjudged our assets, in my opinion.

As liquidator, he explained: 'I cannot be your friend. I have to do the best job I can for your creditors. But the fact that you called me in means I feel a certain responsibility towards you. If I can be helpful without compromising the creditors, I will.'

We left the bank manager a copy of our statement of affairs, prepared by Melvyn after weeks of poring over our books. It didn't make happy reading, especially with the properties assessed considerably below their actual commercial value and stock at the sort of valuation most people put on 'bankrupt' stock: tuppence-ha'penny in other words.

We learned the etiquette of going into liquidation. There is a strict sequence of events to be followed. Firstly, you may not tell anybody anything until you have told your major creditor, which in our case was the bank. Should news leak, warned Melvyn, and the bank found out from lips other than our own, they would 'make mincemeat' out of us.

Then Melvyn phoned the factory. It was their first day back after the break. He spoke to Doreen who looked after personnel and wages and asked her to inform the staff. They were effectively dismissed, and had no further need to come to work until he travelled up for a meeting, at which he would explain the situation to them. Meanwhile, a member of his staff would be on hand to assist anyone who required help in filling out the claim forms regarding wages, redundancy and holiday pay.

Peter and I went at once to Bond Street, gathered together the staff from both shops and made our sad little announcement. And I made two essential telephone calls.

The first was to Sheila Gore, one of the people we had confided in. As a fashion PR she had first-hand experience of clients suffering the same fate. Although it is true to say she had felt we would come through, for she, too, was used to Peter crying wolf, throughout she had urged me that, whatever happened, whatever I had to do to save the business, I shouldn't let myself become an employee. 'You're better off selling oranges from a barrel than doing that after being your own boss all your life,' she said.

The second call was to Bryn Harries, chief executive of Berlei. I told him that something very urgent had come up and that he should cancel any plans he had made for the evening in order to meet us.

The news broke that evening on Radio Derby and our telephone began ringing with calls from incredulous friends asking whether it was true. At once it was picked up by Capital Radio, followed by the newspapers. 'BOTTOM DROPS OUT OF KNICKERS,' said the *Sun*. 'The firm that put the frill into sexy undies has overstretched itself and gone bust.' You couldn't argue with that.

Television news followed with a new angle: complaints from

girls at the factory at the way they'd been treated. But in general the national media were sympathetic, thorough and balanced.

When word hit the news-stands in London, our sale was still in progress, and at once queues formed to stretch the length of Beauchamp Place and a long way down Bond Street as people rallied to buy a Janet Reger garment before it was too late. No wonder some of our friends in the business thought it was all a publicity stunt! Melvyn wasted no time. He walked into both shops, locked the doors on the queues, hung up the closed signs for two hours while everybody changed the labels back to full price, took down the sale signs and opened for business again.

Almost at once, the local Derbyshire newspapers, inspired no doubt by old mud-slinging, attacked us mercilessly. The national press talked of the loss of a good business, for whatever reasons, commiserating with us and the workforce. The Derbyshire papers painted a picture of the Regers as the villains of the piece, fleecing the workers while making huge profits.

One Labour councillor wanted an investigation into the 'appalling conditions' in our factory. In other circumstances, it would have been laughable. The factory and its surroundings are quite beautiful. I took over a factory with a leaking roof and a broken, pitted floor, restored the roof and brought in men to sand and polish the floor until it gleamed. Areas which had been rubbish tips, we renovated and put to good use. We put in money and effort as you do into a home you intend to settle down in for the foreseeable future. And part of it *was* our home, set in a garden that had been totally overgrown and was brought to life by Peter's passion for gardening. The factory had been endlessly photographed and featured in newspapers and magazines, and was the subject of a television documentary. How could it possibly be a primitive dump, as was now being suggested, the people working there poor downtrodden slaves? It was too well publicised.

The stories were fuelled by factory gossip. Hints of sinister work afoot made intriguing column inches. Quotes appeared along the lines of: 'I can't understand it; it's very mysterious. Up to Christmas we were still on overtime and there was loads of work in hand.' True. But we didn't have the money to pay their wages into the new year.

I was afraid of the press. I had seen the press in action so many times: congratulatory when someone is on the up; bitchy when they're down. The Derbyshire press talked of public inquiries and questions in the House, and it printed letters from local readers saying: 'We still haven't had our wages.'

They had been paid three weeks' wages in advance when the factory closed for Christmas on 23 December, but they hadn't yet received their money in lieu of notice or their holiday pay and superannuation. But they had been kept fully informed and told they would receive their money in a few weeks, which they did. Surely even the local press must have known that this was standard procedure in a liquidation, that from the moment the liquidator was called in we weren't allowed to write a cheque.

On the morning the news broke nationwide our landlady, Mrs Regal, knocked at our front door. 'And what about my lease?' she demanded, tense with anxiety. 'I have a lease contract with a company that is in *liquidation*.' It had been a bone of contention that the only form of contract she would consider was a company let. 'I don't want my contract to go to the receiver. I don't want anything like this going on in my house. What are you going to do? I can't have you here *personally*. My solicitors won't hear of it; my accountants won't hear of it; my relations won't hear of it . . .'

Peter told her not to worry, that we would form a new company to provide the company let she required. (Which we did, and she used the opportunity to negotiate a rent increase.)

Bryn Harries of Berlei responded to our call requesting an urgent meeting. The collection I had designed for Berlei had been marketed, orders taken, and was at this point (according to Bryn) 'under the machines', in other words in production. It was a nightmare situation. We must not let Berlei hear of our liquidation via the newspapers. It had to be direct from us.

Over dinner we told Bryn everything, and he was totally sympathetic. We also outlined a proposition whereby if Berlei were prepared to make the contract over to myself or Peter personally, we could approach the bank about the trademark, saying that Berlei would continue the arrangement – not with the company because once the company has gone into receivership there is no way anyone can have a design contract with the receiver – but with one or both of us personally, subject to the bank's approval, since the bank had overall authority at that point. If we could buy back the trademark, we would use the money we earned from Berlei to pay the bank off over a period of four years.

Bryn promised us support: 'Just tell me what I have to do to save this situation.' We had his word on it, he said. Berlei were absolutely committed to this merchandise. They had a lot of money tied up and I needed to deliver the goods. They were happy to do whatever we said so long as this contract was kept going. They valued my design input, the name, the business we'd done so far. At the right moment Berlei would assign the contract to us or to any company that we might control.

Hugely relieved that we were over one hurdle, we felt confident enough to tell the bank we would have £25,000 this year, £50,000 next year and £75,000 the year after that: the sort of money which repays debts.

The cash registers were making music and people interviewed in the queues were saying that they were going to frame the French knickers they planned to buy. Sheila forbade me to go into the shops. She said the press had staked out there (as they had at our home) and I wasn't in the right frame of mind to give interviews, although I did allow myself to be persuaded by the fashion writer Jean Dobson, an old friend, to talk to Diana Hutchinson, woman's editor at the *Daily Mail*.

We kept well out of the limelight while we tried to raise money to buy the lease at Beauchamp Place. That would give us something to hang on to. We had discovered we were entitled to redundancy money along with the staff, and that with a bit of help from the family, who were being wonderfully supportive, raising a thousand or two here and there, we could just about manage to buy it at the values which were at that point being put on it. We would use the room upstairs for sewing, make a small amount of stock and, even if the drawers might be a little empty, create an illusion of activity while we took orders. So, with low overheads, it would be possible to start earning money more or less immediately. Peter and I sat down together and sifted through our staff, deciding which were the best, the most versatile, the most suitable to join us in our new venture.

It seemed that what Melvyn had said on the way to the bank was true; as if a whole lifetime had taken place between the moment we walked into the bank and when we said good night to Bryn later that evening. I felt better at that moment than I had felt for many weeks. Something positive would happen; it wouldn't be total disaster; we'd get something back together again. Peter and I talked and talked all night and finally fell asleep in the early hours. At that moment I was very close to him, feeling more sorry for him than myself.

I've always been an optimist. Even when things get very black and I am depressed for a short time, I always feel that I'm going to find a way to deal with the situation, and usually I do. I tend to say: I'm still here; I'm still alive; I've managed it so far, why shouldn't I manage it this time? Peter's attitude was more pessimistic, just like his mother's had always been. She tended to paint the future black, too. With her, it was always 'the Russians are coming', and the liquidation might as well have been the Russians so far as she was concerned: something bad even if not exactly what she had predicted. But in our rational moments we accepted that our worst fears had been realised. We had confronted them and we felt better for it. Peter found a new energy and began applying his mind to things we could do.

I busied myself following up every possible lead that could help us to get started again. The best advice I had at that time was: get going instantly. If you don't you'll lose the impetus. You'll get used to doing nothing. Start finding ways of managing. Don't lose your name. People forget very quickly. While you're still known, while you're still in the public eye and in the wake of all the publicity, use it to your advantage. Don't wait until nobody remembers who Janet Reger was. So move.

And I was really moving, and learning, and facing up to the mistakes that had allowed this whole sorry mess to happen. Melvyn maintained that however things worked out we would need money to start again on a sound basis; he would give guidance in this direction. We could buy the shop and the factory. There was no problem raising money for property. He recommended several financial sources, and eventually introduced me to my present bank.

Appointments were set up with various companies interested in offering a deal. Along with the vultures who wanted the choicest morsels from the corpse were the more benevolent hawks interested in buying the company with a deal for us to run it. The view in the trade was that we had been misguided, had over-extended, were too inexperienced to handle difficult times, but that somehow we knew what we were doing. We hadn't done too badly in the past. We had set up and, with no money, made a name for ourselves and spread our products all over the world.

We ran around, mostly in circles, but it helped to take away the pain. When you're busy there's no time to sit and brood. It's absolutely exhausting just trying to make life work at such times. In our lighter moments the situation looked fairly promising, and it seemed that the bank would finish up with a substantial part of their money. In fact, it never balanced out but I was told a considerable portion was recovered. And of course we were negotiating with Berlei.

Ten days later the bank announced they were appointing a receiver, which put the fear of God into us. Melvyn, as liquidator, was decidedly miffed, having assumed that, should the bank decide to appoint a receiver, it would be he. We had grown used to him; he was certainly selling the stock off very profitably; and the more money he raised, the better it was for us, leaving less to be covered by our personal guarantees.

A receiver takes priority over a liquidator, who then moves down a peg and deals only with what is left after the preferentials – the Inland Revenue, the VAT man and the banks who have personal guarantees – have taken theirs. The staff come first of all and receive everything that is owing to them, and quite right too. We had almost a hundred and fifty on the payroll at that time; and a great deal of money was owed to us, although regrettably not enough. Senior liquidators all move on the same circuit and there is a professional rivalry between them. Equally importantly, their earnings are related to the money they turn over.

The new appointee installed watchdogs in each shop to ensure there was no dishonesty over the takings. They were pleasant men doing a boring job, agreeable to taking their turn to make tea and checking each day's takings and post, which brought cheques from wholesalers and credit card companies settling their accounts.

The bank gave us twenty-four hours' notice to make ourselves available to this dreadful ogre who was going to loom up over us. Peter and I were terrified at the prospect.

13

The receiver, Phillip Munjak, was not quite the ogre we had been anticipating. But he was resolute. When Peter found reasons for keeping him waiting, he pointed out: 'I'm running this company now. You'll do what you're told, Mr Reger.'

To me, he began by asking what I hoped to get at the end of the day. The company was in liquidation, *fait accompli*. He had been approached by people prepared to put money into the business to keep it going, with an offer for me to stay on as designer-figurehead and to run the production side. Would I be interested in such a deal? I had been told that failure on my part to co-operate would go against me with the bank; they would take a tougher line on calling in our personal guarantees. So I did my best, and agreed that if someone wanted to buy the company and offered me a reasonable salary and acceptable conditions, then I should be happy to talk.

The receiver called in agents to sell everything the company owned: office and factory furniture and equipment; stock, fabric, hangers, labels. Nothing was missed – or so I thought at the time. Estate agents came in to sell the property. He combed the accounts to ensure there were no hidden assets.

He spotted the marks where an obviously heavy table had been standing, and screw-holes in the wall indicating the recent existence of a fitting of some sort. He wanted to know where these items had gone. Very sweetly Doreen, who dealt with wages and personnel, went into battle on our behalf. The table belonged in our dining-room in Wirksworth and was moved downstairs only when Peter needed an office table for a meeting, she explained. The receiver was dubious, but allowed me to win that one. Likewise, our painted corner cupboard. It had been in our home for years until Peter decided to put it in the Wirksworth showroom.

It was like watching a death. Melvyn had closed down everything except the Bond Street and Beauchamp Place operations in order to cut overheads. Now, with one of his staff, I went to Wirksworth to see what had to be done, angry with Peter for refusing to come with me.

I stayed up all night copying the twenty thousand customers' names on our very prestigious mailing list. I didn't dare take the index with me, because I knew that such lists were worth money; the receiver would want to sell it for thousands of pounds. Ours was an efficient though primitive system, and copying each name and address individually on a small machine is a painfully slow process, only marginally faster than writing it out by hand. My one brainwave was to copy on to envelopes, ready for the first mail-out. At a future date we would repeat the process, copying on to a new card index. Nobody ever asked about the mailing list. Weeks later when they held the sale of Wirksworth office furniture, among the items listed I saw: grey filing cabinet, £35. This was the mail-order file. Whoever had inspected it hadn't noted the contents and it was to be sold off as furniture with used stationery inside. All that work to copy the mailing list, and in the end we bought it for £35.

Our flat was cold and depressing; the electricity had been turned off. First thing the following morning, we loaded everything on to a van to be delivered to Beauchamp Place. I wanted to keep the Beauchamp Place shop open as long as possible, to have a presence there, partly because I couldn't bear to say goodbye, but also because it made sense if I should succeed in buying the lease to have as short a break as possible.

The receiver knew I desperately wanted to buy the Beauchamp Place lease, and said he would give me the chance to meet the best offer he received. There were so many imponderables. How could we set about borrowing money without knowing the full extent of our debt to the bank, which depended on the outcome of the receivership proceedings? Whatever happened, we knew we had to set up a new company as had been stipulated by Mrs Regal at Cadogan Gardens, or lose the roof over our heads. We couldn't risk rocking that particular boat.

The one hopeful spark in the murky gloom was Berlei, and as soon as I had Bryn's word on it, I reported back to the receiver that, if the bank would agree, Peter and I would form a new company, make a new contract with Berlei and out of our earnings (to include money from other licensees in the pipeline) repay the bank. Thus the bank would probably end up being paid in full, and maybe leave some over for the other creditors.

The receiver informed us he had been made an offer for the trademark of £100,000. If we could top that, it was ours for £125,000, to be paid over five years. In addition, we would make payments based on a percentage of any royalty income that we earned over and above sums already guaranteed by Berlei. (In the event these proved to be well in excess of the original prognosis. I have learned since what licensees can do with an important trademark and this deal would have benefited the unsecured creditors as well, who would almost certainly have got something out of it.) The bank seemed happy with this proposition, and we felt we were taking the first steps towards recovery.

Nothing had been finalised. Contracts were whirling back and forth between lawyers. But at that point we had an agreement with the bank that they would not call in our guarantees if the deal was completed as discussed. It can take months to finalise a liquidation. In our case it was a year before the line could be drawn to indicate the matter was over. I needed somebody to act for me. Peter's behaviour was very erratic, and I was totally inexperienced at handling anything of this magnitude.

To my immense good fortune I was introduced to the accountant John Corré, who still advises me today and, together with Ronald Norman, the solicitor we'd been using for years, he drew up the contract for the purchase of my trademark.

It was not significant then, but I now see that I was shifting to John Corré and Ronald Norman the role played for so long in my business life by Peter. The agreement ran to many pages of small print that only solicitors can understand, but the main criterion depended on the proviso that Berlei would assign the contract to the 'new' company.

As we have seen, from the moment Janet Reger Creations Ltd went into liquidation and we had collected our scrambled thoughts together, we knew that our only hope for the future was somehow to hang on to Beauchamp Place. Melvyn now gave it a commercial value of £8,000. It had a short lease and anybody else taking it on would need to refurbish for whatever product they were selling. We thought we stood a good chance of raising that sort of money.

Meanwhile, we had concluded our negotiations with the bank to buy our trademark over five years. We knew we were taking risks because of our personal guarantee to the bank, but everyone assured us there was no way the bank would grab back the shop so long as we were able to make the repayments regularly each year as agreed. At this point we all thought Bryn Harries at Berlei was one hundred per cent genuinely behind the deal we were discussing. It wasn't until he started to make offers to me personally that I began to realise he wanted to get his hands on the whole thing. He knew Peter and I had problems in our marriage. It's quite clear to me now that, much as I tried to be discreet about it, there were people very close to us in the business who knew exactly what was going on.

We would need stock for the shop, and design-room space to prepare our own collection and Berlei's, so we decided to buy part of the Wirksworth operation. In fact, all this time I was earning. The shops were taking good money from our permanent 'sale' – not a sale at all: nothing was reduced, but everybody knew the company was in liquidation and sales were buoyant. So the receiver thought it made sense to finish the stock that was cut and half-made and had us set up in the smaller factory in West End, Wirksworth with two machines in the old design-room. I re-employed several girls I thought were good for that sort of operation.

The receiver paid my salary for three months, and Peter's for one. I had never before had my wages paid so promptly. I was used to asking Peter for money as and when I needed it. The previous year we had been tightening our belts and taking very little for ourselves, so this was, ironically, the best personal money I had received for some time. Towards the end of my three months, when I knew I was soon to reopen Beauchamp Place, I took on two further machinists of my own and set to making stock. Everybody always asks, 'How did you get it together so quickly?' That's how.

We also bought back our flat in Wirksworth. For one thing, Peter was madly in love with the place, particularly the garden. We had bought the building as a derelict cluster of cottages with a factory in the back garden. I worked on restoring the house, he on the garden, and it became one of the great loves of his life, so much so that it was breaking his heart to think of parting from it. 'You'll need Wirksworth for Bryn's contract,' he said over and over again. 'And if things get really tough, we could give up Cadogan Gardens and go and live there.'

He loved being in Derbyshire. He dreamed of life on a remote island, or of buying a farm in rural France, and Derbyshire was the closest he ever came to the idyll he fantasised about. He really should have stayed in Israel on his kibbutz as he always said he wanted to do when I first met him. We never got around to going back and it got harder and harder to make the break, but it would have suited him beautifully.

In the best of our golden years we had bought a lovely old farmhouse in a village near Wirksworth and planned to make it our home. Before the collapse of our business, when I had vowed never to live with him again, we sold the house. Peter was very sad, but I had no use for it, alone.

Buying the equipment to set up at West End was complicated. What we didn't buy from the receiver, we obtained by signing a new hire-purchase agreement. I wanted cloth, components, lace, garments in production. The receiver asked £20,000 in total and there was no way I could raise it. The goods were certainly worth it, but it was a great deal of money for us to find. After all, the sale agent would have to find somebody who needed that particular combination of goods, and he planned to sell the materials and finished merchandise as one lot. I did a deal, paid a deposit, gave him a sheaf of post-dated cheques that had to be met out of the shop's takings; £500 a week for thirty weeks.

The Beauchamp Place shop was put out to tender, and the receiver told us that he had been offered £20,000 for it. 'Take it or leave it.' We agreed to exchange contracts immediately with two months' delay in completion. We thought that in two months we could take that amount of money providing we incurred no other bills whatsoever, apart from the £500 a week going out.

I was forced to use the cloth we had. I couldn't buy anything else, but it didn't matter. And actually the shop was closed for only a few days while we went in and tidied it up and sorted out the last remnants of unsold stock: bright purple briefs that matched nothing else in the building. I crammed them all in a box. We'd put them into the next sale.

With the liquidation Brenda's job ended, but she remained in telephone contact with us. One day I overheard Peter telling her of my plan to buy back Beauchamp Place. The implication was, whatever we did, she would once more be one of the team. When he finished the call, I said, 'Peter, the plan does not include Brenda. I want to make that absolutely clear.'

He was shocked. How could I be so ungrateful, so dismissive of all the effort she had put into the company? How could we leave her out now?

'Brenda has earned herself a good living, in a very cushy job which allowed her to arrive for work at ten in the morning and leave at four in the afternoon. You gave her an excellent salary, prestige, a directorship, a flat in London. Don't tell me I have to be grateful to her; she doesn't have to be grateful to us. It was a business relationship, and I don't propose to begin it again. I'm not having her back.'

And then I told him about the detective. He didn't believe me. He didn't think me capable of such a thing. He wouldn't admit I was right, but I cast doubts in his mind.

Finally Brenda and Peter quarrelled. She phoned him at the flat one day when we were trying to restart in business, to say that she was setting herself up to do mail-order promotions, and wanted our mailing list. Peter found it difficult to say no to people, unless it was me. He told her he would call her back. He came into the bathroom. 'That was Brenda. She wants the mailing list.' He recounted their conversation. 'I don't feel like giving it to her.'

This was a change of attitude. 'Why not?'

'Well, why should I give her our mailing list to use for other companies, possibly competitors of ours?'

I was pleased to hear him saying precisely what I felt. It saved another argument.

'What shall I tell her?' he asked.

'Tell her precisely what you've just told me. You're not giving her the list for somebody else's benefit.'

Finally he plucked up the courage to telephone and told her that she could not have it.

We reopened the Beauchamp Place shop in April. All the tourists were back and hadn't even noticed we'd been closed. A few who went to Bond Street asked around and were redirected by the local shop assistants to Beauchamp Place. It must have seemed mysterious to the public, believing we had gone 'bankrupt' – not true, of course; there's a world of difference between bankruptcy and liquidation.

Bryn sent us flowers on our opening day. He was happy for us. We were arguing a little over various points in the contract but in an amicable way. The bank was ready to go ahead on the transfer of the trademark, but needed the new contract signed by Berlei before they could proceed with us. Berlei had given the receiver notice that they were no longer in contract with Janet Reger Creations because they had the right to drop out if the company went into receivership, which it had.

After that, there was a change of attitude. No doubt following our meeting over the dinner table when we had told Bryn of our problems he had gone home, had a good think and started, as people do, to ask himself what more his company could get out of the situation. When he next contacted us a few weeks later, it was to say that all the publicity about the liquidation was not helpful to the Reger image. The situation had changed. Circumstances weren't as favourable as they had been when we originally signed the contract. 'Deliveries are going to be late. I think we must have a six-month extension on the contract.' In other words, don't expect any royalties for a while. And, while they were about it, Berlei would like a few extras included in the new contract. As well as Great Britain and Europe, he wanted us to include America.

We said: 'Anybody who hadn't heard of Janet Reger before the liquidation has heard about Janet Reger now. The publicity hasn't been all negative. Janet hasn't come out of it as a wicked old crook from whom no one will ever want to buy again. On the contrary, we've had a very sympathetic reaction from the press. The tone has been, What a pity this company made such beautiful things and how sad it couldn't survive. The liquidation hasn't put anybody off buying the merchandise.'

We agreed to the extra six months; we agreed to give him America and he went away to redraft the contract. It came back with numerous additional new clauses we hadn't agreed as well as the ones we had, such as a reduced royalty for the first year. The last straw was his clause saying that we could produce underwear only for ourselves at Beauchamp Place; any other sale we wished to make would require his permission first.

We told him that this was really not on. We said that he couldn't expect us to spend a small fortune purchasing our trademark and then have him control our business, telling us to whom we were allowed to sell. We had to earn money to pay for the trademark. And we had to purchase our trademark back or he couldn't go on with his licence agreement.

During one of Peter's down moments – we were still living together, fighting most of the time – Bryn asked me to discuss one or two production problems over lunch. Afterwards, he put to me a not very well veiled proposition: that he would buy the Janet Reger trademark, and then he would set up a small section in his factory that I could run as a sample-room and a place to make couture garments to retail in Beauchamp Place, which he would also buy. I would be made a director with a huge share of the equity.

I asked about Peter.

'Peter?' said Bryn. 'Oh, he's brilliant at languages. Let's send him off to be export manager somewhere.'

'No, Bryn, I can't cut Peter out; it's as much his baby as mine. I'll obviously think about your proposition but it must have a deal for Peter and even then I'm not sure. We're very independent. We've had a lot of offers and so far nobody has been able to come up with one that makes us feel really free, and since yours is obviously going to be the lion's share, you'll have control. After all, you'll be putting up the money.'

'I'd do fifty-fifty,' said Bryn. I found that quite unbelievable. I told him I'd think it over and we parted.

He continued blustering, and wooing, and rewriting the contract. Each time it came back, some of the points we'd agreed to delete were still there. Some points we had agreed had gone. Yet every time the clause remained about my not being able to sell without Berlei's permission.

14

Out of the blue I received a letter from the receiver's assistant (known to us as 'the receiver's little hero') saying it had been brought to his notice by interested parties that we were using the Janet Reger logo and trademark, which, we must realise, was an infringement. I found this odd since during the several months we had been trading at Beauchamp Place, he had actually visited us many times. His agents had even sold us carrier bags and labels, on which our name was loud and clear.

We were beginning to feel buoyant by this time. Business was good. We were managing to pay our bills on time and had plenty of cloth in stock, which meant I wasn't forced to purchase any more immediately, although there would soon need to be a change from the sea of red satin which engulfed us for the first few months. At least that was better than the sea of red and white striped fabric left over from the mail-order project. We had some cream satin, and masses of lace. I am at my most ingenious with lace. I can always make it look different.

We felt quite confident, and believed that sooner or later Bryn would finalise the deal. Apart from anything else, it was a good proposition for both sides.

I was hurt by the tone of the letter from the receiver's assistant. After all, we knew each other and were on first-name terms; he had been seeing us almost daily for months. Why write, why not pick up the phone? I rang him. 'What the hell's going on? You know damn well I'm about to purchase the trademark any minute. The whole purpose of this operation is to enable me to pay the bank. This is ridiculous. Do the bank want to get some money from me or do they want to block my ability to earn?'

Actually, he said, it isn't the bank who's complaining.

'Who are the interested parties in the trademark, then? There's only me.'

'Not exactly,' he said. 'Berlei are an interested party.'

That was the first intimation I had that Berlei were going to trample all over me and disregard my interests totally from then on. I knew Bryn was trying to get better terms on his contract, but people do that sort of thing in business when they believe they have the advantage.

Peter phoned Bryn.

'Oh, no, no,' said Bryn. 'No problem . . . I just happened to make an enquiry. You know we do have this licence. We ought to have a meeting.'

He arrived at the meeting with his solicitor and his adviser, not his regular accountant but a man whom we later learned is an expert on liquidation. Bryn had asked to meet us earlier in the afternoon, before the business meeting, to go over some details of the launch, and we met. Nothing untoward was mentioned, so we were unprepared for what followed.

Bryn and his solicitor sat quietly, letting the adviser do all the talking. He was, literally, a heavy, and incredibly aggressive. He began by demanding: 'Why do you expect my client to underwrite *your* business?'

My accountant, John Corré, replied by saying he thought that exaggerated the situation. 'My client and yours had a business relationship which they were both happy about. Both wish to continue, and all we're actually asking him to do is to change one word on a contract. Instead of Janet Reger Creations, to change it to Janet Reger Boutiques.'

'We don't see it like that,' the adviser replied. 'We see it that we're guaranteeing you money to pay the National Westminster Bank.'

'No, you're guaranteeing to pay us exactly the same money – in fact a bit less, because we've been negotiated down – that you agreed to pay in the original contract. That we choose to pay the bank with it is our business.'

We wouldn't give an inch at that point. We felt we had already given so much.

The meeting finished very abruptly. 'This is our position,' said the 'heavy'. 'Think about it.'

'And this is our position,' we replied. 'We won't budge.'

Bryn said: 'We'll see you later anyway. We'll talk about this again next week.'

They left without the usual pleasantries, which John said was part of their negotiating strategy. They wanted to make us nervous.

That night we were to attend a trade ball as Bryn's guests. The ball was in the Members Room of the Royal Zoological Society at Regent's Park. Bryn had taken a table and invited quite a few important buyers. Obviously he wanted to be seen with us; he wanted the buyers to see that we were still alive and well and doing business. In a way I was the feather in his cap. It was not a function I would normally attend, and he knew this, but since we thought we were in business together, it was natural that Peter and I should wish to give him our support, and it had been arranged for weeks.

Peter didn't want to go to the ball that night, and John agreed that it wasn't a good move. Sheila was also invited, and we telephoned her to report the afternoon's events, to say that we would not be attending and that we felt extremely nervous about Bryn's reliability.

'You've got to go,' said Sheila. 'I've told the press you will be there. If you make him look a fool it will only antagonise him.'

Her persuasion won us over, very much against our better judgement. It was a miserable evening. I felt our smiles were grimaces, and it was a strain to meet so many people we had known for years in the trade. Their reactions were divided between, 'How lovely to see you looking so well', carefully avoiding any mention of the ordeal we had been through. And, 'So sorry to hear about your troubles. How are things going now?' as if they were meeting someone recently bereaved. Gloss over it, or be blunt and come straight to the point – that was the predicament. The majority chose the first and easier option.

I had made an effort to look good and wore a special outfit made for my niece's wedding the year before, which had a skirt in a tinselly material in blue and silver, a blue silk off-the-shoulder blouse trimmed with beads and a wide silver cummerbund. I wore my hair up, gripped by a comb that had been made to match with silver and blue flowers and delicate dangling ribbons. After all the trauma of the liquidation and the publicity I really made a big effort to go there looking like a million dollars and was pleased with the result. Peter always looked wonderful anyway: his clothes immaculate, shoes polished. He was what you'd call a snappy dresser, handmade shirts and suits, nails manicured, hair freshly washed. He was fastidious about his appearance in every way even if he was sometimes a bit of a slut around the house. But I was so miserable the entire evening it was hard to be sociable. Peter was never sociable anyway, and he particularly loathed that sort of evening.

I had reason to be unhappy. I felt insecure about Berlei. We had a shop, a factory employing four girls and a cutter, but were not yet picking up any wholesale accounts. Money was so tight I couldn't even afford to supply the shop properly and couldn't have coped with producing a wholesale collection, either financially or timewise. All these meetings were so time-consuming. Every week, when I should have been running my business, I was sitting in meetings with banks, accountants, solicitors, Bryn Harries. And now Bryn had raised the spectre that things were not as we had believed, and we had reason to be worried about his behaviour.

There we were, accepting Bryn's hospitality, putting on a brave face and feeling that we were present under false pretences, being nice to his and our customers. Buyers, like fashion journalists, don't know what liquidation is about. Why should they? Fashion journalists know fashion, store buyers know their merchandise, turnover, profit ratios. They're expert at the things they do. Why should they know how the City functions, how banks operate? I didn't know either until I became involved with it.

The buyers thought they were buying from Janet Reger, and since the products bore the Janet Reger name it was reasonable to assume Janet Reger and Berlei were happily united. I had to project myself, be happy and sweet-natured and exude confidence, when I actually felt like kicking Bryn in the teeth. It was one of those nights when we went home and sat talking, and finished up having a row as we so often did.

Meanwhile, the bank sat holding its contract and waiting. The signing had to be simultaneous. The bank had to know we had

141

guaranteed income; Berlei couldn't sign with us unless we owned the trademark. The plan was that all interested parties would meet with lawyers and would sign.

We were all set, and had arranged one final meeting on the Thursday. The following day I was due to fly to Munich, where we had problems with the bank over our overdraft there. Aliza was managing the Munich shop, which was a separate company so not directly involved, although the Munich bank knew that we, the shop's sole supplier, were in liquidation. They became concerned, got in a panic and immediately demanded a meeting in Munich with somebody senior to Aliza who was twenty-one.

Peter didn't want to go to Munich, so I planned to spend the weekend with Aliza, give her some cheer and comfort, and then together we would meet the bank, which she had so far been handling very well. For the first time I realised she was a thoroughly capable adult. It was quite funny when, during that meeting with the Munich bank manager as he paced around his office rather aggressively, he said, 'You do realise I have the power to take all your stock?' Aliza replied, 'But wouldn't it be better left where it is? I'm doing good business and paying money in every day. You're not going to be able to sell the merchandise in the bank.'

So there I was, planning to go to Munich on Friday afternoon's flight after everything with Berlei and the bank had been signed and sealed. Bryn and Maurice, his sales director, arrived at Beauchamp Place on the Thursday and we went upstairs and sat around the black dining table we had rescued from Wirksworth. There was champagne on ice and we had sent out for lunch to save time. The contract was in order – except for the clause prohibiting our selling to anybody else.

'Oh, that idiot of a lawyer,' said Bryn. 'I'm sorry, Peter, he has failed to follow my instructions.' Whereupon he took the draft contract and crossed out the offending clause in front of us.

'I'll get back to him this afternoon. The contract is on his computer. I'll have him take it out and it will be ready for signing tomorrow first thing. I'm sorry about this. I know we agreed weeks ago that the clause must go. Don't worry, it is an oversight. It will be done.'

Bryn phoned his solicitor to ask how long it would take him

to remove the offending clause, and a meeting was arranged for ten o'clock the following morning at Bryn's office in Slough. Peter was to sign for us.

That evening, Peter suddenly said: 'Do you know, Bryn said he would be bringing his solicitor to tomorrow's meeting. I think we should have our solicitor there, too.' We managed to track Ronald down and he agreed to accompany Peter to the Berlei office the following morning. In the event it didn't make much difference to the outcome, but it did provide us with a witness.

As I was leaving Beauchamp Place for the airport on the Friday, Peter arrived by cab. I hadn't expected to see him back so soon. He was clearly very upset.

'I've got to talk to you. We have a problem.'

I had a plane to catch, so Peter drove me to the airport. On the way he recounted the morning's events. The first thing that had astonished him was to find, on his arrival, that the receiver's assistant was there. This was unnecessary and inappropriate. Bryn's solicitor produced the contract, handing a copy to Peter, and sure enough the contentious clause was still there.

At this point Peter knew they had no intention of taking it out. He looked Bryn in the eye and said, 'Bryn, you know I'm not going to sign this, don't you? We've given you so much already. This contract is very disadvantageous to us compared with our original contract, which you were happy with. You now have advantage after advantage. We are not giving up the right to run our own business. We've made it clear. I'm not signing unless this clause is taken out.'

Ronald Norman had been kept in the picture all along, every time the contract was changed or not changed. In his opinion all the haggling and discrepancies suggested all was not as it seemed.

Bryn spoke: 'The way I see it is this. Why should my company underwrite you? And if you're not prepared to go along with me, then I'm doing something else.' He addressed his next remark to the receiver's assistant. 'Mr Receiver, I'm offering one hundred thousand pounds to buy the trademark, cash on the table. You don't need to wait five years for it.'

Now the pretence was over.

Our accountant, John Corré, had been suspicious all along, and had said, after one meeting at which Bryn's team was being rather aggressive, 'These are your friends?' But he also agreed that, because of the stance the bank was taking, we had no choice but to try to hammer out a deal with Berlei. We had our backs to the wall.

The receiver's assistant turned to Peter. 'Can you counter that offer?'

'No,' said Peter, 'I really can't.'

Then Peter said to Bryn: 'I can't stop you. If you've got the money to do it, do it. But I'll tell you one thing, you certainly won't have any co-operation from us. Neither Janet nor I will have anything to do with it. And you may not particularly need me, but to use a designer's name you need the designer. And my wife is a very, very good designer.'

Bryn replied: 'Don't you worry. Janet will understand and will do a deal with us.'

'I know her better than you do,' said Peter, 'and I assure you she will not.'

He left me at the airport and went straight to Ronald Norman's office to find out what our legal position was. After all, we were trading in Beauchamp Place with the name Janet Reger slapped across the shop front. Peter wanted to know what we could and couldn't do. Was there still some salvage deal that could be done with the bank? He must also speak to Sheila Gore; perhaps publicity would shame the bank or Bryn Harries or the receiver into a change of heart.

We agreed that he would phone me for a discussion soon after I arrived in Munich, and as I reached the hotel the phone was ringing. He told me that, according to the lawyer, we could go on using our name so long as we didn't use the actual logo. There was no reason to stop calling the shop Janet Reger as that was my legal name, but we could not call the company Janet Reger Creations or use the old logo. That would belong to Berlei if they went ahead and did the deal, but there was still time to intervene. Ronald Norman would speak to the receiver's lawyers and see what could be done. We shouldn't give up hope completely. And we should try to activate a little media support if we could because it couldn't harm us, and banks don't like this sort of publicity.

By then Peter was very depressed. The day's events had left

him totally shattered. He had not been able to contact Sheila Gore and was still trying. A few hours later he phoned again.

'Janet, we're really in trouble. Sheila is not with us.'

'Don't be ridiculous,' I said. 'You've got it wrong. You know how you misinterpret sometimes.'

'I promise you Sheila is with Bryn. I talked to her about it and she made it absolutely clear there is no way she will say a word against Berlei. She is one hundred per cent on his side and is supporting Berlei in this.'

Before the company went into liquidation we had given Berlei permission the previous December for Sheila to handle the press launch of the Berlei Janet Reger collection; it made sense. Bryn then asked if we were agreeable to Sheila handling all Berlei's public relations although it is not usual practice for a public relations company to handle competing clients in a field; we gave it some thought but had to say no. Indeed, it would have been extraordinary had we said otherwise. Sheila appeared to accept this with her usual equanimity.

Peter repeated their conversation, remarks that Sheila was later to reiterate to me. Sheila argued that she could hardly go to the press and disparage Berlei after handling the Berlei Reger merchandise. She said she would lose face if she had to criticise anything Berlei did now. Besides, she had been talking to Bryn Harries that day (which was why Peter had not been able to reach her on the telephone) and her advice to me was that she thought I ought seriously to consider Bryn's offer. She said that Bryn had been telling her all his plans and he was going to make me a rich woman.

'But Sheila,' I said, 'you were the friend who said to me months ago, when somebody else was offering me a deal, "You'd be better off selling oranges from a stall in Oxford Street if you're used to being independent." And now you're telling me to put myself in Bryn's hands after what he's just done to us.'

She protested that I was misjudging Bryn, to which I responded by asking her whose side she was on.

'Well,' she replied, 'as a matter of fact, I've signed a contract with him. I didn't have one with Janet Reger Creations any more. There you are in liquidation . . . ah yes, I know you've formed a new company [this in response to my interruptions] but I didn't know if you were going to be able to pay me anything.'

I said: 'Sheila, we've *never* had a formal contract, you and I. I'm amazed after all these years we've been together that you've signed a contract with Bryn knowing we didn't want you to represent Berlei.'

'Janet, let me talk to you. It's silly wasting all this money on the phone. You're coming back to London on Tuesday. We'll have a meeting then and talk it through. I've got a lot of ideas. Bryn doesn't mean you any harm. Keep an open mind, and look on me as the mediator.'

Back in London we had the meeting. Sheila reiterated that she felt we should throw in our lot with Bryn Harries. And we said how hurt we were that she should have signed a contract with Berlei without telling us. This was friendship as well as business. If she had been worried about her future and money, we would have understood only too well, being in the same situation ourselves. If it was something she felt she had to do, we'd have understood. 'We're hurt', we said, 'because we feel you've had a foot in each camp. We've been confiding in you, asking your advice, being totally unaware that you have a contract with the person we are trying to deal with.' A person, incidentally, whom we felt had tried to take advantage of us. It wasn't heated. We were too upset for that. We had worked together all those years, were friends, had been on holiday together. We'd lived through her romance, her engagement, her wedding, her buying the connubial cottage. I was making her tissue boxes to match her curtains. We were friends.

There were harsh words but no shouting match. 'How can you speak to me this way after all I've done for you?' cried Sheila at one point.

'Sheila, you've done nothing for me that I haven't paid you for,' said Peter. It wasn't strictly true but he was deeply hurt and shocked.

We went back to the bank. Was it really too late? Had the deal been signed and sealed? But there we found a curious change of attitude. Suddenly they were being kind. They didn't want to treat us badly, although there was no way they could now entertain the five-year repayment plan, having been offered cash. But since Janet Reger was my name in the first place, they would be prepared to accept £75,000 – or at least talk about it.

146

John Corré and Melvyn said there had to be a catch; something was not quite right with Berlei's offer. No receiver would turn down £100,000 in favour of £75,000. We determined to try to raise the money, and played for time. The bank had stipulated a limit of one week. But it was far too much for us to raise from family, friends or well-wishers. People had already rallied magnificently. Family had proved more supportive than I could ever have hoped for, but even if they could raise it, £75,000 was the sort of money that could break you if the deal goes wrong. When somebody lent us £3,000 or £5,000 we were confident we could pay it back. It wasn't somebody's house or life savings; it was money they could afford to lend us and were generous enough to do so. But £75,000 was a different matter.

One of my brothers-in-law suggested he get a consortium together to raise the money and leave us in charge; another said perhaps he could pull in a collection of small loans. People were being extremely helpful, and we had precisely one week to do the deal. At the end of the first day, we knew in our hearts that we had lost. I went home that night and said to Peter, 'It's done.' We didn't talk, we just sat staring into space. Peter suddenly got up at about midnight and said he was going out. He took the car and drove around for hours.

When he returned he looked a little better.

'I'm going to kill Bryn Harries,' he said.

I told him not to be so silly. 'We'll survive. I can still trade under my name; that's legal. We'll find a way out of this. We just have to.'

In the end it was a legal hassle that went on for almost three years, while I had to live with the odd sensation of knowing that my own name was somebody else's property.

Peter actually went so far as to join a shooting club, although he never actually attended. He was going to buy a gun, and to buy a gun you need a licence, and to get a licence you have to join a shooting club, and to get that far you have to be interviewed by the police. The policeman was very charming. Oh yes, Mr Reger, how nice to meet you. He sat in our flat, no doubt thinking Peter was a very sporting man who wanted to learn to shoot.

He had to get a licence because he intended to buy a gun to kill Bryn Harries. That was the little boy in him. A man's gotta do what a man's gotta do. I knew he wouldn't shoot Bryn. Peter was a talker and totally non-violent, except verbally. He could say the most dreadful things, be horrible and inflict the most frightful pain with words. But he always found it very hard to match his words with actions.

15

I vowed not to co-operate in any way whatsoever with Berlei or Bryn Harries. I'd sign nothing. However, I reckoned without the bank. Sign or else.

Now it emerged that Berlei's offer to buy the trademark was conditional. If I signed the contract, limiting us to selling only in Beauchamp Place, Berlei would allow me the right (renewable) to use my name there for seven years at a nominal fee of £1 a year. Berlei would then hand over £100,000 for the trademark and the bank would be happy. If I refused to sign, Berlei would pay only £25,000, for without my goodwill the trademark was worth much less. The bank naturally wanted the full amount. If I refused, they would be likely to demand I pay off my outstanding loan immediately. They held all the cards and were entitled to. I had no choice, yet I continued to resist, buzzing like a bee in a jamjar.

In September, in the midst of all the traumas, Peter suddenly decided he couldn't cope. He needed a holiday; he would visit Lisl. But Lisl had the builders in, and Peter needed the holiday instantly so he sprang it on me: 'I'm going to Sardinia tomorrow.'

I didn't like the sound of this. Peter never went anywhere on his own, and I was suspicious. He had been very little support to me since the Beauchamp Place shop reopened. His only contribution – this was his period of sitting unwashed and unshaven by the television all day – had been to bring a great pot, beautifully planted up, as a shop-warming gesture. Ironically, I had just delivered a lecture to the staff on being stringently economical, not wasting a farthing, all that sort of thing, when in walked Peter with his pot and told them they must be careful to water the plants every day as he had just spent £45 on them. Not exactly appropriate when we were on a serious economy campaign. (Actually the pot was far too big for the shop. We kept falling

149

over it, and eventually I took it home, where it continues still to trip people up.)

His plans to draw money for a Sardinian holiday when I had my suspicions it was with somebody else, made me even angrier. I couldn't leave the business. I certainly couldn't spend money on the luxury of a holiday. Peter said he was happy to go alone; he needed time, space, a change of scene to be by himself 'and sort things out' which, when he had thought of going to Lisl, had made sense. She is very down to earth and sensible, and I knew she was on the side of our marriage. She has always liked me. If anyone could help him get his feet on the ground, it would be Lisl.

But the minute he mentioned Sardinia, I knew he would be taking Pamela with him. The Pamela situation wouldn't go away. He was still seeing her, even though I was living with him. After I'd left she never actually moved in with him; he drew the line at giving her a key to the flat.

I did a little detective work. I knew she worked from home, so I tried calling her and, whatever time of day it was, there was only her answering machine. I wanted *not* to believe it, so I kept trying in the hope she might answer. One evening the telephone was answered, and I was relieved. But it wasn't her voice. I asked to speak to Pamela. Pamela was away in Sardinia until the weekend, the voice said. Did I care to leave a message?

No message, thank you. I put down the receiver.

When Peter phoned from Sardinia we had a pointless shrieking row. He had told me he would be home on Sunday, but when I checked with Gatwick I learned there was no flight from Sardinia on Sunday, which could only mean he was returning to London on Saturday and would be spending the night with Pamela before coming home to me. I packed his case with a few items he would need, because I knew he would have only summer clothes with him. I put the case in his car and his car keys in an envelope, together with a note telling him I had changed the lock at Cadogan Gardens, and on Saturday night sent it by taxi to Pamela's flat.

Early on Sunday morning Peter came banging on the door, demanding to be let in. I told him to go away. 'What about my post. I want my post,' he said. I passed his mail through the chained door. It was ludicrous. I'd thrown him out and all he

150

could think of was his correspondence! But that was Peter, always ludicrous. The first time I left him after Mustique he had stood over me as I packed my bags, saying, 'Why are you going, why did this have to happen to us?' as if it was not his fault, but rather that fate had dealt a dreadful blow out of the blue. I often wondered why Pamela put up with the situation, unless she was in love with him.

I switched on the answering machine and let the phone ring. On Monday he turned up at Beauchamp Place, asking to be allowed into the flat during the day while I was at the shop. 'I'm moving out,' I told him. 'I don't want that flat. I don't have a single happy memory there. It's been nothing but misery. I'll find somewhere to live. And what's more, I don't want to be in business with you any more. I don't want anything to do with you. I want to buy you out of the business and I want a divorce.'

He was furious. There was no way he would agree to a divorce, but I told him he didn't have any choice. 'If you don't want a divorce soon, then we can have one in five years' time anyway. It's up to you whether you want a clean break now or want to drag it out. But there is no way I'm coming back to you. I've had it. I'm not negotiating with you. I don't want to talk to you. Find somebody to represent you and talk to John Corré. I want to buy you out.'

He was making threatening noises: I'd be sorry. I'd be ruined without him. I'd finish up with nothing. Then he left.

He asked Melvyn to intervene, to persuade me to allow him back into the flat; he had nowhere else to go during the day. Pamela worked at home. He would have to sit in her bedroom all day while she painted clients' toenails and tinted their eyelashes. It put him under an obligation to her. Tough, I replied, his activities were no concern of mine. I would move out as soon as possible and he could have the flat back then, and not before.

When you're upset you tend to seek help from someone you think you know, and I went back to the same estate agent who had found me the Hyde Park Street flat two years before and said I would like something similar.

What a strange coincidence, she remarked, that I should crop up at this moment. The very same flat was once more available. The owners had lived there since I left and were now leaving for

151

India within the week. They were asking more rent, but were now sufficiently desperate to accept a reasonable offer since I had been a good tenant before.

I agreed to take it for two years, at the previous rent, but stipulating that I must be allowed to paint the living-room, kitchen and bathroom in my own choice of colour. The existing colours were shiny flamingo pink in the living-room, black and canary yellow in the kitchen and a red and emerald bathroom.

They hummed and hawed about my suggestion. I pointed out that in two years' time the flat would be due for redecoration anyway, so if they liked what I'd done they could save themselves a job, and if they didn't like it they wouldn't have lost anything. It was all signed and settled and I moved in that same week.

Everybody told me that once you start divorce proceedings, things become very unpleasant about the objects you own. I was determined I was going to make everything very clear about our joint possessions and their worth, and before I left Cadogan Gardens I made a complete inventory of the contents and a separate list of the items I had taken with me to furnish my new flat. I reorganised the flat in Wirksworth, using some bits and pieces from Hyde Park Street which I didn't like to save the cost of storage.

I also went to the bank and withdrew exactly half the money in our personal account. I wanted to be scrupulously fair. And then I told Peter I wished to buy him out and that we should appoint an independent valuer to assess our business. I planned to make an agreement to pay him over a period of years.

I was still committed to paying the rent at Cadogan Gardens, for which we held a company lease, and it was proposed that this would continue and the amount would eventually be deducted from the money I paid for his share of the company.

I was efficient, cool, outwardly calm, resolute. Part of me was totally committed to starting a new life without Peter. If, tucked away, lurked a faint hope that what I was doing would scare the daylights out of him so effectively that he would change and we would get back together on new terms, then it was barely considered consciously. We had gone too far along the breakdown path. I was at the end of my tether and couldn't endure our marriage any longer.

Those last few months had been unbearable, when the hostile atmosphere in the flat was so miserable that I used to go out walking, dreading going home. The desire to leave Peter had been building up, but always the business crisis demanded my time and energy and the personal problems were shelved. I had flat-hunted spasmodically. Being shown around a flat I would suddenly get such a surge of depression at the prospect of what was involved in moving out, and breaking up the marriage for a second time, that I would have to rush out quickly before I burst into tears in front of the estate agent, sometimes even the owner.

During that time, on the rare occasions when we tried to talk, we had discussed our marriage problems. He wanted me to stay with him, love him, take care of him, be his wife, and just turn a blind eye to his affairs. Indeed, if I had any sense I would make friends with any woman he fancied, so I wouldn't feel so left out and hurt. He lived in his own world. Now I was half-relieved that I had found the strength to go and leave behind that dreadful atmosphere. Hyde Park Street became my little haven. I painted it prettily and made it mine for the couple of years I was there.

I wouldn't see him. I forbade him to come to the shop and, although he ignored that once or twice, I wouldn't have anything to do with him. My accountant was negotiating the value of the business.

For many weeks I prevaricated about signing the trademark agreement. All my instincts strained against it and in vain did my accountant and solicitor try to soften the unfairness of it. Now we had reached ultimatum time. We were sitting in Ronald Norman's office, or rather they were sitting and I was pacing the floor, when John, flicking through the dreaded contract, suddenly looked up and said: 'They've made the same mistake they made before. Look, isn't that so, Ronald?'

Two heads bent together and looked up with beaming smiles of enlightenment. Unbelievably, throughout the contract, it referred to Janet Reger Boutiques Ltd. It was the same old stumbling block. They had tied the company to the contract, not the contract to me as an individual.

Simple. We'd found a loophole. All I had to do was wind down the company and trade under my own name. They had no contract

153

with Janet Reger. I had the perfect out, whenever I was good and ready. I signed knowing full well that I was tied to nothing.

I reached an agreement with the bank whereby the bank agreed to reduce my personal debt to £10,000, to be paid back over an agreed time span. The bank got its £100,000 from Berlei, and the National Westminster and the receiver now bowed out of the arena. But the battle between Berlei and Janet Reger was not yet over, although for a time there was an uneasy lull.

We had several valuations of the business because Peter argued about every one. 'This business is worth at least a million pounds,' he kept saying, and everybody laughed at him.

At first he declined to negotiate at all, flatly refusing to talk about divorce. 'You have one husband, one wife. There is no such thing as divorce,' was his way of closing his mind to such an unpleasant subject. We knew what the factory was worth; we had bought it only a few months before. We knew what the shop was worth for the same reason. Stock? There is never any argument about stock: you value it on the day and that is it; it has its set price; everything is on record.

Then there was the matter of goodwill. We didn't really have much of that. In fact, my solicitor told me that I didn't have to give him anything for goodwill because if it went to arbitration, which would happen if we couldn't agree, nobody would take the goodwill into account because we had lost it. I didn't want to be nasty. I wanted to be fair, and in all fairness it was his business too. Apart from the last few months we had always worked together, and a lot of the ideas were his. We were a good team. I did still love him. And I really always hoped that somehow we could get together, although I didn't know how. There were times of despair when the last thing I wanted was for us to get back together, and other times when I just felt so miserable I was prepared to agree to almost anything to be back with him. We had been married a long time and, although it was a very difficult relationship, there was a lot of holding on. We somehow needed each other. One of our friends once said it was a case of the old cliché: we couldn't live with each other and we couldn't live without each other.

The company was valued at something around £250,000 to

£300,000, then the debts, mortgages and loans were deducted. Peter came to a meeting, banged his fist on the table and said, 'There is no way I'll agree to this. These are liquidation prices, not real prices.'

'Not at all,' said Melvyn. 'These are prices paid on the open market. You know that well enough. You're being silly. Take it and be sensible if you want out.'

'Who said I wanted out?' said Peter. '*She* wants out. Either she agrees to my terms or I'm not leaving.'

He stormed out of the meeting and vanished. Nobody could get hold of him. Aliza called me to say he was in Austria, and although I tried to reach him, he proved elusive. When he did reappear in London, albeit briefly, he behaved in an outrageous and quite uncharacteristic way.

Aliza and I had decided to take a holiday during the Christmas break. I was exhausted, physically and emotionally. As usual Christmas trade was good, so we could just about afford to take ourselves off to Mustique with the windfall I had earned by collaborating with a newspaper on a series of articles.

When we returned I discovered that in our absence Peter had been to the bank and helped himself to £20,000 from the business account, most of our hard-earned takings. I hadn't taken his name off the account. We hadn't settled the sale of the business yet and, although I had often been advised to remove his signature from the cheques, it would never have occurred to me that he would do such a thing. It really wasn't in his nature.

He did it for spite, to give me a hard time. I phoned Lisl and his mother. Peter refused to come to the telephone. 'He has no right to take business money. It's stealing,' I said. I was shocked and angry. We later settled it. The money was deducted from the amount due to him from the sale of his shares in the business.

He was short of ready cash at that moment and was earning a little buying and selling pictures with his mother, and also on commission. But he was knowledgeable and was beginning to do quite well.

Aliza, on my instructions, went to the bank in Munich and had Peter's signature removed from the account, which, when he discovered what she had done, made him very angry.

When you've spent your life with somebody for more than

twenty years and suddenly you're on your own, it is like a death. In some ways it is worse than death, like finding yourself crippled. You've always been able to walk and suddenly you can't. You're not functioning properly.

I believed I had done the right thing and would have been silly not to have done it, but I kept feeling that maybe things could work out differently; that anything would be better than being on my own. I never felt that for long. There were times when I was relieved and decided that life was easier without all the aggravation and heartache. But at the same time it was miserable, lonely, and I missed him a lot.

My family were my closest friends and support. I saw nobody else socially. I was in a bad way, probably ill, taking tranquillisers and sleeping pills. I didn't want to go out or do anything. My family would ring and say, Come here. Do this. Do that. And I always replied: 'Afraid I can't, I'm going out' or 'I've got other arrangements for this evening' or 'I'm going away this weekend.' They were all lies. If my family ever believed me, they must have imagined I was leading the most frenzied social life.

At work it was better. I could function there because it involved my total concentration, and I didn't need to think about Peter. Then I would go home and close the door on my little sanctuary, be as miserable as I liked without anybody knowing and pitying me.

Recently I came across a letter Peter sent me. I had to smile at the memory it evoked. When he had returned from his Sardinia idyll with Pamela, I was sorting everything out in the flat. I didn't want to leave it looking a mess, so although I divided the furniture and possessions, I moved everything around so that it wouldn't look bleak and miserable when he got back. And I looked in the freezer and saw there were some string beans. Peter was totally unable to perform in the kitchen; he could hardly pour himself a Coca-Cola or a glass of water. It was stupid to leave those. He'd never know what to do with them. So I made a big saucepan of his favourite Austrian bean soup, with potatoes, sour cream and caraway seeds, and left it in the fridge. Alongside the inventory of everything I'd taken, everything I had left there and everything that was still in Wirksworth, I left a note saying: 'By the way, the bean soup in the fridge is fresh. I made it today. You might as well have that, it's the last thing I shall ever cook for you.'

Shortly after I left him Peter wrote thanking me for leaving the flat looking so nice, and for the bean soup that was delicious. And apologising for overlooking my birthday. Perhaps we were doing the right thing. A separation might help us to sort out our problems. We would be together, eventually.

16

Business was good in Beauchamp Place. I made two decisions: to start wholesaling again and to find myself a public relations officer. Since Sheila's departure Peter and I had decided we couldn't afford someone to handle publicity, and I was therefore perturbed when I received a call from a television researcher who, in passing, referred to 'your PR'.

'I don't have a PR.'

'Oh, isn't Sheila Gore your PR?'

'No, she's Berlei's.'

'Oh, I see. I thought she was Janet Reger's.'

A few weeks later the television programme went out and Berlei got the publicity. Obviously I needed a public relations person, and as I was wondering how to find one, I quite literally bumped into the fashion journalist Bonnie Spencer, who, when asked, at once recommended Christine McCarthy to me. At the same time Berlei's publicity machine had circulated a press release which began something like: 'Good news. Berlei have rescued Janet Reger.'

It wasn't surprising, given the machinations going on behind the scenes, that even the trade press – who ought to be well informed – carried varying accounts of the Berlei strategy. From where I stood, it was more of a rape than a rescue! Christine and I countered with our own press release pointing out that no, we hadn't been rescued by Berlei, far from it. Hiring Christine caused another row with Peter – he felt this was a ridiculous waste of money. We sank into another long silence. Christine certainly walked into a battle zone when she joined us!

I wrote to several of my old wholesale customers to tell them that I was now in a position to supply a limited number of customers, and to ask if they would be interested.

At last I had organised my business affairs. I wound up the

company called Janet Reger Boutiques that I had owned with Peter and set up a new firm, which I named Designs by Janet Reger. My main reason for the change was the Berlei problem. My new company had no contract with Berlei. As for Peter, he was on sticky ground should he object. I was prepared to make a money settlement with him although I was not legally obliged to; he did no work in the business and was merely a shareholder in a debt-ridden company. If he wanted to sue me, any lawyer would tell him he was wasting his time because I was making the change for very sound financial reasons: I wanted to wholesale.

It didn't take long for Berlei to find out what I was doing via the trade grapevine, and to write a strong letter warning me that I was in breach of our agreement and threatening an injunction. But John Corré and Ronald Norman had already prepared my answer. The clause in our initial contract which had proved such a tight knot to unravel now worked to my advantage. Janet Reger Boutiques was no more.

In response to Berlei's threatening letter, my solicitor wrote to say that I was using my name in a *bona fide* way and there was nothing Berlei could do about it. I had responded to their initial complaint, had painted out the Janet Reger name above the shop and had it repainted in ordinary capital letters. They had given me six weeks to stop using the logo, but I couldn't manage it in the time. It meant new receipt pads, bags, tickets and making sure that none of the old Janet Reger labels remained. Changing labels on garments is terribly expensive but I tried to phase them out in the six weeks. (When I asked the receiver's assistant why he should have sold me the bags in the first place if I was not permitted to use them, he replied that he thought I might like them as souvenirs! £2,000's worth?)

We had taken great care not to write letters on the boutique's paper but on paper headed with my name only, and signed by me. All our advertising was done on a personal basis: 'Mrs Reger' would like you to come to see the collection, not 'we' implying the company.

There followed a silence. Temporarily. They were planning the next attack, which took us totally off guard. The receiver wrote bearing an injunction accompanied by a report from a Mrs Somebody-or-other.

In search of evidence of our transgressions, she had visited the shop and spotted a black vase that nobody had noticed and of course it carried our logo. She had then enquired whether we had a visiting card. It is not something we're asked for very often. After a search, the assistant, helpful but unsuspecting, rummaged in a drawer and produced a visiting card. It bore the old logo. The 'customer' took it away as evidence. Armed with the ammunition they needed, Berlei slapped an injunction on us within twenty-four hours.

My solicitor advised me not to panic. We could go to court and obtain a stay of the injunction, pending a hearing in a few weeks' time. Meanwhile, I must get rid of the vase, go through the shop and check there was nothing else bearing the old logo. We had committed a misdemeanour by not ensuring that already, but nobody was going to close us down for it.

But it didn't end. The handle on the shop door in the form of a dragonfly had been there so long we all touched it every day without even noticing it. This too was quoted as evidence of our intent to 'pass off' as Janet Reger, when everybody knew of course that Berlei were Janet Reger.

As letters winged to and fro, legal bills mounted horrifically. We were now getting litigious, a new word for me. Letters accusing me of crimes concerning doorknobs, old business cards, presenting myself as Janet Reger when Berlei were and our replies kept the lawyers busy. But they could no longer sue me for being in breach of contract for they realised they had made a mistake there so they left that one alone.

Legally Berlei were on weak ground, but by this time they were becoming increasingly hostile. Bryn had been very unlucky with Janet Reger. The goods I designed for him had sold reasonably well (although I as the designer never received a penny royalty), but he had to follow up with a new collection. He took on a designer who had previously worked for a Marks and Spencer producer. It all cost him a great deal of money. And he had me to contend with, also proving costly, because whatever I was paying in lawyers' fees, he was paying at least as much.

One ludicrous aspect of the entire Berlei affair was that the new collection actually cost them more in the end than paying the royalty would have done. To design a collection – employing a designer, designer's assistant and the cost of working space and samples – would add up to at least £50,000. Bryn had a far better deal with us. I simply couldn't see how it wasn't in Berlei's interests to work with us from the outset of liquidation. There is a sound rule in business: never think about what the other person is getting out of a deal, think about what you're getting. Berlei couldn't accept this.

Christine meanwhile was talking to the press, who knew me well and were very sympathetic. They were featuring my garments in preference to the Berlei Janet Reger. The *Daily Mail* fashion editor Jean Dobson, taken by Sheila Gore to see 'the new Janet Reger collection' at Berlei, looked at it in some disbelief and asked: 'Sheila, is Janet still working?'

'Yes, of course she is,' said Sheila.

'But she didn't design this, did she?' said Jean. An experienced fashion writer reads a designer's work like handwriting, and it was obvious that this was the work of a hand other than Janet Reger's.

Not only were Berlei not getting the press coverage Sheila wanted but the stores were unimpressed, too. When the new collection went on sale in Harrods, I sent one of my girls to buy a complete set and we all pronounced the garments dreadful, ill fitting, badly finished. Then the range suddenly vanished out of Harrods; presumably the buyer had sent them back. The merchandiser later told me that she had decided any Janet Reger in her department from now on would have to be Janet Reger personally, not Janet Reger from Berlei.

I was angry at the proliferation of 'Janet Reger' products emanating from the Berlei licensing agreement. Most manufacturers realised it was worthless putting a designer's name to merchandise the designer hadn't so much as glanced at, but around this time numerous 'Made in Macao' items slithered on to the market, to the possible detriment of my professional reputation. I went home and wept after seeing a particularly uninteresting dressing-gown in dingy blue velour hanging on a rail in Selfridges. It was priced at £69.95! Had it been £19.95 it would have represented reasonable value, drab though it was. When I went back for a second look it had gone. I think the buyer must have had second thoughts.

All this was to form part of our case. While I felt that on the design side I was winning, I could not predict the outcome of the long-drawn-out legal battle that might have to be fought in court, and which meant meetings with my solicitor at least once a week preparing to answer numerous preliminary court hearings, all postponed on the day pending new evidence to be presented by one or other party. It seemed that everything I earned was immediately passed on to lawyers and accountants.

Peter remained in Austria, and made his peace with Aliza. Our efforts to reach settlement were at a standstill. On one of my visits to see Aliza in Germany, I met up with Christina, my friend from Mustique. She lived in Venezuela and had shown up in Munich to care for her sick mother. Between her duties at home she was helping Aliza in the shop and of course knew all about the situation between me and Peter. I suggested she might like to help me in Beauchamp Place during the summer, filling in for staff holidays. She was already familiar with our merchandise. What could be better?

Around Eastertime Peter called me, saying he wanted to see me. What was I doing right now? It was a Saturday morning and I wasn't doing very much except being miserable.

'I need to talk to you,' he said. 'It's very, very important. Why don't you come over?'

When I refused he said, 'Then I'll come and visit you.'

I didn't want to finish up in either of two ways: another screaming, flaming row, which I didn't think I could take; or his persuading me to go to bed with him, which might be a temporary panacea but it had happened so many times before that I knew it couldn't solve anything in the end. If we were going to talk, it had to be somewhere where good sense and moderation could prevail.

'No, I'll meet you out.'

He came to pick me up and we went for a walk. It was a fresh, sunny, cold day, too cold to stay outside. We ended up walking along the Bayswater Road to the Royal Lancaster Hotel, where we talked over tea.

He told me he was very unhappy and that he wanted me to come home. Couldn't we make things right? It didn't have to be like this.

'What about all these females?' I wanted to know. 'What about Pamela?'

162

'Gone, gone, gone . . . all gone,' he said. 'Gone her own way. I don't need anyone, only you.'

It wasn't only the women. There was also his attitude to me, his moodiness, the fact that he constantly dictated my every move, made me feel I had to ask permission to use the telephone. We discussed things in a reasonable way without any quarrelling, Peter being the persuasive Peter I knew so well. But he looked so desperately unhappy, and pleaded with such honest conviction that he could and would change his ways, that I began to believe what I suppose I had always wanted to believe: that there was, after all, hope for us and our marriage. On rare occasions Peter had been known to say 'Sorry', and this was one of them.

Maybe things *could* get better. I told him I wasn't prepared to go back to him at once. There were some aspects I needed to think through, and I wanted to sort out where we were going from here. I didn't want to go back to the old situation, the old fights. We must have a new understanding.

He took me home because I wanted to be alone. I was churned up inside and needed to think. He left me at the door and we agreed to meet the following day.

On Sunday he called for me and, as I let him into the flat and he looked around my little sanctuary with some of the bits and pieces we had chosen together, he became very emotional and started to cry. It was the only time I ever saw him cry. 'Wherever you go, you make everything so nice,' he said. 'That's one of the things I really miss about you. I just like being with you.'

'Yes, but obviously not enough,' I said.

He protested that he wanted only to be with me, that if I could show just a little tolerance I would see his indiscretions meant nothing, were mere male instincts. 'If you loved me the way I love you, you would want me to have my little pleasures that don't matter anyway. I want to share my experiences with you.' This was a recurring theme of his.

We talked and talked and finally agreed to try again. We would begin by living apart during the week and spending our weekends together. It was a start, at least.

17

When Aliza stayed with me Peter would never visit; the tiny flat was far too crowded. So she saw him at Cadogan Gardens. One day after having tea there, she decided to drop in on a friend nearby. Her friend's mother, the writer Shirley Eskapa, had just published *Woman Versus Woman*, a humorous view of how to stop your marriage breaking up when you have a flighty husband. Aliza's friend's brother Roy, a psychologist, passed this book on to me to read.

It was lying around during one of Peter's weekends at my flat. We were having breakfast, always a volatile occasion, for we were both at our most excitable in the mornings. He picked up the book. Why not borrow it? I suggested. It was full of common sense about holding families together.

He opened the book at the first page, his glance falling on the opening paragraph in which the author advises women not to leave hastily *just* because the husband is having an affair. It states that men do these things and, while the book doesn't condone the man's behaviour, it suggests solutions or ways to deal with it. Peter seized on this opening line as vindication of everything he had always advocated in his own defence.

'See, I've always told you that you get too upset about things. It's just a natural male instinct.'

'Read the book, Peter; then we'll talk about it,' I said. He stormed off, very angry.

A few days later my friend Christina arrived from Munich to help me with the shop. She had never been to London before, so I took her sightseeing. She was receiving a generous allowance from her husband pending a divorce settlement. In the event, this happy state ended with a fall in the value of Venezuelan currency and its effect on her husband's support. That summer she went from being a wealthy Venezuelan lady travelling around Europe on an allowance from her husband to being penniless. As the value of her currency plummeted it seemed as if somebody had taken her money and divided it by ten.

In any case, I was busy escorting her around London, and Peter accepted this with equanimity and no displays of his old possessiveness. He knew she would be going home and that we would take up where we had left off. Once he gave Christina the benefit of his advice on how to handle her husband, and she replied that she *had* handled him: she was filing for divorce!

Once, after Peter and I had quarrelled on the telephone, she said: 'You know, Janet, it's over for you and Peter. You've left. Why are you still quarrelling with him? When you leave, all that should stop. You only fight with someone when there is something to save; there's nothing to save in your marriage.'

Another day she suggested I should do something for myself. 'You can't go on like this. Why not take one of these courses?'

I didn't know what she was talking about. I had vaguely heard of est. I had consulted therapists and psychiatrists with and without Peter; but nothing had really helped. I listened to her describing how, when she left her husband Kai she went to a friend in Florida and for four weeks she did nothing but sit in her house and cry. 'And then I got myself together. I got some help, and look, I'm fine now. I wouldn't go back to Kai now whatever happened.'

She had grown-up children and our circumstances were similar in several ways, except she hadn't worked for years.

Kai was an entirely self-made businessman. Christina had helped him when they first started out, but he was up and running and made money very quickly; by the time we met them, they were extremely rich. They had a magnificent house in Caracas, another on the beach with servants and cars; and a beautiful house in Mustique. They mixed with rich ranchers and politicians; he loved to socialise, and required a wife adept at running the house superbly and organising the social whirl to go with it. This Christina did to perfection.

One evening when Aliza and I were alone, we answered a knock at the door to find her friend's brother Roy and another man, Sam. Would we like to join them for a curry? It was an enjoyable evening. I took an instant liking to Sam. He was years younger than me, but it didn't matter. Conversation was more of a flood than a flow. He projected so much warmth and *joie de vivre* it made me happy just to be in his company; there was absolutely nothing sexual or romantic about it.

A few weeks later Sam invited us to a dinner party. There were some people he wanted us to meet. I was in one of my more depressed moods and it took all Aliza's powers of persuasion to make me change, put on my make-up and drum up a vestige of enthusiasm.

I arrived in the middle of a deep discussion about a seminar due to start the following day. Sam and another man, Leon, were trying to persuade Roy and Aliza to enrol. Sam was quietly persuasive, Leon enthusing wildly about what a beautiful experience it had been for him. I wasn't sure what they were talking about, except that *it* was a course in self-discovery and would cost £200. It sounded a stupid way to spend money. Aliza was resisting. Roy was keen to go; as a psychologist he had a professional interest.

Aliza said to me, 'Mummy, why don't you go?'

Roy was urging: 'Do go, Janet,' and I knew he wanted a companion.

Sam was saying: 'Just do it. Just do it. Just do it.' I looked at him and thought, I wonder whether he has this wonderful calmness because he was always like this. Or is it because he's done the course?

'Okay,' I said to Roy. 'Pick me up tomorrow. We'll go together.'

There was even a money-back guarantee should you be dissatisfied, providing you finished the course. It was spread over six days: Wednesday, Thursday and Friday evenings, all day Saturday and Sunday, and a Monday night discussion review. I had nothing to lose, so I gave them my cheque.

Insight originated in Los Angeles. Arianna Stassinopoulos (also a customer of mine) found it in New York and brought it to England. Among the new recruits, one enthusiastic disciple, Ruth Lederman, carried on the work in England.

This was their first London seminar for two years and several in the group had been waiting a long time for this moment, their

166

enthusiasm kept on the boil by small workshops. Others had done the course before, and were 'auditing': doing it for a second time. We were a mix of types – doctors, businessmen, housewives – and ages. The youngest was eighteen, the oldest a lady in her seventies. John Cleese and his then wife Babs were there. By the end only three had dropped out.

The atmosphere was highly charged. Roy and I were conspicuously restrained, sitting quietly – not together; the first rule of the seminar was not to sit beside anyone you knew – unsure whether or not to join in the frequent bursts of clapping that followed the most prosaic actions. It seemed to us that someone had only to say hello to receive a round of applause.

Very soon a small, suntanned, neat-suited man took the stage. This was our Californian facilitator, Russell. He proceeded to explain the rules and guidelines of the seminar, smiling a lot and displaying perfect dentistry as he elaborated on what we could and could not do over the next five days and repeating the same theme in various ways. It was excruciatingly boring. The break came just in time to stop me falling asleep. Rule two: every time you came in after a break you had to sit in a different place.

For the rest of the evening we played a long-drawn-out, pointless game. This consisted, it seemed, of choosing a colour; marks were awarded for choosing the 'right' colour. A guessing game. I was thoroughly fed up, confused and irritated by the time we left. We had also been instructed not to talk for an hour on the way home, so Roy and I promptly got in the car and talked all night.

They called it the Game of Life. Everybody thought they had to win it but later it seemed I had misinterpreted. I felt cheated about winning. It was as if I had not been given fair instructions on how to play. I am very competitive by nature. It took me a long time to see that there *was* a point. In fact I saw it fully only during the next year. Insight was to equip me with a new, better approach to my life. Nothing could stop bad things happening to us, but we could be taught how to handle them. There was no guarantee of eternal happiness, but we could learn how to cope with the unhappy experiences, and how to avoid the avoidable.

Somebody asked how long would it take to achieve this state of mind, and the facilitator replied, 'How long does it take to wash the soap out of a bottle?' You put in the soap. You let the water run through until it runs clean. It takes however long it takes.

They talked about the quality of life, and getting what you want out of life in a way that won't hurt anybody else, in a way that is beneficial to everybody.

One of their ground rules was to use everything to your advantage. Whatever happens to you, however awful, however difficult, use it to learn from because you will get an advantage in the end. Instead of wailing and bemoaning your fate or going out and causing damage, sit down, say to yourself, This is the situation I'm in. What am I learning? By taking that attitude you turn things around within yourself.

I started the second evening already in a bad mood. One of the rules was to be on time. They played a short snatch of music for one minute before the beginning of a new session. When you heard the music, you had a minute to take your seat, so punctuality was paramount. We would have been on time, but we couldn't find a parking space. We rushed in just as someone closed the door in our faces. I had a row about that, and then Roy and I slunk in and sat down at the back.

The facilitator was asking whether anyone wanted to share their experience of what they had done yesterday. And people began to talk about the Game: what he said, what she said. I took no part. I couldn't for the life of me see what they found to talk about.

We began to do 'exercises' involving a partner not previously known to us. I still couldn't see where this was leading, but I went along with it. One exercise was called Victims. Russell began the session by telling us how, when he was a student pedalling his way to college, a big expensive car came tearing down the road, speeding, and knocked him as he turned into the road. He was sent flying from his bicycle.

It was our turn. You sat facing your partner. One at a time, each told the other a true account of an occasion when he or she had felt victimised. You were told to look the other person directly in the eyes, to touch if you wanted to, hold their hands, for instance. But say nothing, no 'Oh, you poor thing, how dreadful for you,' and afterwards no comment of any kind.

168

I told how I'd been burgled a few days after I moved into the flat in Hyde Park Street, a really upsetting experience. After a few minutes Russell stopped us, and it was the partner's turn.

Then Russell repeated his original story, this time including facts he had omitted, such as that his bicycle had a wobble he had been too busy to get fixed; and that the road he was turning into was actually one-way although all the boys from college habitually used it as a short cut.

Then we had to retell our stories, taking a critical look at the initial account to see what we had left out. As Russell put it, nothing he could have done would have prevented that car being in that place travelling too fast, but there were aspects of the incident for which he was responsible, and which had put him in the position of victim.

In my case, I had noticed that the door of my flat was a little worn and I had been meaning to put a Chubb lock on it. It was an interesting lesson in accepting responsibility for what happens to you, rather than blaming everything that goes wrong on somebody else.

Each game or exercise took a different form. There was no way that you could cheat by spotting the formula. We examined Guilt and Resentment. Russell explained that they are the same emotion: resentment is directed against others, guilt against yourself. It is anger at your own inability to cope. The cause and the emotion are the same. At this point I began to feel a little more interested, although I still failed to see how it would do me any good. After all, I'd read countless books on the subject of self-help and what good did they do? But the Guilt and Resentment proposition was a revelation. I had never heard this connection expressed before and it rang all the bells with me. I was full of resentment at the time, and to a certain extent guilt, too. I wasn't behaving well to Peter, but at the same time I felt justified in my actions. I was in a mess and wasn't thinking about anything clearly.

No answers were presented: we found them for ourselves. Not quite at that moment, but we went home with something to think about. Some people became emotional at times and assistance came from the line of helpers, all ex-graduates of Insight, sitting at a table at the back of the hall. Lectures and demonstrations were punctuated by games. Everyone had the chance to share experiences if they wished. There was no pressure. In fact, on the first night Roy refused to play the Game of Life. 'I'm not playing anything so stupid,' he said, and sat out.

After the second session I went home feeling that I had not wasted my time. Aliza was still up so the three of us shared supper together. (I had forbidden Aliza to breathe a word about Insight. I didn't want people – her father in particular – thinking I'd gone quite mad.) 'It was much more interesting tonight,' I told her now. 'I'm glad I'm doing it.' I still couldn't see that it would help me; neither could Roy. But we hadn't been bored and Roy especially liked the course because there were lots of gorgeous girls. 'A very good way to pull,' he joked. 'All this mingling and touching and learning about total strangers.'

By Friday I was looking forward to the evening. I had become friendly with several members of the group, including Stuart, a doctor with whom I always shared an ashtray during breaks. He and his wife Giselle are now among my closest friends. After Friday's session our little crowd sat drinking coffee and chatting until late, and when I got home Aliza was asleep.

I went to bed feeling very stressed. Despite having enjoyed chatting with my new friends, I had been forced to think in a way that was uncomfortable, to recognise the sort of messes I'd made. I was obliged to agree that things weren't quite as I had seen them at the time, that sometimes I could have handled situations better. I thought about that morning at breakfast when Peter had commented on Shirley Eskapa's book, and how stupidly I had handled it.

I felt very miserable. It seemed that I had created so much mess in my own life. Why couldn't I have known all this before? I didn't see how it could really change me now. I went to bed depressed. Nevertheless, I was quite looking forward to the weekend. At least for once I was doing something positive. One of the things Aliza had said to me when she was trying to persuade me to sign up for the course, was: 'Well, Mummy, the worst thing that could happen is that you might meet a few interesting people. And you can do with that right now in your life.'

And I thought, I *am* meeting interesting people. I'd stopped thinking they were all nuts.

On Saturday I was up and about and ready to leave home very

early. This was strange after such a late sad night. It was like waking from a wonderful dream – you can't remember it but it leaves you with a feeling of euphoria – the first morning in years that I had not awoken feeling tearful and as often as not actually wept before I finally got myself together.

It was a sunny, mellow October morning. I got a taxi immediately; the park looked beautiful. I felt on top of the world. I didn't ask myself why. It just felt good to be alive.

It was only when I got there and moved around greeting people – we had all sat in the same room for three evenings and were well used to one another by now – that I suddenly realised: everybody feels like this . . . And then, they must be brainwashing or doing something to us here. Everybody feels like I do, enjoying the day and feeling good about it. There was music playing and some people were actually dancing before the session began. This was 9.30 a.m. We might have all been tipsy on champagne. In fact, it was water only on the course; no alcohol or recreational drugs. If you had a headache you were encouraged to try doing without medication: that way you could learn a lot about healing.

We had become a close-knit group, had learned a great deal about one another, including those serious problems that some were currently facing, which had in effect made us very supportive.

We experimented with telepathy. You had to concentrate on somebody you knew, and your partner had to tell you the first thing that came into their head. Mine said: 'Laughs a lot, a teasing person, small with masses of dark hair; her favourite colour is a pale pastel.' Aliza wears pale pink all the time. When somebody asked Russell why such a test should be so accurate, he answered that human beings have a perception, a power of communication we don't realise or feel day to day. He allied this to hidden strength, and quoted the story of a frail woman being able to lift a truck that had pinned her child to the ground. How could she find such strength? We must never forget, he said, that we all have hidden power and strength and they can aid us when we are in need.

Some people wept. I cried, too; not for myself, but for the woman saying about her son: 'How am I supposed to cope? My son is on heroin and he's only twenty years old.' We felt very

171

close to one another, identifying with one another's problems.

The session ended and some of us went off for a meal together. It was late when I fell into bed. I had still not seen Aliza and had had nobody to discuss it with outside the seminar since Thursday evening when I was still very sceptical. Roy by this time was feeling quite elated too.

Sunday was an amazing day. I understood what Christina had been telling me that summer. I felt strong. Aliza came in the evening to the friends' party that marked our graduation.

'My God, Mummy,' she said, 'what have they been doing to you? You look absolutely wonderful. You look twenty years younger.' She immediately signed up for the next seminar. 'I mustn't miss out on this.'

She also told me: 'Daddy has been phoning all weekend and I told him you'd gone away. He phoned at least two hundred times.'

That Sunday I was sorry he wasn't there with me. The course had clarified my muddled thinking about Peter and especially our marriage. Now I knew that I was going to sort this out with Peter or finish it. The choices were actually mine. I could give them to him and it would be up to him which he accepted. I knew what I wanted, and if he didn't want the same thing, it was totally pointless even to carry on together.

I went to work on Monday morning feeling that a totally new person had come out of the seminar. And people were saying to me, 'You're looking good, you're looking wonderful. What have you been doing to yourself?'

Then Peter phoned. 'Where the hell have you been?'

'I've been doing a course,' I said. 'I've been busy.'

'What sort of course?'

'Look, I can't discuss it now, but perhaps I can see you tomorrow and we'll talk about it.'

'Why tomorrow, what's wrong with tonight?'

'It's the final evening of my course tonight. I'll see you tomorrow.'

He was very argumentative on the telephone but I wasn't going to have a fight with him. I was in that calm space. I didn't want to fight. I didn't even find it difficult to remain cool; it seemed natural. 'Peter, even if I had time I wouldn't want to discuss it with you now. Why don't we talk tomorrow?'

I agreed to go to the flat on Tuesday evening: a promise which did not stop him phoning in the interim at fairly regular intervals to hurry things up.

That evening people were talking about how their Monday had been. Since Friday afternoon they had hardly seen or spoken to a soul except for their classmates. We had been through so much self-discovery that it really did feel as if we had left our old selves behind and begun Monday morning as new people. The meeting was to discuss how the first day had been. I did not pronounce upon it, but I had been elated all day and felt I had handled the day well, including my first difficult situation, which was Peter trying to pick a quarrel.

I arrived at his flat. He was very proud of a huge picture he had just bought and immediately began talking about it. Eventually he said: 'So tell me about this course.'

'It was about growth and self-awareness,' I replied.

'What did it cost?'

'Two hundred pounds.'

'Now I know you're an idiot. Mug.'

'Peter,' I said, 'do you want to know about it or don't you?'

He made a dismissive grunt.

'It's a pity you don't,' I said, 'because actually I got so much from it. Perhaps it would do the same for you.'

'Well, if you're so gullible you let yourself be talked into paying two hundred pounds for feeling great, we'll see how long that lasts.'

Fool, idiot, stupid, shit for brains . . . He let fly abuse, pressing my buttons (as I had learned) because he knew what wound me up. And he was frustrated at not having the desired effect.

'If you will just be quiet a moment and listen to me, you might learn something. On the other hand, you don't have to. But I don't want to stay here and listen to abuse. I don't need it. I don't like it. Make up your mind. We can sit here and I'll tell you what's been happening to me for the past few days, but without having my words flung back in my face; or we can sit here and talk about something totally different; or we can go and have dinner; or I can go home. It's up to you. You choose.'

It did nothing to halt his flow of invective. He was annoyed

173

that I had actually done something without him. He had to make it negative. He never liked me to show any independence.

Summoning all the dignity I could, I calmly stood up. 'We're not enjoying this very much,' I said. 'I didn't come here to fight with you. I don't enjoy fighting; that is something I have learned this weekend. I don't have to shout and scream to get my point over. I'm not listening any more.'

'You could at least stay and make some dinner,' he shouted after me as I left.

'Call me tomorrow if you're in a better mood,' I replied.

I could tell he was shocked. I had never before walked out, except in anger. It was a small achievement. Yet in the car driving home, I felt miserable and let down. I had hoped he would listen. I would have liked him to notice that I was behaving in a more mature way than usual, and that this was a better way, and perhaps he could learn it too. But it wasn't right for him then, and I felt sad. But I refused to let it depress me.

I concentrated on other things. I had decided I was going to start, in a small way, selling to other shops again as well as in Beauchamp Place, where business was now better than it had ever been, for as well as our old customers, we were now seeing all those who used to favour Bond Street.

During that autumn of 1984, Peter contacted me, aggressively demanding his share of the business. I had made up my mind about this and I stuck firm. He was to negotiate through my solicitor, and any settlement reached was conditional on divorce. I wanted a divorce; I didn't want to see him any more. We'd met, we'd tried, it didn't work.

He went trotting round to my lawyer's, making his demands, and my lawyer pointed out that I, his client, didn't *have* to give him anything, but felt a certain moral obligation. That was when Peter found out we had changed the name of the business, and my reasons for doing this. What an idiot I was, he said, to pursue the Berlei battle. 'Doesn't she realise she's lost it?'

He wanted his share of the business and he was talking in millions, but we certainly were not. Look, said the lawyer, nobody would pay anything for the goodwill of a company that is in litigation with another company over its trademark. He told Peter:

174

'Be more realistic. My client is willing to give you something, but she is not willing to have you come out of the deal better off than she is herself.'

I also offered the proposition in reverse. If Peter preferred, he could have the business, and do for me what I was offering him. I would accept that. I thought that fair, but Peter didn't see it that way. He was totally illogical when he was angry. Both lawyer and accountant said there is nothing worse than somebody handling their own affairs because they always get emotional. There are facts, and these are what decide the issue. Everyone breathed a sigh of relief when Peter got himself a solicitor.

Thus we reached an amicable agreement. I paid Peter a lump sum immediately, with an arrangement to pay additional sums, annually, over the next five years. In return for this he would make no further claim on me or anything I earned, and would instigate divorce proceedings, by mutual consent, in the new year.

He sent me and Aliza a Christmas card, which we found rather strange as he had been telling the lawyer to warn me he would have his revenge. It was all talk. I knew he would never harm me.

The agreement was signed and sealed and I paid him the first sum of money – the second, actually: the first he had paid himself! I should have breathed a sigh of relief that at least the fighting was over, but I felt terribly sad. It was Christmas Eve. One of the girls said that she had seen Peter drive up to the shop and park, but he didn't come in. He just sat in his car. She went out to ask if there was anything she could do. 'I just wanted to wish you all a happy Christmas,' he said. 'Will you go in and tell the girls I wish them Happy Christmas?'

18

The Christmas holiday, with its associations of happy families, Aliza's and Peter's birthdays and our wedding anniversary, threatened to depress me. Aliza and I scoured the cut-price holiday advertisements and came up with a week in Rio. It might as well have been a week on the moon for all I cared. We took it.

Brazil was a wonderful place for a holiday because the Brazilians are such beautiful people. I felt in tune with myself and others. I was beginning to put behind me the events which had caused me so much suffering, and learning to cope with things that could still cause me pain; to use it to grow and learn from rather than sit at home crying as I had been doing.

This was where I had my moment of truth, *vis-à-vis* the Game of Life. I was in a street market, and I saw small children sleeping in cardboard boxes. I also saw what a wealthy country Brazil is. There is so much food that fruit literally falls off the trees; so much jewellery; so much potential and actual wealth. And these poor little children were sleeping in the street. I suddenly had a revelation: so that was what the Game was all about. Competitiveness is so ingrained in us that in every situation we feel we have to win; our side must win. And I suddenly thought, life's not about that. And I knew what Russell meant by 'everybody wins'. Winning is to achieve the highest possible score for everybody around you. And I realised how much better off Brazil, which is a beautiful country, would be if there were no children sleeping in cardboard boxes. Because those children are the people who disturb the peace. They steal; they force the rich to have guards in front of their houses and hotels. Not to guard against violence, but from thieving. To protect them from these poor little children who have nothing.

*

I came home looking forward to a few highlights already in the diary. Life was suddenly hopeful. Although my business was still a headache, with the copious litigation, and although I was sad about Peter, I wasn't dramatising the situation or feeling hysterically miserable, but recognising this to be a natural sadness at parting after sharing my life with a man I had known since I was very young and had loved and cared for all those years. My attitude was that of course I was sad, but I didn't have to let it ruin my life.

I was beginning to go out socially, and even to enjoy such occasions. Stuart and Giselle and others from Insight had become very good friends. Things were picking up. I even had a few dates! It was not necessarily what I might have chosen for myself, but when there isn't a better choice, get on with the second best. Above all, I felt much more in control of what was happening to me.

Peter was in Austria again. Lisl asked me to join them there, so that we three could sit down and talk things over. It was incomprehensible to her that Peter and I were apart. I declined. He wrote telling me he had met up with Aliza and commented on how beautiful she looked. He didn't mention that he had quarrelled ferociously with her; I found that out later. He wrote several times, reiterating his theme of 'Let's be friends; we don't have to be apart all the time.'

It was Easter week. Something strange began to happen, my phone ringing and the caller hanging up: not instantly, but listening first. I knew it was Peter. I kept saying 'Will you speak?' but he wouldn't. After a week of these calls he rang me at the office asking to see me. I refused but he was persistent.

'Janet,' he said, 'I've made the most dreadful, dreadful mistake and I want to see you. I must talk to you. Just give me half an hour . . .'

Against my better judgement, I agreed to meet him in Richoux and he caught me on the way there. He had arrived ahead of me and had begun walking in the direction he knew I would take. We bumped into each other in Knightsbridge. I was shocked at his appearance. Since I'd last seen him, he had become so thin, so old and weary-looking. I felt really sorry, yet in another way I was pleased to see him. I had missed him.

Over coffee he said he wanted things to be different. From his talks with Lisl had come the realisation that he had been a horrible husband to me. He wasn't asking me to come home straight away, but could he just see me sometimes? 'I'm not seeing anyone else,' he said. 'I promise. Let's try to make it work.'

'Peter,' I said, 'this is very difficult. I keep putting you behind me, and you keep coming up in front again. I can't live like this. It's been going on for three years now: together, apart, together, apart . . . Our marriage was pretty lousy even before we split up. What are we trying to get back to?'

'Please,' he said, 'I promise you it will be different.'

I was inclined to believe him.

I had a dinner date that evening that I couldn't cancel.

'Leave early,' said Peter. 'And come straight round.'

I did. I stayed the night. Then it was all on again. We were back together.

Since he had been alone, Peter had taken on the most delightful man called Joe. Aliza used to refer to him as Daddy's nanny. He kept the house clean, did all the washing and ironing, took the pictures to the auction rooms and bid if required. He was big, coffee-coloured, part Venezuelan (we never worked out all the other parts), with a quick sense of humour and amazing knowledge.

When I heard Joe arrive in the morning, I decided he wasn't going to like this very much: running a bachelor establishment and suddenly the wife comes back. But Joe walked straight into the kitchen where I was having coffee, and said: 'How nice to see you. I know who you are because I've seen your photographs. I'm so glad to see you here. We've been very sad without you.'

I felt I had come home. This time it would be better – except there was still Pamela. Peter swore he wasn't seeing her, but that didn't stop her telephoning, initially that first weekend at 2 a.m. She was ill, or a friend had died. She yelled or she cried, anything to get him to go round to her flat. I suggested he might say 'Go to hell.' After all, he had never minded screaming at me when I displeased him. But he spoke in reasonable tones, and was sweet, kind and gentle. It made me cross; she knew I was there. She knew he had been through a lot and was trying to bring about a reconciliation with me.

It rankled too that he would not speak to Aliza. She was living with me. 'What do you want – that we both come back to Cadogan Gardens and she'll live here without you speaking to her?'

'We'll deal with that when we come to it.'

He wanted to know about Insight. I introduced him to Stuart and Giselle. He liked them, found them intelligent and interesting, and decided he would attend the April Insight course. It seemed to help.

Pencilled into my July diary was a trip to Brazil to talk business with a swimsuit manufacturer. Peter didn't want me to go. He missed me, and our togetherness had its funny side. There was one weekend, arranged by my public relations manager, Christine, when I had to host a writer and photographer from *Options* magazine at Wirksworth. Officially we were living apart, so Peter spent the weekend dodging the journalists and hiding in the spare room. We really laughed at ourselves. We were getting on very well except when Pamela phoned or when his silly squabble with Aliza blew up.

I told Peter what a wonderful country Brazil was, and that I knew he would love it. He was looking for something to do and I felt that this land of opportunities, with so much to see, might prove the inspiration he needed. The fare then was £400, and I offered to pay the hotel expenses. Although he still protested that it was bound to be a disappointment, he began to be enthusiastic about the prospect of travelling to South America.

The trip started with good news. Just before we left, we read in a newspaper that Bryn Harries had been fired from Berlei. The company was having severe financial problems which were laid at Bryn's door. David Pinkney had taken over as managing director, pending a new appointment that was to be announced. Both John Corré and Ronald Norman considered this an interesting move. Wait, they advised me. You will hear from Berlei. Peter, when he heard, had a similar view: 'You might actually win this.'

He made his peace with Aliza, who drove us to the airport. My plan had been to travel alone, to meet the swimwear manufacturer and attend to our business. Then I'd made arrangements to travel to Manaus, meet a friend and do a trek into the jungle with her, return to Rio, collect my samples, wait for any necessary alterations, and then leave for home. The only change was Peter would be with me instead of the friend. She understood.

Peter was not a good traveller, hated flying, was tetchy on the plane and ratty when we arrived at the hotel to find our room not ready. Awaiting me was a lunch invitation with the man I was to do business with. When I called my contact, Louis, and explained I was with my husband, the invitation was at once extended to include him. As I replaced the telephone, Peter began: 'I'm not having lunch with you both. I'm not sitting around while you two talk business.'

He did, however, relent, behaved perfectly and enjoyed himself. There followed several relaxed days. He pottered around Rio when I had to see Louis. While I dealt with my samples, he researched all he could on the jungle. He had been brought up on Rudyard Kipling's *Jungle Book* and had never outgrown the romance of the story.

We had a tiring flight to Manaus, but our hotel there could not have been more perfect. I placed a call to London; the line was bad. I kept conversation to the minimum, just to give Aliza our location details. As I finished I was aware of Peter's brooding sulk. What on earth was wrong? If I didn't know, he wasn't going to tell me. Hours of coaxing and persuading later, I managed to extract the truth: he was offended that I hadn't asked him whether he wanted to speak to Aliza.

So that part of the trip got off to a bad start; but once we moved into the jungle, staying in a little wooden hut and going out trekking each day, he was as happy as a child. And so the holiday progressed, with Peter alternating between happy moods and black ones, which came and went without rhyme or reason. We had saved a special restaurant for our last evening, but at the last moment Peter decided it wasn't his sort of place and surely I should have known. By this time I could do nothing right and every remark I made prompted an argument. It hurt. I was already thinking along the lines of once more packing my bags – not that they had ever been entirely unpacked.

During our days in the jungle we had talked a lot, and I asked Peter if he would agree to our having some sort of therapy together: marriage guidance, perhaps, or something similar. He wanted to know how we went about arranging that. I suggested he ask his doctor, knowing that anyone recommended by his doctor stood a better chance of being acceptable to him than a therapist proposed by me. He did not refuse, which I thought was a good sign.

Heading home after several weeks together of what should have been perfect holiday conditions, I was reaching the conclusion that we were beyond marriage counselling. Peter was all right as a boyfriend. When he became too impossible, I could leave. When I enjoyed being with him, I could stay. On our return to London we took a taxi, first stop Cadogan Gardens. He got out, I stayed inside, and the taxi pulled away towards Hyde Park Street.

One Saturday afternoon Peter called. He was with 'this woman who thinks she can help us'. He had been talking to her most of the day, and she would like to meet me. This was after a week of his not speaking to me, but I was quite pleased; he was never going to be easy but at least he was trying to do something positive.

I agreed at once. She came alone and stayed for several hours talking to me. Then she asked Peter to join us and we talked all night. I felt that she was making matters worse, and I didn't get on with her. But at the same time I felt I had to make the session work, if only for Peter's sake. After all, he had selected her.

It struck me as rather unprofessional that she constantly referred to her own problems, confiding at one point her own mistake in walking out on her husband because of other women. Too late, she said, she realised she had acted hastily. Now she was alone and didn't have much of a life. He had remarried with a new family. 'For me the time has passed; there is nothing I can do about it. You have this opportunity; your husband wants reconciliation.'

She was making the decision entirely my responsibility.

It was daylight when she decided we all needed to sleep. She didn't want us to see each other until we met to continue our talks that evening. She and Peter left, and I fell into bed.

I was woken at noon by Peter calling to invite me to lunch. During his stay with Lisl she had taught him to cook and one of the attractions he offered, should I return to live with him, was that now he could share in the cooking. It had always been a bone of contention that he was so unhelpful in the kitchen, yet so demanding.

181

I reminded him we were not supposed to speak to each other. 'We won't talk, just have lunch.'

'Don't be ridiculous, that's impossible.' I had to laugh, but I felt if we were going to do this, then we should do it properly.

So at five o'clock both of them arrived at my flat. Curiously, the emphasis had shifted. It had begun with assurances from Peter that everything would be fine if I went back; I was still angry that Pamela was part of his life and couldn't see why he refused to get rid of her in words she understood and would take seriously. That had been my point all along. Now it seemed that Peter, encouraged by the presence of a third person, wasn't making any promises. 'I'm not having *women* tell me what to do,' he said.

It was the first time I had lost my temper (except once when I pretended to, which doesn't count) since Insight. I was upset with myself for getting so angry, but he really wound me up and I screamed at him. He stormed out, saying he didn't want to continue the therapy, followed soon afterwards by the woman. Much later I found out that our 'therapist', whom I understood to have been recommended by Peter's general practitioner, wasn't a marriage guidance counsellor at all, and certainly had not come to us via his doctor, but was in fact one of Peter's many former girlfriends.

The day I arrived home from Brazil, Aliza had made an appointment for me to meet a prospective customer, Marion Potasnik whose husband Michael wanted to open a Janet Reger shop in Dallas. I felt elated. Something was happening with Berlei; and here was what looked like being a really wonderful outlet for us in Texas.

David Pinkney got in touch with me: 'I don't know whether you know who I am?'

'Actually, I read about you a few weeks ago.'

He laughed. 'I thought you might have done.' He went on to say that he felt we were in a situation which we could both live without. It was costing us a lot of money and he thought it was really ridiculous. He would like to meet me without any lawyers, any professionals, and try to have a reasonable person-to-person discussion about what we could do to prevent this stupid waste; and to find a solution that would 'make you happy as well as us'.

I said: 'I'm very happy to meet you for discussion, but I also read in the article that you are an accountant, and I'm not. I'm a simple, ordinary person who runs a business on a day-to-day trading basis and I would like to bring my accountant with me. He's a very reasonable, sensible man.'

'Oh, all accountants are reasonable, sensible people,' he said. 'I don't mind your accountant at all.'

Over a few meetings David Pinkney put forward a proposition. He offered to reassign the trademark to me so that I would once more own my own name. In return for giving me the trademark free of charge, Berlei wanted a share of any licensing income. He had taken on a licensing agent (I later discovered they had already organised numerous licensees), and in this way Berlei could earn back from the Janet Reger name.

In these licensing contracts there is always a clause to the effect that the licensor has 'total unchallenged right' to use that name. Now, because there was litigation going on around the trademark, they could not sign the contracts and were forced to procrastinate.

At that stage in the legal battle, Berlei were suing me for 'passing off' and my defence was that by using the name Janet Reger they were deceiving the public. I had been to counsel, and counsel had delved into the files and come up with similar cases in the past, on which we could base our case. We were gathering evidence that the name was associated with me personally.

According to Pinkney's proposals, although Berlei would give me back my name, they would still run the licences. The licensing agent would receive an agreed percentage and they would give me ten per cent. Berlei would keep the rest for ten years and then the trademark would be entirely mine.

We began to iron out the details in negotiations. My percentage began at ten per cent but would go up to thirty-five per cent, and at that I was quite prepared to agree. Apart from anything else, I stood to save a fortune on legal costs. This way, at least I would be earning something, and eventually the trademark would be mine completely. My accountant advised me to agree. All that remained was for contracts to be finalised and signed. In one way, Peter was pleased; in another he was almost resentful. He kept saying, 'I don't know why you want to knock yourself out with all this. Just get on and make your underwear and let them be.'

'But they're not letting me be. I've got to fight.'

Now it looked as if the end was in sight and I was going perhaps not to win, but to gain an advantage in the short term and to win eventually. And to own my own name again, which from a purely emotional point of view was good.

Peter had fallen in love with Brazil. He had found it perfect in every way, and not only did he want to live there, but he felt that he had found valuable untapped scope for tourism – another of his great concepts, the first for many months.

During our stay he had been enchanted by the jungle and all its fascinations, and frustrated that the only place to stay was 'this lousy hut where they serve tinned food'. This he felt was where the opportunities existed: to provide the sense of rustic adventure with a little sophistication. He talked of organising what would be 'a permanent jungle party'.

He had delved into it very seriously while we were there, made friends with our guide, spoken to the local travel agent to work out ways of organising trips to suit all tastes from the adventurous to the sedate. Back in London his enthusiasm did not flag.

His plan involved subletting Cadogan Gardens, furnished, to show a profit, and using this money to go to Brazil and build his lodge for tourists. He said he would sell all the paintings he had accumulated over the past year. I should sell the shop and we would go together to Brazil. It was quite a nice idea, like turning the clock back to our starting out together. I could see why it appealed to him, but I was frightened and, particularly, I was frightened of being stuck there with him and no one to turn to.

'Don't you think it's a bit rash to sell the shop?' I asked. 'It's not just the only source of my income, it's the only source of yours, too, for the next five years.'

At the time Beauchamp Place leases were going for around £60,000. His idea was to invest that money at ten per cent, plus the rental from Cadogan Gardens, and this would keep us and enable him to establish his business in Brazil. In the Manaus area, a little bungalow with a couple of bedrooms could be bought for under £1,000 at that time, and simple wood-built properties were selling for £700. It wouldn't have been a problem, except that neither of us knew a thing about tourism or the hotel industry. But I encouraged him to pursue his idea. He had nothing to lose.

Hyde Park Street was too small for both Aliza and me, and I was thinking of buying a flat. The business was going reasonably well. I'd managed to save a little money which I could use as a deposit, perhaps helped by the family, who all thought it crazy that I was paying two rents: Peter's in Cadogan Gardens, and mine and Aliza's in Hyde Park Street. With that money I could be paying off a mortgage.

Peter made the decision to sublet the flat, go to Brazil and put his idea into practice. I could join him later, for a holiday if not permanently. He was still talking of the new start we would make. But first he was off to Majorca for a couple of weeks. There was a woman involved . . . 'But nothing like that, she's just a friend,' he protested.

'Obviously, Peter, you're extremely anxious to get our marriage working again. But you do what you want to do,' I said. I could see he was getting into a depression again.

Peter asked Mrs Regal's permission to sublet and was refused. He begged and pleaded, offered her part of the extra money, but she was not interested. Because she lived on the premises, she watched the comings and goings of her tenants, and recognised the local estate agent when he called. Peter later described her tearing up the stairs, fists flailing at the door, demanding to know what he was up to. Actually he wasn't up to anything except to take legal advice as to whether it was within the terms of his contract to sublet. This seemed unlikely.

He had to find some other way of financing his Brazil trip, which was not to be dismissed as one of Peter's mad ideas. Actually it made sense. It was sound, and, who knows, could have been the making of him.

He asked my help. Because he couldn't sublet the flat, and as the flat I was buying had just fallen through, he suggested Aliza and I take over Cadogan Gardens for the duration of the lease. He was disposing of his paintings and wanted to instruct me what to do with any unsold after he had left England 'for ever' as he put it.

He was quite ill after his inoculations, and felt very sorry for

185

himself when I went to discuss his paintings. He showed me the book in which all his pictures were catalogued, and gave me instructions concerning each one. 'And all these little pictures,' he indicated some landscapes on the stairs, 'whatever you do, I don't want you to sell those. They're not worth anything at the moment. The artist died recently and in a few years' time they will be quite valuable, but don't sell them now.'

'I'm not going to sell anything unless you tell me to,' I said. We were no longer quarrelling, but were having calm, slightly bitter conversations about practical matters. He had booked his ticket for the following week.

When it was time for me to go, I offered to stay the night. I didn't like leaving him alone, obviously depressed. No, he said, he would be quite all right. 'See you next week.'

'Peter,' I said, 'I really feel very concerned about you going.'

'As well you might,' he said. 'The jungle is no place for a white man. I might die of some terrible disease. And then what are you going to do?'

'Well,' I said, 'I'd come to the funeral.'

I feel terrible about that now.

19

On Saturday the no-talking telephone calls began again, which Peter had admitted to making when they had happened before. I knew he was very distressed. I spoke to the silence. 'Peter, I know it is you. Talk to me. Do you want me to come over? If you do, say so.'

I was getting very churned up, feeling half-inclined to go to his flat. On the other hand, he had been so precise about not wanting me to stay on Thursday night that I hesitated. For all I knew, he might have a girlfriend there, or maybe it wasn't him at all. I couldn't be entirely sure either way.

The calls continued all day Saturday and throughout the evening. I felt so tense and nervous I couldn't go out of the house. And then I got really worried and tried calling him, but all I got was his answering machine so it didn't seem as if he was at home. I left messages. Then the silent phone calls stopped and he didn't return my messages. I was torn between fear and anger that he might have just gone off with some girl for the weekend. Or maybe he had taken an earlier flight to Brazil and hadn't stopped to say goodbye.

Eventually I drove to Cadogan Gardens, where there was no sign of his car. I rang the doorbell and got no reply. I left. On Monday I telephoned him throughout the day, but there was no reply. Neither did Joe answer, which was unusual. Peter must have gone off somewhere and given Joe the day off. Or he had gone to Brazil, Joe had left and there was a letter in the post telling me all this.

Aliza had been away for the weekend. Now she, too, was concerned. On Monday evening we went to Peter's flat together but no one was in. Joe's bound to be there tomorrow, we said; but he wasn't. I tried Mrs Regal but she wasn't there. I finally made contact with her on Wednesday morning.

'I know you've got a key to the flat and I absolutely need to get in,' I said. 'I think my husband's either gone away or is ill.'

'He must be away,' she said. 'He didn't cancel the newspapers and I've taken them in because I don't like newspapers lying around.'

I managed to interrupt her tirade about the newspapers. 'Mrs Regal, I'm a bit concerned. I must get in the flat. Will you please let me in.'

'As far as I'm concerned it is your flat too, your name is on the lease. I will let you in but I'm just on my way out now; you will have to come this evening.'

Throughout the day I continued to phone his number, and at six o'clock Aliza and I presented ourselves at Mrs Regal's front door. She handed over the key and hovered on the landing below as I went to open the door. The key wouldn't go in the lock. I peered into the keyhole and could see the key in place on the inside. The hall light was on. I began to bang on the door, yelling through the letterbox at him. I knew something terrible had happened. I knew what he had done. I just didn't want to believe it.

I said to Aliza: 'We'll have to get the police.'

Mrs Regal was beside us. 'What's the matter? What's the matter?'

'He's in there. He must be ill and can't open the door. The key's in the lock.'

'Oh no,' she said. 'It's a safety device. I have one the same. You can put it in so nobody else can use your key to get in.'

'No, Mrs Regal, he doesn't have anything like that.'

'He's probably bought it without you knowing,' she said.

I said: '*Please*, Mrs Regal, I'd like to phone the police. I've got to get in there. May I use your phone?'

'No, I won't have the police here. I'll give you an address. You can get a locksmith tomorrow morning.'

'Mrs Regal, I know he's in there and he's ill. He hasn't got a safety device. He'd have shown it to me if he had.' (Even as I spoke I was picturing Peter with a safety device, showing it off like a new toy.)

She refused to allow us to use her telephone. We jumped in the car and drove to the Chelsea police station. My mind was racing. They're going to think I'm a neurotic wife checking up on her husband; they won't take any notice of me. But they didn't think that and they did take notice.

'I haven't spoken to my husband since Thursday. He should have called me on Monday. He calls me every day, several times usually. His door is locked from the inside. He has attempted suicide before. I'm really frantic that he's done something stupid. I've got to get in there.'

'Just a minute . . .' The three of us went back to Peter's flat, and the policeman managed to dislodge the key using a piece of wire. He opened the door and went in first. Peter was lying on the stairs.

Aliza and I started to follow him in, but he said: 'Will you wait. I have to go in on my own. Please wait here.'

We just sat outside the front door, not speaking. It seemed as if I had sat there in silence with Aliza for ever until the policeman came back. It was probably only a few seconds.

'He's here,' he said, 'and I'm afraid it's what you thought.'

I said: 'But is he all right?'

'I'm afraid not; he isn't all right.'

I could suddenly hear this wailing screaming sound, and it was me. I was still sitting on the stairs. Aliza was silent. It was as if she were a long way away. I was aware that the policeman was speaking to me but I couldn't understand what he was saying.

They found a glass by the phone in the bedroom and pills spilled on the floor. Peter had taken a massive dose. He used to save pills by the bottleful, and I threw them away periodically. I'll never know what he was doing on the stairs where he died. Perhaps he had changed his mind and was trying to get help. Perhaps he had left the bedroom – the telephone in his bedroom was faulty – to call from the other telephone. Perhaps he wanted to call me, or was about to answer one of my calls.

I think he died on Saturday, 28 October. He had planned it to the extent of giving Joe three days off, saying that he and I were going away for a few days to sort things out between us. Joe turned up for work as arranged on the Thursday morning.

Peter was wearing a shirt and his underpants. He often walked about at home without trousers. Woozy from the drugs, he had tripped over an ornament he kept at the top of the stairs – I was always nagging him about it – and was too weak to get up when he fell. He hit his head and bruised his leg. The blow to his head knocked him out completely. He died there. Perhaps if he had answered my call or called me I could have helped him, even after he had taken the pills. He had done it before and recovered.

With the banging on the door, shouting through the letterbox, forcing the lock and crying, there had been a lot of noise and commotion. Then I was dimly aware of sitting in a neighbour's flat, and he was giving me a brandy. Aliza was still silent and deathly white. She seemed to have shrunk, and was pitifully small. My eyes focused on the table, set for four people.

'Oh Arthur, we must go; you're having a dinner party.'

It was the only thing I remember saying from the moment the policeman told me Peter was dead.

'Don't worry about that. You sit here as long as you want,' Arthur said.

Mrs Regal was buzzing around our open door. 'What's happening? Where are the spare keys? I must have the spare keys.'

The policeman was very firm. 'Madam, would you mind going back to your flat. Leave this to us.' He was not allowed to let anybody into the flat and had informed the CID, which has to be done in the case of death by anything other than natural causes.

In a state of shock I sat with the brandy in my hand as men walked up and down the stairs and into the flat to attend to Peter, passing Arthur's front door which was on the same floor. It worried me that Arthur's dinner guests would soon be arriving. I mustn't inconvenience or embarrass him.

Then somehow I found myself downstairs in Mrs Regal's flat – she must have invited us in – still clutching Arthur's brandy. She was clearly concerned about Peter's suicide, and what was to happen to the flat. The policeman told her that she would get her keys back in good time and that nobody was allowed to enter Peter's flat until the CID had completed their investigations.

The policeman took charge. 'I don't want to leave you here,' he said to us, 'and I don't think you should go home to be on your own. Is there someone I can contact for you? It would be a good idea if somebody was there with you.'

It hadn't dawned on me until then that there was anything else in the world to be done. I felt that my life had come to an end. That was it, nothing else mattered now. Everything was over.

I was answering the policeman's questions automatically. I phoned my sister Barbara from Mrs Regal's flat. John answered the phone, his usual cheery greeting. 'Hi, Janet. Everything all right?'

I told him. 'We'll come at once,' he said. And they did.

The police offered to drive us home but I had parked on a yellow line. 'I can't face dealing with that in the morning,' I said. 'Perhaps somebody could drive my car?' The policeman was apologetic. No, they were not allowed.

Aliza and I drove home at five miles an hour. Gradually the implications, all that had to be done, were sweeping over me.

Aliza said: 'Mummy, what are we going to do about Oma?' (*Oma* is German for grandmother and was the name Aliza used for Peter's mother.)

The phone was ringing in my flat. My other brother-in-law, unaware of what had just happened, was calling for a chat. I broke the news.

Aliza and I sat in stunned silence as my sisters Barbara and Sandra and their husbands John and Stewart arrived and began making tea and coffee and sandwiches, sorting out the fridge and making phone calls. The doctor came and gave Aliza a sleeping pill. I hadn't taken sleeping pills since first going to Insight. There were some left in the cupboard and he told me to take one but I didn't. I stayed awake all night, going over the events as I have done so many times since. I could have gone to Peter and saved him. I've worked it out now. When he called me earlier that year and said he had to talk to me, when he kept phoning . . . I knew by his drawn, haggard look that he was depressed. If I hadn't kept our date at Richoux that day, he would probably have done it then.

I kept seeing the empty cigarette packet lying in his ashtray. Brazilian cigarettes. He always used to do that when he'd run out of cigarettes: go through his pockets and see where he'd left an old pack. So those were the only cigarettes in the house. When he finished them he took the pills. I think at that point he phoned me, trying to alarm me into going over to his flat.

He left no suicide note. But he put a message on his answering machine. When we found it, most of it had been wiped out. He wasn't very clever with machinery. I think he had intended to put it on the outgoing tape so that I would hear it when I called in. Somehow he messed around with the tapes so that his message ended up right at the end of the incoming messages. We had tried the machine because the police told us that this is often done by suicides. In fact, they had taken away the outgoing tape and found nothing.

Six months after Peter died, we were advertising for a cleaner. There were many callers, and we played the messages back. Right at the end, semi-taped over by one of the callers applying for job details, came those snatches of Peter's voice that had not been erased. It was the tail end of his message to us, a sentence or two saying how he knew what it was like to have a good life and to be loved; and now he didn't have that any more and he didn't want to live without anybody to love and to love him. And then there was a reference to something he had apparently said earlier in his message, that he wasn't going to stay around. There had been a lot more said, I could tell. When Peter decided to say something, he had his say. It was a shock after all that time to hear Peter's voice coming out of a machine. He could never master technical things, and it always made him cross that I seemed to succeed where he failed. Not that I was cleverer than him, but I always begin by reading the instructions. Peter didn't have the patience for that.

There is never a day I don't think about Peter. I may be at work, attending to a particular task and I think, this is the way Peter used to do it. Strange things evoke his memory. Eau Sauvage, his cologne. I can't smell it without thinking of Peter. I used to dream vividly, but since Peter died I have seemingly stopped dreaming, which is very odd. My doctor says I haven't stopped dreaming, I have stopped recalling my dreams.

I kept his pen, his ring and cufflinks. Aliza kept the odd tie or two. He never wore a watch. He used to say he didn't need one, that he always knew what time it was. But the truth was he was constantly asking 'What's the time?'

There was a moment that night, standing on the stairs listening to the policeman, when I experienced a sense of my whole life passing before my eyes. They say this happens when you are drowning. I saw a picture of our whole lives together and suddenly it was over. There was a complete story, which began and now was ended.

The things that became clear in my memory just for a few seconds, had nothing to do with what was going on then and there. These images continued throughout the evening. I saw just how Peter looked, what he was wearing when we met in Israel. I saw him the way he used to come and meet me after work, how he used to stand with his hands in his pockets. Meeting me off the train when I first visited him in Munich; our wedding, having Aliza, the holidays. Very vividly I recalled Italy, a holiday I had forgotten about, with baby Aliza. There was nothing of the business aspect; only the essence of our personal life together like a picture running in front of my eyes.

For the most part my brothers-in-law attended to the funeral arrangements, but there was the problem of Peter's mother. Then Aliza had the inspired idea of telephoning Clemmie, a former boyfriend living in Munich – their romance had given way to genuine friendship – to ask him to go and see Mama personally. A telephone call from London seemed so brutal. Clemmie would not break all the news at once, but would tell her Peter was seriously ill in hospital and to come at once. We felt that to tell her he had died, at her age, and then for her to travel alone to London, was cruel. Far better she should be with us. Clemmie said he or his mother would be prepared to travel with Mama to London. Lisl was in hospital with a leg injury and Clemmie undertook to visit her, too.

Suddenly I remembered the appointment at noon on Thursday with Berlei to go through the draft of the final contract, which we had already agreed and which they were keen to get signed. It had gone completely out of my head. There was no way I could go to that meeting. My public relations manager, Christine, contacted my solicitor, told him about Peter's death and asked him to cancel the meeting and explain in confidence the reasons why. We hoped to avoid alerting the press at least until the funeral was over.

Aliza slept that night in my bed, and for a month after. We couldn't face being alone. When she eventually returned to her own room she said she was afraid that, if she didn't make the break, she would end up fifty years old and unable to sleep without her mother!

My sister Barbara arrived at the crack of dawn. Goodness knows how but she had managed to find a shop open and was weighed down with bags of groceries. 'People will be calling in,' she said. 'And you have to keep your strength up.'

She left to drive to Reading to collect my mother who wanted to be with me. Sandra arrived, carrying two shopping bags full of food, essential, she said, 'Because people will be calling in, and everyone must eat . . .'

An hour later Christine arrived and unpacked a huge carrier bag of food. 'You know, Janet, I was thinking you would need some food in the house. You won't be feeling like shopping, and people will be calling in . . .'

We saw the funny side of it, and laughed hysterically. Barbara and Sandra produced savoury fish balls *ad infinitum*. To this day Aliza can't look at a savoury fish ball.

Clemmie phoned to say he had checked with Lisl's doctors and been advised that although Lisl was in pain and confined to bed, she was in a fit state to be told the truth. He would drive to the hospital at St Johann, speak to Lisl and await my mother-in-law, whom he had not been able to reach at her home but was due to visit Lisl during the afternoon.

Clemmie knew Lisl reasonably well through his association with Aliza. He knew my mother-in-law less well. She had never cared for friendships, seeing them as time-wasting distractions. Her attitude had rubbed off on Peter, who never, in all the years we were together, learned that family life is about loving and sharing and that close friends are drawn into that. He never understood that you could actually love several people without loving one of them less. To him, love was a rationed thing. There was a finite amount available, and if I gave it elsewhere there was none left for him. When you grow up in a large family you just keep finding more love to give.

Lisl was distraught and phoned from her hospital bed, weeping pathetically. She agreed it was kinder to tell Mama, initially, that Peter had suffered a heart attack; she would find out the truth soon enough. For purely practical reasons, it would not be possible for

194

Mama to fly to London the same night, so Clemmie had booked the first flight the following morning. She took the news badly, and as he drove her home he was worried about leaving her there. Would she like his mother to stay with her? No, said Mama, she would not have strangers in her house. She would prefer to be alone.

When she telephoned us in London it was not to enquire after Peter's condition, but to say that she had changed the flight Clemmie had booked her to a later one. He must be crazy and think she was made of money for there was a surcharge on the first flight of the day. In the event it wasn't going to make a jot of difference.

Joe had arrived for work, let himself into the flat and knew at once something was wrong. There was the bloodstain on the carpet, the sense of a place abandoned. He tried to reach me at the office and they told him what had happened. He phoned me. He was crying in shock and disbelief. He came to the flat and sat there all day, going over and over his hurt numbed feelings.

'I really loved him,' he said. 'He was difficult at times, but underneath that he was kind.'

It was true. Peter for all his faults was always good to people if they had problems or were in trouble. There was a gentle side to his nature that he never liked to show, because he thought it looked like weakness. Obviously Joe had discovered it, too. And Joe blamed himself for Peter's death. It seemed that he had volunteered to go to Brazil with Peter, and then changed his mind. He had let him down and this was the result. We told him not to be so silly. Of course it wasn't his fault.

Barbara went to meet Mama's flight. She hardly knew my mother-in-law, so Aliza went too. Mama was grim-faced. 'Are we going straight to the hospital?'

Barbara said they were taking her to my flat first. I dreaded this moment. Stuart, my doctor friend, had come to help. When he heard the news and telephoned me, he asked, as everybody did, if there was anything he could do. I said I would be grateful if he could be there when my mother-in-law arrived. She might get hysterical and faint; she was well into her seventies. I wouldn't know how to handle it. So Stuart came.

We decided among ourselves that since Mama was unlikely ever to read about the inquest, all she had to know was that Peter's pill-taking (which she knew about) had had a bad effect on him, had affected his heart, and that was why he had died. It was more or less the truth. We would not tell her that it had been a deliberate overdose. We thought it was a feasible story and the one to give her the least distress. If somebody dies of a heart attack, you can't blame yourself. Most people have a certain amount of guilt when somebody close dies; with a suicide, everybody feels bad. Joe felt guilty; my sisters felt bad; my brothers-in-law felt guilty. If, if, if. If we'd known we could have done this or that; we could have saved him from himself. For a mother I think that suicide is probably the most dreadful thing that could happen.

And so I told Mama this semi-lie. She began to cry, first loudly, then quietly. Then she seemed to pull herself together and stop. Stuart sat with her. 'Would you like me to give you something to help you sleep? Nothing will take away the pain. But after you have had a good night's rest, you will feel much stronger to cope with it in the morning. You have had a dreadful shock, and a tiring journey. It's tough at any age. At your age I would recommend you rest now.'

She declined. 'I don't take pills. I don't need injections. I won't fill my body with chemicals.'

She did, however, demand a bedroom, and went to bed in Aliza's room. My mother sat with her, holding her hand, listening to Mama's diatribe about Peter. His extravagance, his disobedience (as a child), his refusal to take his mother's advice, his smoking, his pill-taking, his stupidity with money.

My mother, who hardly knew Mama, sat speechless as she dragged up the most absurd criticisms of her son. 'When he went to a restaurant, he used to give the waiter a bigger tip than the bill came to and they used to laugh at him.'

It was a stupid exaggeration. If he gave a tip it was a generous one, when we were earning the money. And even when we were hard up he was always as generous as he could afford to be. He believed in sharing money around. His economic principle in life was that if you earn you've got to spend. It keeps the money circulating. It helps make everybody else rich. There was a certain moral truth in it. Let the lucky, successful ones share with those who work hard for less money.

196

I kept hearing snatches of this through the door, and occasionally my mother would say: 'Oh, don't say things like that about him.'

'Mama,' I said, 'one of the nicest things about Peter was his generosity. He had enough faults without making that out to be a fault too.'

The men were attending to things like the death certificate, the coroner's court, the undertakers, the synagogue, the cemetery. Aliza and I were walled up in our separate grief, only dimly registering the arrival of visitors and the constant telephone messages.

According to Jewish custom, Peter would have been buried the day following his death, but because the circumstances required coroner's permission since there would have to be an inquest, it was Thursday before details had been attended to, Friday before the authorities would release the body. Jewish funerals are not allowed on Saturday, so the funeral took place on Sunday.

Mama, after the first day's outpourings, displayed a calm, contained exterior. On Friday morning she announced that as she was in London she might as well go to Harrods to buy her favourite brand of tights. We invariably performed this errand for her. It was useless saying that in Munich you can buy just about anything under the sun. Mama swore these tights were available only at Harrods. Ditto Johnson's Baby Oil, which we were asked for whenever we went to visit; you can buy it at small extra cost in Munich.

Aliza was instructed to accompany her, and certainly the walk through the park did her good. However, in Harrods, Aliza was overwhelmed with grief and broke down in tears. She trailed along behind Mama, weeping uncontrollably, to the consternation of the assistant at the hosiery counter. Mama toyed with a selection of tights, then gave up and turned away. 'It's no good. I can't concentrate,' she said. Clearly she was upset.

There was a moment of near insanity when Mama began berating Aliza for being unsuitably dressed. She objected to Aliza's clothes being too glamorous. 'Mama,' I said, 'those *are* her clothes; what is she supposed to do, go out and buy something ugly to wear this week?' The offending outfit was a tracksuit, the mainstay of everyone's wardrobe, pulled out when you don't even want to think about what to wear.

But Mama was well and truly wound up. Aliza's lack of respect showed how little she cared for her father. 'You never cared for him, that's what killed him,' Mama shrieked at Aliza. Then she turned on me: 'What are all these people doing here?' she demanded. 'These people' were my mother and two sisters, and I wanted them; they were a great comfort.

She went to bed for the rest of the day. I looked in on her several times. She was sitting up in bed reading *Teach Yourself Turkish*. I didn't know whether to laugh or cry. When she finally emerged from her room, she told us to book her a flight home. She would not be staying for the funeral. 'I don't want to go to the funeral,' she said.

'I understand that, Mama,' I replied. And I did.

She decided she wanted to go on Sunday morning, thus creating the maximum inconvenience for all concerned.

Sunday, 5 November 1985 was bitterly cold. It was even worse than the days that had gone before. There are no flowers at a Jewish funeral; everything must be as plain as possible, with no embellishment. The philosophy is that you go out as you came in; that there is no distinction in the eyes of God. Whatever you have accumulated in this world no longer counts; it is left behind. The coffin was unadorned; you knew what was in it. I thought of Peter, wrapped in a prayer shawl, and stood trembling. I wanted to jump into the hole when they started to throw the clods of earth.

I seemed to register very little except my sense of horror, and one thing that stood out. Immediately after the funeral, a prayer is said, usually by the deceased's male relatives. My brothers-in-law stood up, being the closest males as Peter had no brother or son, and with them a cousin who had been quite close to us when we were in our twenties. We had drifted apart. Now he came forward to pray for Peter. I wondered how Peter would have felt about that, and it touched me more than anything else.

I had hardly noticed who was there, except to wonder at the number of people. As we were walking away from the graveside, a woman rushed up to me and almost fell into my arms, crying. 'I'll never forgive myself,' she was saying. 'Oh Janet, this is terrible . . . it's all my fault.' At first I didn't recognise this little round lady with golden hair, her face buried in my coat. It was Sheila

Gore. She had highlighted her hair. I hadn't spoken to her for almost two years; neither had Peter.

'Sheila, stop. It's nobody's fault,' I said. 'Everybody's trying to feel guilty. It doesn't help.'

She came back to Sandra's house, still upset. 'If only I was still with you,' she said. 'Peter needed me. I would have been able to help; I could always make him snap out of his mood. He always listened to me. I made him take notice . . .' It was true. He had respect for Sheila.

She was genuinely upset, to such an extent that it became slightly incongruous, with me comforting her. But it broke the ice between us. Although we never regained the close friendship we had lost, she was very considerate to me in the weeks that followed.

News of Peter's death had hit the newspapers. Berlei were being very sweet. David Pinkney had sent word via Christine that I was not to worry, we would have our meeting when I felt up to it. I ignored what was going on at work. My landlord, in France on his way back from India, phoned to say he needed to know when his flat would be available. He was most sympathetic and didn't want to pressure me. We had to do something about Cadogan Gardens.

Joe had cleaned it, and packed all Peter's clothes. I went to meet him there and we walked around the flat together, both crying. Joe was too big to wear Peter's clothes, but took a few things for a friend of his. He packed the rest in suitcases.

I asked Lisl and Mama if there was anything they wanted, thinking they might ask for a ring or candlesticks or something similar. Lisl said she would like his ski sweaters. Mama said she would be pleased to have his ski underwear, which was very fine quality.

By the time Aliza and I could face sorting out the things they had asked for, the cases had been packed for weeks and, as we lifted the first lid, there flooded over us a sense of having Peter back in the room: the smell, the feel of his clothes. Our tears flowed and we sat on the floor, our arms about each other.

Aliza kept his lambskin coat for herself for a while but hardly wore it. I kept some shirts. She took the rest, in suitcases, to the synagogue in Kensington for them to distribute to charity. The rabbi did not know us; we weren't members. Nevertheless, he wrote a kind letter to Aliza, comforting her in her recent bereavement; she acknowledged his letter and told him what had happened to Peter. He wrote back a spiritually uplifting letter. They developed a correspondence which meant a great deal to Aliza at the time.

20

Aliza was in a bad state, the more so because her relationship with her father, generally stormy, had been irrevocably damaged by the Pamela affair.

From the minute Aliza was born Peter loved and adored her, although at the same time he was jealous of the time I had to give her. She was Daddy's Girl from the age of a few weeks, when she gave him that great big smile. When she was old enough, he was always on the floor with her, playing tickling, pinching, pulling games as though she were a little puppy. And she reciprocated, endlessly teasing him. If he was reading a paper, she would sneak up and poke her finger through, then run away and hide. Even when she was quite grown up they used to romp around, screaming and shrieking.

As she grew old enough to have her own friends and Daddy was pushed into the background, he started to make rules and regulations about what was and what wasn't allowed, and since he wasn't very consistent this created friction. He was strict about boys, make-up and clothes, the usual issues. 'You're not going out looking like that,' was a frequent cry, even when she was at an age when most children have a certain amount of freedom. It was futile for me to tell him that all the girls were wearing the offending article at the moment. He'd tell me not to interfere. We had a lot of fights over Aliza. Sometimes I erred on the side of over-tolerance because he was being overly strict.

He made difficulties about her boyfriends, once with justification when Aliza brought home a man old enough to be her father. He closed his mind to the prospect of Aliza getting married: 'She doesn't know what life is all about; she's only a baby; she's got to make a career first . . .' He was always full of reasons why Aliza didn't need a husband. I suppose his idea of an ideal husband for her would have been an agreeable, innocuous person, who would move in with us, wouldn't mind being bossed around by Peter and wouldn't threaten Peter's control of Aliza. He liked to control the people he loved. He was happiest in any situation that involved just me, Aliza and him. He'd never buy more than six of anything for the table, because he didn't like the idea of having more than that number to dinner.

In the months after Peter's death, Aliza's face became gaunt as she lost weight. She was constantly tired and craved sleep, getting up at midday, dragging herself in to the office and trying to work but lacking any concentration. By four o'clock she was too tired to continue, so would go back home to bed, where she would remain until noon the following day. This was the pattern for weeks. She herself knew it was abnormal to sleep so much. I persuaded her to see her doctor, who in turn recommended her to a psychiatrist because, he said, she had been through a very traumatic experience, made the more so because she had been on bad terms with her father when he died.

One of the things that upset her terribly was that she felt Peter said goodbye to everybody except her, which in a way was true. With hindsight, I realised that on the Thursday evening when he was telling me about the pictures, he was saying goodbye to me. And as Joe was leaving, Peter suddenly said, 'Have three days off, Joe. I won't be needing you. I'm going away with Janet. Have a good time,' and he clasped his hand and put his arm across Joe's shoulder. Aliza was upset that she had quarrelled with her father over petty issues and that the last time she had seen him, when he had called for me at the shop, they had passed with barely a nod.

Her psychiatrist had previously been consulted by Peter, and was well informed about the complexities of our family life. Aliza was greatly helped, although it was to be a year before she felt well again. Her doctor said it was quite common for somebody with a problem they cannot face to go to sleep. That was something Peter always did: when he couldn't stand the way things were, he used to sleep. And that was what Aliza was doing to block everything out.

Although there was much to attend to with the business, I didn't go to work for some time. I'd been in to the office once or twice and had to go home almost immediately. There was the unfinished business with Berlei to think about, and I couldn't face making a new appointment. I had promised to be in Dallas in early December for the opening of the Janet Reger stockist there. But I couldn't even step outside my own front door without bursting into tears. While I was in the flat I felt secure and Aliza felt the same. We couldn't bear the thought of leaving the house, and went out only when it was absolutely necessary; and every now and again we attempted to go to the shop.

My landlord, justifiably, was starting to put pressure on me to move. It was by now the end of November and we had to make a quick decision, to move out or renew the lease for a further year.

Joe tidied up the flat at Cadogan Gardens, and I had the carpet on the stairs replaced. When all that was done, Aliza and I had a look around and decided this was where we wanted to be. This was where we felt most at home, and close to Peter. It felt good. We rearranged things to suit ourselves and moved back in.

It was the last Thursday in November. Joe came to help us with the move. I had grown very fond of him, with his good nature, his cheerfulness, his fund of amusing anecdotes. A handsome man, widely travelled, he had been involved in photography, in art, had run a restaurant, and was a superb cook. I couldn't afford to employ him, and was worried about him finding a job. That day Joe seemed unwell, which we put down to the shock of Peter's death and to his recurring gout.

I wasn't surprised when he didn't come in the following morning, assuming he was having a restful day at home. He had no telephone but had previously given me a number where I might leave a message in an emergency. On Monday when he didn't arrive at the flat, I decided to call the emergency number.

However, a friend's call superseded mine.

It was bad news. 'Mrs Reger, Joe died.'

I thought someone was having a sick joke – this four weeks after Peter died?

Joe had gone home to bed. When his friend called on Friday, he took Joe home with him. On Saturday the slight pain in his side had become so serious that an ambulance was called. Joe was admitted to hospital and died a few hours later.

I have always felt bad about Joe. I sent flowers to the funeral and a note of condolence to his friend. It was only months later that Aliza and I began to feel upset. It was as if being stunned at the shock we felt no hurt.

Aliza said: 'Daddy *took* Joe. He couldn't stand being on his own; he took him for company.'

Previously, she thought, Peter 'wanted' her.

That last weekend, Peter parked his car some distance from his flat which was why I had not seen it when I had gone round to his place. The Daimler remained there for more than a week before we decided to move it, and Aliza combined this task with collecting a friend from Heathrow.

On the way back she experienced a feeling that Peter didn't want her to drive his car, and she was afraid that there was going to be an accident. The urge to stop the car and abandon it where it stood was almost overpowering, and she slowed down to a crawl. A few days after that she begged me never to drive the car. She drove it only once again, to the garage for servicing. It was shortly after Joe died. This time she felt unthreatened. 'Now Daddy has Joe, he doesn't need me,' she said. We were neither of us at our most rational.

It would have made sense to sell my car and keep Peter's. Mine was the older of the two. I didn't. I sold his. I never felt right in it.

In Cadogan Gardens it seemed as though Peter wanted us there. It felt like coming home, except that we had not thought of it as home before. We had complained that it was dark and gloomy, especially the hall. But after Peter's death it was different, as if it had been haunted not by its past but by its future, and once that happened nothing else could hurt us. In as much as it was possible to feel happy or peaceful at all, we were almost happy in Cadogan Gardens. When we moved in, we saw it as a temporary expediency; when we were forced to leave a few months later, we had grown very attached to the place and would have given a great deal to be allowed to stay. But Mrs Regal was intractable.

All this time there was the Berlei appointment to think about. It was up to me to make a telephone call to arrange a meeting, but I couldn't face it. Then there was our big new American customer to consider, and my promise to attend the opening of the shop in Dallas at the beginning of December. The owners had sent me a club-class ticket to New York. I was incapable even of calling a taxi at the time, so there was no way I could get on a plane for Texas. But Christine McCarthy, who out of the goodness of her heart was making a point of calling in at the office to handle day-to-day problems, took one of the calls from our Dallas customer, who was beginning to get anxious when there was no news and no stock.

We had arranged to dispatch the merchandise at the beginning of November and, at the time Peter died, had been pulling out all the stops to finish the order on time. That's the nature of production: it's always later than you think!

Christine told the Dallas customer that Peter had died, and that this was the reason I had been unavailable at the office. But, she said, everything was in hand, and there was nothing to worry about. But what about all the press coverage, interviews and photo calls? Janet Reger was billed to be there, in person. 'Don't worry,' said Christine. 'She will be.'

'And Janet,' she said later when she reported back to me, 'I think you *should* go. It is really important. We're talking about seventy-thousand-pounds' worth of business here, and that's just the beginning. You can't let them down, you've got to do it. What's more, it will be good for you; it will take your mind off Peter. I'll organise everything.'

I had nothing to wear. Christine went to Caroline Charles, Joseph Azagury and Benny Ong and asked them all to send clothes round. As I clambered in and out of one outfit after the other, she made remarks like, 'Take it off, I've seen you look better'; 'Have that in a size larger' – or smaller. I'd lost a lot of weight for grief is a great appetite suppressant. She planned my wardrobe for the trip, then practically packed my bags for me and put me on the plane to New York.

It was only a month since the funeral. I was still dazed, the more so because I had just been stunned by yet another bombshell in the Berlei saga.

21

I arrived early evening in New York, where a limousine transported me to a lavish suite at the Pierre on Central Park. On the Sunday evening Marion Potasnik and Rosanne (her splendid public relations lady) flew in from Dallas through a snowstorm.

We began work on Monday, doing interviews with *Harpers*, *Vogue*, *Elle*; and after three days of press shows, we agreed that so far the trip had been highly successful: we had achieved the press coverage we had set out to achieve.

We flew on to Dallas, to be met at the airport by Marion's husband Michael, an absolute charmer. By this time I had decided I didn't care for Marion. I had met her several times when she came into Beauchamp Place to discuss business; now after three solid days in close proximity, not just on business but having dinner together, I had concluded that she was hard and bitchy.

Their order was worth £70,000 to us. They had paid a deposit but the bulk of the order was to go through on a letter of credit. However, when the goods went out it was at the time when I was lying in bed weeping, feeling ill and miserable, and they left the factory without anybody there realising we had to call in the letter of credit.

Immediately I raised this with Michael, pointing out that the goods had been shipped directly to Dallas while I wasn't at work. But the girls had been marvellous and got it all out on time, and here I was doing the publicity. Did he think he could arrange to have the money transferred? As we hadn't called in the letter of credit, the money had to be there.

'Don't worry,' he assured me. 'It will be waiting for you when you get back to England.'

Three days in Dallas proved therapeutic, with the pressure, distance and distraction from normal life. I felt myself regaining strength. I stayed in the best hotel, the Mansion on Turtle Creek, where Michael kept his own port and champagne in the cellar. You can park anywhere in Dallas, but Michael would drive right up to the front door and give the doorman $5 to park his brand new Rolls-Royce three yards away. This is Texas; everything is over the top and the Potasniks loved it. Marion, a girl from Essex, had already adopted the Texan drawl.

My suite was decorated in chocolate and peach. Everything was king size; the bedroom was larger than my entire flat in London. Flowers, fruit, chocolates and perfume were provided in my room. In the bathroom, the spare loo roll was draped in peach satin ribbon tied at the top in a huge bow. 'Wait till I tell Peter about the loo paper,' I thought, imagining him having a good laugh. I found myself, as I had done the first time I visited Brazil, constantly wishing that Peter were with me.

Never before had I seen such opulence and wealth. As well as the Rolls-Royce the Potasniks had three BMWs, including one for the maid. Marion's numberplate read LAYLA, the name of their lingerie shop; the one on Michael's Rolls-Royce was MP 1. There was also a Range Rover which Marion used to drive to the stables where she rode her own horses every day.

There were four thousand square feet of house, with marble floors and marble doors. I think they would have had marble windows if you could have seen through them – marble is a big deal in Dallas. And of course there was a swimming pool.

I am a great clothes buyer, so was Peter, and I am accustomed to the buying habits of the rich, but the conspicuous clothes buying of the Potasniks beat anything I had ever seen. In New York Marion wore a different fur coat every day – and they were all the most expensive furs. Mink was to go shopping in. Her clothes were from Valentino and St Laurent, and I never saw her in the same outfit twice. When she showed me around the house – she was obviously longing to show it off and I was intrigued to see it – there were rooms devoted to clothes; his and hers. Rails of clothes ran the length of each room, and the walls were lined with shelves filled with shoes, handbags, shirts, hats.

Michael was what is described as flash. I liked him. I didn't like her. She had a whining voice that got on my nerves. But she was extremely attractive to look at, and almost twenty years younger than her husband (they had a three-year-old child). Of the two he was by far the more attractive personality, warm and witty. Although she was pretty, and beautifully groomed and dressed, she had a discontented mouth. All she talked about was money, what she had bought, where and how much, name-dropping designers: 'I got this dress in Chanel last week. I bought these shoes in Charles Jourdan. Do you like these ear-rings? Valentino . . .' If she slummed with a local designer it was qualified with, 'Well, she *must* be very good; lots of wealthy people go to her.'

And she used me as her English celebrity. By having me at her lunch party, she was able to invite the local queen bees who normally buzzed higher than her little hive of activity. As it was, several of her guests weren't too subtle about letting her know she wasn't in their social register; they were just there to welcome the British designer. One actually said: 'Can't stay long. Just here for the soup. We're due at so-and-so's for the main course.' They had their soup and went on to the next restaurant. Much as Marion irritated me, I was appalled by the bad manners of some of her guests.

Marion boasted that her previous man had been an Arab prince. She was Michael's third wife. Everybody liked Michael; his staff adored him; his bank adored him. I took out references before we did business and his bank gave him such a glowing reference that my bank said they had never come across anything like it. He had charm, presence, education and, by Texan standards, was not at all flash. On the surface everything was kindness and hospitality. I suppose if I had been in my normal alert state I would have paid more attention to the danger signals.

They showed me their two shops. One, the lingerie shop, was in a classy mall; think of the television soap opera *Dallas*, and that says it all. The other shop was in a more middle market mall, but sold jewellery at prices from $50,000 upwards. This was incongruous – the merchandise and the location didn't add up. I mentioned this to Michael because it struck me as strange. He brushed away my comment and said that they stocked such fabulous things that the shop's reputation drew the clientele from all over Texas.

He told me something of his background. He had owned a successful limousine-hire company in London in the seventies but became disillusioned by high taxation and the Labour government. He sold out and went to Canada, where he started up an insurance company. Visiting Texas on business, he realised that this was the place of the future and moved all his assets there. I didn't query this story.

But I did query his account of how he got into the jewellery business. Somebody who owed him money and couldn't pay gave Potasnik the jewellery instead, he said. What could he do? To sell it to the trade would devalue it; to give it to Marion to wear would probably make her happy but wouldn't help him to recover his debt. So he opened a jewellery shop. It was a well-honed anecdote, recounted no doubt scores of times, and did not convince me one iota. I wondered whether the jewellery store might be his way of laundering illicit money.

After a few days with my friend Marlene in Los Angeles, I returned to London buoyed up for the Christmas rush.

The Dallas money had not arrived. It's hard to call Dallas; the time lag works against you. I finally got through to Michael's financial director, Robert, who couldn't understand why the money wasn't waiting for me; he had certainly authorised payment. He would chase it up at once, he assured me, and call me back. He epitomised the trustworthy Scot. (My mistake; Michael and Robert turned out to be a quite untrustworthy double act.) But he didn't call me back. I called Dallas. He was out; Michael was out; Marion was out.

A day later Robert called to say the money had left their bank. If it hadn't reached my account, where was it? They needed time to sort out the muddle which they blamed on their bank. Unfortunately, Michael was in New York and not contactable, so meanwhile Robert would telex some money to me immediately and I could expect to receive it within twenty-four hours.

My bank manager said that telexed money, because of time differences, was more likely to take three days to clear, and not to panic. He would advise me as soon as the money reached my account, which he estimated would be Friday.

It hadn't arrived by Friday. I spent the weekend trying to get through to Dallas, by now seriously concerned. On Monday £10,000 arrived, not the £70,000 due. I immediately rang Dallas again, and after trying all that day and the following day, made contact with Robert at last. Because Michael wasn't around, he said, he had sent 'something to tide you over'. But he only had authority to sign cheques up to £10,000. Michael was sorting out the rest for us but it would take time.

'Robert,' I said, 'if I have money in my bank I can pick up the phone and send that money anywhere in the world at once. If you haven't got the money, will you tell me now so that we can come to some arrangement as to how you are to pay me. Please.'

They had already reported how well the shop was doing and had reordered. No problems at all, he insisted. I had nothing to worry about; they had plenty of funds.

A few days later their cheque arrived for the outstanding amount. As I paid it in, at the very last moment before the bank closed for Christmas, I breathed a very big sigh of relief, and okayed the expiry of the letter of credit when the American bank queried this outstanding item on the ledger.

I spent a quiet Christmas with my family. Peter was very much in our hearts and minds. Boxing Day was his birthday, New Year's Day our wedding anniversary; it is a week haunted by memories. I have a dear friend who suffers dreadfully at Christmastime, yearning for the past. She makes almost a cult of it, refusing to get over the sad things which have happened in her life. There will always be reminders: Christmas, birthdays, anniversaries, another day with a reason to mourn. Bad as I felt, I realised that this must not happen to me, that as time healed the pain, so must I learn to cope and not live in my own misery.

It was all too raw that Christmas, but since then I have made sure that I make my own arrangements if a holiday is coming up. I don't sit around and mope and feel sorry for myself. It's very easy to make grief a habit; then you finish up, years on, still in deep mourning. People get fed up with you, however kind and sympathetic they are at the beginning. You have to get over your grief if you ever want to start living again.

When I returned to work, the Dallas cheque had been banked and appeared on my statement. I dispatched their January merchandise. I was feeling optimistic: I had been back in business for nearly three years; I had money in the bank and no serious debts apart from the sums I had borrowed, which were under control; and I was meeting all my payments. I knew my bank manager was pleased with me. I had asked him to give me an overdraft of £15,000 when I received the Dallas order, as I needed to finance that, and I had repaid this when I received the Potasniks' cheque.

I soon had reason to worry. My bank manager called to say: 'Janet, we have a problem. The Dallas cheque has been returned, marked "refer to drawer".'

'What does that mean?'

'Well, in everyday language, it's bounced.'

In all good faith, knowing the circumstances, knowing me, and in view of the superb references furnished by the Dallas bank on Potasnik's standing, the cheque had been credited to me before it had been cleared on the other side. My bank manager suggested that there could be a reasonable explanation. He advised me to re-present the cheque and meanwhile contact Dallas to ask Michael for an explanation.

By now I was frantic. I had been merrily spending the money. I had paid for my expensive new wardrobe for the Dallas trip. I had treated Aliza to a ticket to St Moritz to spend Christmas ski-ing with friends (the fresh air would do her good, we thought – it didn't, she came back with bronchitis).

I started at once to contact Dallas, but I knew there could be no explanation other than the obvious. I had been had. No bank would bounce a business cheque without referring back to their client, especially one held in such high esteem as Michael Potasnik. And, having been alerted, why didn't he cover the cheque to prevent it bouncing?

After twenty-four hours sick with anxiety, I made contact with his office, which gave me the usual run-around. I bitterly regretted not noting his home telephone number; it took several days to trace. Robert offered the information that Michael was incommunicado in Florida, and that he himself was utterly astonished at the bounced cheque. 'This is a little country bank. They make mistakes. I'll phone them and give them a talking to . . .'

There developed a smokescreen of Robert allegedly phoning Michael, Michael phoning the bank, Robert reporting back how angry Michael was, Michael putting a banker's draft in the post at once, Robert and Michael telling me I mustn't worry; money would reach me tomorrow but of course tomorrow never came. They even sent me details of the draft number. The phone calls

211

lasted a week. My home bill alone for that quarter was £900.

When the draft materialised it was for £8,000.

By this time I knew they were not to be believed. I needed to salvage what I could. During one of my conversations with Michael I asked him bluntly: 'Do you have a money problem? If so, please tell me. I've been there; I know what it's like to find oneself in a difficult position. If that's the case, don't let me waste all this time and money chasing you, just be honest, tell me you can't pay right now and we'll talk about how you can pay later. Perhaps you should send some stock back.'

Still he insisted: 'Janet, there isn't a problem. We've just been a little over-extended lately. I'm owed a lot of money. It's just a matter of time.'

Part of our deal had been that I would not supply any other outlet in Texas, and Dallas lawyers had acted for me when the contract was drawn up. I now decided to inform them of events, and they took appropriate action which was to deliver an ultimatum in writing. If the amount outstanding was not paid to the law firm by the end of that week, a court order would be issued and goods seized.

Michael phoned me. Not from Dallas – he was always elsewhere. It was another of his stalling 'Don't worry, Janet, it's all in hand' calls. 'Too late,' I told him. 'It's dragged on too long. The excuses have worn thin. The lawyers have taken over and you can expect a visit from the sheriff on Friday. I want my money.'

'And you shall have your money. It's already on its way. You will receive it tomorrow.'

Tomorrow came and £1,000 arrived. I was furious. I rang the shop, but there was no reply. I rang his home; the maid answered. I told her he must telephone me the moment he returned home, whatever time of the day or night. He didn't.

The following day I called again, timing it for 7 a.m. in Texas. Marion answered. Michael had gone to his club, she informed me, to play tennis and work out. No, she wouldn't give me the name of the club; Michael wasn't 'available' at his club.

This was the red rag. 'He's available enough when he wants my merchandise. I want to know when he will be available to pay for it.'

'Don't you talk to me like that,' she retorted. 'How dare you?'

'Until I get my money, I'll talk to you how I like, Marion. Will you please get hold of your husband and tell him that if he doesn't call me back *immediately* with a very good explanation as to why he hasn't paid me, you are going to have serious problems because I have already set things in motion.'

'If you were more businesslike and spoke to me in a civilised way, then perhaps you would get your money,' she replied.

'What! I kept my part of the bargain, delivered your order, showed up in Dallas at the most stressful time in my life, kept my commitment to the last detail. You are the ones who have been unbusinesslike!'

It was like being told to speak nicely, then I might get the money due to me. With one last threat that the sheriff was poised to act on my behalf, I rang off.

Before long Michael, smooth and charming as ever, was on the telephone. 'Janet darling, I hear you've had some words with Marion.'

More apologies, more soothing words. He had received the summons. The money would be deposited with my lawyers by midday on Friday. It wasn't. The next step was to put a lien on his stock. This 'fixes' the goods; nothing may be moved from the premises until the court makes a decision. In theory, it effectively ties up the assets.

Michael was one jump ahead, however. When the sheriff arrived to issue the writs, the Potasnik house was deserted. Robert's house was deserted, stripped bare of furniture, cars, families, nanny. The remaining household staff turned up for work, unaware of any problem. At Michael's thirteen businesses staff turned up too, and at twelve of them it seemed at first to be business as usual. At the jewellery shop, however, there was not so much as a single diamond chip to be found.

At Layla's the manageress, a meticulous woman whom the Potasniks had persuaded to leave a prestigious job at Saks – particularly unkind as she was bringing up a seven-year-old child – found open drawers and disarranged shelves. She checked the stock; many of the most expensive nightgowns, negligées and underwear were missing. Surprise, surprise, they were all in Marion's size.

Michael, Marion and Robert had vanished. Everything was

213

already assigned to the bank, which meant personal guarantees and first charge. The bank stood to recoup after the preferential creditors, which are the same in America as in the UK: tax authorities and staff. Anything left would be divided among the creditors, of whom I was one among what seemed like most of Texas and Florida plus parts of Oklahoma.

The truth emerged bit by bit. Michael owed the bank $8 million. An electronics company in Florida had invested millions in one of Michael's dubious businesses. Since he opened the underwear shop he hadn't paid rent, the decorators' bill, the mortgage on his house or Robert's. His Rolls-Royce was rented. He took it with him; it disappeared without trace.

The limousine company he had allegedly sold when he left London had gone into liquidation owing thousands, yet he had arrived in Dallas a millionaire. The bank in Texas made enquiries. Banks don't take lightly to being defrauded of millions, and their representative kept me informed, so the reason emerged for Potasnik's glowing references. His was a small country bank. When Potasnik first walked in – well dressed, well spoken, every inch the affluent, successful businessman – the manager was impressed. Introducing himself as Mr Potasnik from Toronto, he explained that he had been so impressed by this city that he felt sure this was where his future lay. He was in the insurance business and wanted to move all his assets to their bank. To start with, he would transfer $2 million immediately.

A short time later $2 million arrived. As the bank manager said: 'Never in all my years in the bank have I come across a customer who had two million dollars in *cash*.' He was suitably convinced. Over the next two years the account fluctuated, sometimes needing an overdraft facility. Michael's trust fund in England sometimes paid a little late.

The money came in because new investors were being found for dubious businesses. Moving money created effect, allayed suspicion, attracted more money. Everything operated on credit; nobody got paid. As the layers of deceit peeled away, debts emerged of many, many millions of dollars. These were confidence tricksters *par excellence*, and they got away with it.

The Texas bank sold my merchandise to somebody else. I had an unexpected, unagreed overdraft. I tried unsuccessfully to trace the Potasniks. Marion had mentioned the town in England where she grew up, but this led nowhere. There were so many victims of the sting, all of us telephoning each other; people like Rosanne, the public relations lady who had done such an excellent job and had incurred considerable expense on their account. It made your blood boil to think that Michael had even conned his staff out of their wages; if he had just sold the diamond ring he wore on his little finger he could have paid the entire staff.

I'd recognise them anywhere. Michael bore a strong resemblance to a man I know in London. I remarked on it at the time, and it keeps a picture of his face clear in my memory. After three days in Marion's company in New York, and five in Dallas, I'd know her again.

The Berlei battle was on again. I'd lost all my stock in Dallas. Eating in San Lorenzo one day the proprietor's wife Mara said to me: 'Do you know, I think someone put a curse on you. When I go to church tomorrow I shall have you blessed.' I don't know what she did with that blessing, but it worked. Eventually.

22

The day before I left for Dallas I had been due to have a meeting with Berlei. The contract was ready and now was the time to sign on the dotted line. My Joseph Azagury outfit needed an alteration and Joseph was to fit it before my meeting, then have it ready for collection after I had finished at the solicitors' office and been to the hairdresser. It was that sort of day.

I had one foot out of the door when the telephone rang. It was John, my accountant, calling from his car on his way to work.

'Janet, you're not going to believe this. I've just had David Pinkney on the line, and he tells me that if we want to sign the contract, we've got to go at once and sign it now. Because they are just about to go into a meeting with their bank, and if the outcome of that meeting is not successful, and the bank refuses to go on supporting them, they will have a receiver there by midday.'

I couldn't believe what I was hearing.

'I couldn't believe it either, but it's true,' said John.

'Just a minute, John. Do I *want* to sign?'

'There are advantages,' said John, 'and disadvantages, which I have talked about with David. We must have an immediate meeting with Ronald and decide what we are going to do. There is very little time.'

As it happened I had already arranged to meet Ronald in Knightsbridge. Among Peter's things we had come across a key to a safe deposit box, and an appointment had been made for the box to be opened in the presence of a solicitor. Having done nothing for a month, I was experiencing an action-packed eve-of-departure day.

It took all of one minute to open the box and examine the contents: one out-of-date insurance policy. (I had to go on paying for the box, regardless, until probate was established and I was permitted to take the contents away.)

Meanwhile, my brain was ticking over and my instinct was telling me not to sign the Berlei contract. Over coffee in Richoux, John, Ronald and I examined our options.

From David Pinkney's viewpoint, my signing was an advantage. It would be another asset. The position remained very much the same: Berlei had in their possession a collection of 'Janet Reger' contracts which they could not sign. In order to do so, they had to declare that the licensor (Berlei) had 'complete and uncontested right to licence the name'. Litigation was proof that this was not so. They had an asset, for which they had paid £100,000, which was losing value because of our litigation. With my signature they would be able to say, 'We have an income of forty per cent on this trademark, even though we don't own it, over the next fifteen years.'

That was what they stood to gain. The benefit to me in signing was also relevant. As David Pinkney pointed out, once the news broke that Berlei were in receivership, the vultures would descend on Berlei, and somebody else would buy the Janet Reger trademark unless I had already protected it by signing the agreement.

My argument was that, whoever bought Berlei (assuming somebody would) was also buying Berlei's percentage in the takings of that trademark. And right now, the trademark was up for grabs. Maybe *I* could raise the money to buy it.

Financially I was feeling secure. I had this wonderful new customer in Dallas; business was looking good. I felt confident I could raise the money to buy the trademark, which would surely go cheap because of the surrounding litigation.

John agreed. He felt we might even get away with making a silly offer, such as £5,000, although we might have to go as far as £20,000. His instincts were not to sign. Mine were one hundred per cent not to sign, and I was glad he agreed with me. I stood a good chance of getting the trademark back that way and we couldn't see that anyone in their right mind would want to buy litigation.

We told David Pinkney that we had decided not to sign at this stage, but if they were still in business when I returned from Dallas, then we would revert to our original agreement. Flying to

America, I read in the *Evening Standard* about Berlei going into receivership.

We submitted our silly offer to the Berlei receiver. When I asked Melvyn – who better knew the machinations of a receiver's mind – he thought I'd offered too much. They might even had given the trademark to me, if I'd asked nicely!

Everything stopped for Christmas. In January John and I presented ourselves to the receiver and his team. They laughed uproariously at our £5,000, which they said gave a new meaning to the phrase silly offer, and told us to go away and try harder.

By the time they came back to us I was not feeling rich any longer, having been conned in Dallas. I had had some serious chats with my bank manager, who agreed to let me continue the overdraft, which I had promised to clear with the Dallas contract. He could see that money was coming in steadily; the merchandise was selling well in Harrods and a new customer in New York was doing well. The bank manager had faith in me, and didn't blame me for the Potasnik treachery; bigger people than me had been stung by him, including the Texas bank. Barclays were very supportive; they could have demanded repayment of the overdraft at once, but they didn't.

I knew that this would be the only chance I would ever have in my entire life to buy back that trademark. I would raise the money somehow. Maybe the family would help.

I had never been to an inquest. I don't know what I'd expected. The person finding the body is required to attend and I wasn't going to subject Aliza to the ordeal. The coroner phoned me the day prior to the inquest to say he would meet me before it began and go through the procedure in private.

It didn't occur to me to ask someone to come with me. Either of my sisters or Christine McCarthy would have done so. I felt I'd received so much help and support I was loath to ask for more. In any case, I didn't think I would need it. I didn't tell anybody about the inquest and I went alone.

As I climbed the stairs looking for the room where I was to meet the coroner, a man approached, hand outstretched.

'Mrs Reger?'

'Yes.'

'*Daily Express*, Mrs Reger. May I ask how you feel? Are you upset?'

'Upset? How do you think I feel?' He was polite enough, but it wasn't a question I could answer just like that, and I hadn't expected to be talking to reporters.

The coroner rescued me and led me into a small office. He explained that I would be asked in simple terms why I went to the police to request assistance, and that all I needed to answer was that my husband had suicidal tendencies and I believed he was inside the flat, possibly unconscious or worse. He told me I would not have to go into any personal details.

The next day at the inquest, it was as the coroner had said. The policeman gave evidence, followed by the police surgeon. We heard a description of the drugs in Peter's body, that there was evidence he had not eaten for several days, although there was ample food in the flat. A statement from his doctor, who had been prescribing pills for sleeplessness, was read out.

I answered questions and heard my own voice echoing from a distance. Who were all these people sitting in court? What were they writing down?

The coroner gave a verdict of suicide. As I got up to go, the people busily scribbling downed their pens and hurried after me. Outside there was a crowd of photographers. I couldn't trust myself not to burst into tears. Please, not here, not now.

A strong hand took my elbow and drew me, forcefully, away from the crowd. 'Janet, this way, stay with me.'

It was Pauline, the 'therapist' Peter had produced to sort out our marital problems. She led me out, shielding me with her body. We came out on to the street and I looked across Horseferry Road, recognising a familiar building: the Insight office. I hurried in. They gave me tea, and I took refuge there until the panic had died down within me.

I went home and thought about something the coroner had said. 'Your mother-in-law is rather strange, isn't she?'

I agreed, but why in particular?

He said that she had telephoned him to inform him of her suspicions that Peter had been murdered. 'I cannot pre-empt the verdict,' he told her, 'but please set your mind at rest. I am sure it will not be one of murder.' I pitied her. But that, and her later

219

attempt to contact Pamela – she asked Aliza for Pamela's telephone number; she wanted to befriend her – seemed reason enough not to speak to her again.

Berlei had appointed a licensing agent, Leslie Creasey, whose attitude was: 'My licence is with Berlei. If you get the trademark, you'll have to take me with it.' I told him I was in no position to discuss this with him. It was another thorn in the flesh as far as I was concerned; there were so many.

As rumours of Berlei's crash rippled through the business world, rivals began to take a lively interest. Vantona's Janet Reger bedlinen was building up nicely. Berlei had received around £30,000 in royalties that year – a sum that was continuing to grow – despite the aggravation and litigation. But if they were doing that well with absolutely no support from me, other companies took the view that perhaps it would be worth their while to buy the trademark from under Vantona's nose.

Suddenly my trademark was in demand. Vantona were in the bidding for it but, because of the litigation, wanted first to do a deal with me. Their major opponent was the firm of Peter Black, a public company which, before Berlei's crash, had entered into negotiations with Creasey to market Janet Reger slippers. This company, headed by one Thomas Black, also distributed bedlinen. They were trying to woo me, as were assorted financiers, and each day brought a new proposition from somebody offering to cut me in on a share of the action, should their bid for the trademark be successful. By doing a deal with me, they were ensuring they would not come up against me in the as yet unresolved litigation.

My solicitor took the view that I must negotiate with the various offers on the table, if for no other reason than to stall for time while I tried to raise the money to buy the trademark myself. A flat refusal would alert competing bidders, and I was up against the big boys here; there was no way I could compete in cash terms.

Everybody was offering similar deals. Sign up with them, they would buy the trademark and guarantee me a percentage as income from licensing. Vantona's royalty to Berlei had proved the potential. It was the percentage I would receive that we were negotiating, but the best deal in the world was still a deal and would not give me my own trademark back.

Various minor characters who had expressed interest dropped out when the stakes began to get too high for them. This left Vantona and Peter Black, who both had genuine reasons for maintaining interest and could clearly see the commercial advantages.

Dealing with these two made my machinations with Berlei a year before seem child's play. They seemed hell-bent on tying me up in knots. My meetings with Thomas Black were particularly stormy. It was a tense time, played against the backdrop of my frantic phone calls to Dallas and my nagging anxiety that, for the first time since our liquidation, I was running an overdraft that I had no prospect of clearing in the very near future.

Berlei's receiver's team were keeping us informed, and the day came when they announced that they had received offers of at least £75,000 for the trademark, and there was no doubt this could be increased. Were we still in the running?

John said: 'We're just going to have to telex back and say we'll pay £100,000.'

It was madness. I had nothing, and no idea how I could possibly raise so much money. At the same time, this would be my one and only chance. There was absolutely no likelihood of companies like Vantona and Peter Black going bust, so the idea of my later trying to buy the trademark from *their* receiver was stupid and I knew it. So we telexed my offer of £100,000. The receiver accepted, with the proviso that the money must be on the table by 18 February 1986.

Waiting in the wings was a bevy of prospective licensees, contracts at the ready, lined up by Berlei's licensing agent, Leslie Creasey. Later I discovered that these contracts had progressed to the point that Leslie had told the licensees they could begin to market products, but initially he told me: 'I've got so many deals up my sleeve for you. If you are successful, I'll help you and give you advice if you agree to keep me as licensing agent once you get your trademark back.'

I refused to commit myself. I kept everybody sweet by talking to all of them but didn't agree to anything, while I did everything in my power and pursued every possible opening to raise £100,000. And even that figure wasn't a certainty. How was I to know it would not go even higher? What was to stop the receiver conducting an auction with my £100,000 offer as the opening bid?

Meanwhile, everyone was pressing me for decisions. Vantona wanted an assurance that if they bought the trademark they would have my co-operation. Thomas Black was pestering me to sign a contract with him guaranteeing that I would work with his company if he purchased the trademark. I was harassed about the Dallas situation and anxious about my overdraft. I was so miserable I wouldn't have cared if I had died then and there. It was as if I'd suddenly had enough. I couldn't see any reason to carry on living apart from the fact that Aliza needed me.

And I had to find money. My bank manager said that, much as he would love to help, this was not the sort of loan a clearing bank could undertake. Property loans were one thing, but they wouldn't be happy about financing the purchase of a trademark.

I discovered hitherto unsuspected capabilities as I careered about the City, talking to bankers, institutions, private financiers. There were innumerable prospective backers but they all insisted on tough conditions. Each and every offer on the table required equity in the trademark and horrendous pay-back terms. Because everybody knew I was absolutely desperate for the money and that time was not on my side, they were offering hard bargains as people are apt to do when they know the score.

I listened as they talked of what 'we' would do – as in 'we' would open shops nationwide; but the 'we' meant they. I was going to be playing a minor role while they were going to run the show. That's business and they weren't wrong to want the biggest share for themselves, but I didn't like it. And I knew that the moment I was the owner of that trademark, I could raise money on a much better deal.

As the days passed, and the date for paying the £100,000 drew closer, I could think of nothing else. Where I had once felt ready to give up and die, I now felt driven by the determination to own my own name. It was the only thing that mattered. Whatever it cost, I did not for a moment doubt the trademark's worth, in terms of both material value and in the satisfaction of feeling whole once more. It was my baby and I had to have it back. My conviction was shared by my accountant and my solicitor. I was lucky to have such good advisers; without them I would have been totally lost.

In itself the trademark was a means to an end, but at the same time I had the sense to recognise that buying it would provide a solution that would eventually put an end to my financial miseries. I never doubted that if I could raise the money it would be possible to pay it back, and I have been proved right.

Mr Black had been keeping up the pressure to make me agree in writing to the deal he was offering. On Monday morning of the crucial week in which I had to finalise the purchase, he telephoned from Heathrow on his way to Milan and let rip a volley of abuse, complaining about my solicitor's inefficiency in not responding to his telex. (Ronald of course was holding back on my instruction.)

Mr Black's tactics were aggressive. Vantona were always courteous even when they were being tough, but they made it very clear that if I didn't co-operate they would go right over my head. They had the money. It was nothing to them to buy the trademark. They just didn't want to upset me, and would like to work with me harmoniously. But they could manage without it, too. At least they 'threatened' politely.

We fended off most of Mr Black's phone calls, except the one from Milan airport on his return journey, when he told me in the most forceful terms that I was employing the most inefficient solicitors he had ever come across in his vast experience of business.

February 17 came, the day before the ultimatum expired. Contracts were drawn and completion fixed. Family and friends had rallied around and together had produced a total of £25,000. This left £75,000 to find. I *could* have had this if I was prepared to do a deal that in effect gave my backer more of me than it left of me for myself, a minority shareholding in my own name. I *would* have done it if I had been forced to: better half a loaf than nothing to eat. But I wanted to be free. I had had enough of belonging to others.

John had arranged a meeting with another bank for the morning of 18 February. I didn't hold out any hope for this last-minute try, but I needed the money by the afternoon, so I had nothing to lose.

On Monday night I couldn't sleep. As I paced to and fro, my

mind went over and over my problems – not just the trademark but the Dallas situation, Aliza, Peter. I tried the radio and the television but couldn't concentrate on them, I was in such a stew of anxiety and panic.

As dawn came my mind started to clear. Stop this, I said to myself. Stop going round and round in circles, achieving nothing. Sit, think, be rational. What is the best possible deal? What are you actually asking for?

As my thoughts cleared I realised my big error. Of course, I'd been telling myself the money was the crucial issue. It wasn't. The most important factor here was time. All I needed was a three-month loan, even one month would do. By that time I would own the trademark and could then negotiate a much better deal with prospective financiers. They were not to know I was only financed short term, if I was apparently negotiating from a position of strength. If somebody would lend me the money to tide me over it would *buy* me time – the most important consideration.

With Vantona's royalties of £30,000 a year it wouldn't be difficult to repay £100,000; there was healthy scope for further licensing; apart from Dallas I had demonstrated a good trading year; I owned the property in Derbyshire. Prices in that area had risen quite considerably since the purchase two years before. I had maintained the repayments regularly, using the sale of one of the flats to pay back part of the loan and earning an income from letting the other flat.

My mind was crystal clear and I stayed up the rest of the night rehearsing what I would say to my bank manager.

As soon as the bank opened at nine o'clock, I was on the telephone.

'I want to talk, please listen,' I said. 'When I've finished, think about it for a bit, and then come back to me as soon as possible. I have to do the deal today.'

And I went through the points that had seemed so logical in the small hours of the morning, and, in the cool clear light of day, seemed logical still.

He listened. He didn't say yes; he didn't say no. 'It has to go out of my hands now,' he said. 'Give me an hour and I'll get back to you.'

Forty-five minutes later he called. 'We'll do it. And we'll do it over three years.'

They moved fast. By midday contracts had been drawn up, and the assistant manager was in my solicitor's office with the papers for me to sign. I signed. The assistant manager telephoned the receiver's solicitor to say that I had signed. Barclays transferred the money. The receiver's solicitors were also Barclays customers, which made the transfer even easier. The receiver assigned the trademark to me. After all that anguish for all those years it was over. The weight was lifted.

I went back to my office after I'd signed, hardly believing what had happened. At three o'clock that afternoon my solicitor phoned to reiterate that it had all gone through. Nothing could possibly go wrong now. I opened a bottle of champagne in the shop and the girls, Aliza and I celebrated our happiness.

I now had to inform the various interested parties that the game was over, and I'd won. Vantona were absolute gentlemen about it. They knew I didn't have any money, that I must have borrowed and needed their royalties to repay the loan. They realised my property could never be used to repay it, since without my factory or my shop I would have no business. So they put two and two together and came up with the right deal for them, and we have worked together amicably ever since.

Mr Black came straight to Beauchamp Place from Heathrow on the Friday morning. I am ashamed to say I was looking forward to this confrontation. He didn't waste time on preliminaries: 'I've had it with your solicitor. I've been messed around long enough; this is as far as it's going. Either . . .'

It was too early for customers. The girls had discreetly slipped down to the basement, where they could eavesdrop in comfort. I tried to interject. But my 'Just a minute, please let me say something,' was drowned by his tirade.

Eventually I managed to blurt out: 'Please let me say something. It's important.'

He stopped in mid-flow. 'What do you want to say?'

'There's nothing really to discuss. I've already bought the trademark.'

'What do you mean?'

'I've bought it. It's mine. I've done it.'

He was startled. 'You've bought it? Outright?'

'Yes, I raised the money. I've paid for it. It's mine.'

His angry expression turned to one of disbelief, then amazement.

Silence for a minute. Then: 'You mean there is nothing more I can do except negotiate with *you*?'

'Did you ever have any other choice?'

'I suppose not.'

He left.

I was told of a fortune teller in Los Angeles who would give a reading over the telephone. She was reputed to be a most extraordinary clairvoyant. The friend who gave me her telephone number was a complete disbeliever; he thought at first he had been set up, so accurate was her knowledge. When he heard the first truths about himself, he roared with laughter, but his tune changed when she began telling him things that were so private she could not have heard of them through a third party.

She took calls only during the morning, LA time, for she was too tired to work in the afternoon. You paid for your consultation by sending $10 in an envelope to the address she gave at the end. Eventually she stopped consulting by telephone; it took too much out of her. If we want to see her nowadays we will have to go to LA.

Aliza tried it first, while we were in the thick of the Dallas drama. The clairvoyant identified what we were going through, and added: 'This man will be caught eventually, but you will not be involved. He has gone out of your life. His capture will be the result of another matter.'

Six weeks later I had my trademark back, and we had reached an agreement with Vantona. On impulse I telephoned her.

I introduced myself and said I had her number from a friend.

'Hi, Janet, who's your friend?'

'Aliza.'

There was a marked silence, not just a little pause. Then: 'You're Aliza's mother. You're not her friend, not *just* a friend. A mother can be a friend, but first and foremost she's a mother. Don't try to fool a psychic.' It was an amazing start.

'I sense a lot of turbulence around you,' she said. 'You've had

226

a lot in the past and it isn't over yet. After you've moved, it will get better.'

'But I'm not moving,' I said.

'Oh yes you are. You're moving and it's going to be in the near future. You're not thinking of moving house, and you're not going to like it, but you're going to move.'

'I've just moved,' I told her, 'and it was in very stressful circumstances. I think you're seeing the past. I'm planning to be here a while.'

'No,' she said, 'it's not the past. I see that too. But you're going to move again, quite soon.' Then she said: 'Because of all this turmoil going on, I'm finding it very hard to get anything else, but there is one thing I can see. You have a very, very important meeting shortly, either Friday this week or Friday next week.'

I did have a meeting planned for Monday with a prospective underwear licensee, with whom I hoped to do a deal that could be very important.

'There is a meeting in the near future,' I said. 'It's on Monday.'

'Forget about that one,' she said. 'You're wasting your time. Nothing will come of that. It's Friday, most definitely Friday.'

I went to the Monday meeting. I was very interested in making it work. But later it all fell through; nothing came of it. After the meeting, John Corré said to me: 'By the way, Vantona phoned. They need another meeting before they sign the contracts. The only time they can manage, and I can manage, is ten o'clock next Friday. I told them I'd confirm that with you.'

That meeting proved very important to me. Vantona developed the Janet Reger bedlinen so successfully that it now earns me an annual sum on which many would retire . . . and frankly I sometimes wonder why I don't.

And I did have to move soon afterwards, as the clairvoyant had predicted.

23

Leslie Creasey had lost no time in informing me that, in buying the trademark, I had bought him with it. 'On the contrary,' I said, 'your contract was with Berlei. Either it expired when Berlei went into receivership or it was sold to Courtaulds, who bought Berlei. Your contract was to promote and manage the Janet Reger trademark with Berlei. Go to Courtaulds and tell them they own you, but quite how they are going to fulfil their part of the contract I don't know. However, if you want to negotiate something with me I'm happy to talk to you.'

He also made the promise: 'The day you sign with me, within hours I can deliver thousands of pounds in upfront fees.'

It wouldn't have been difficult for me to negotiate directly with potential licensees, a list of whom had been produced by Vantona in a marketing booklet naming complementary Janet Reger products in the pipeline, which represented contracts as yet unsigned because of the litigation. Nevertheless, I felt an obligation to co-operate with Leslie, all things being otherwise acceptable, and was quite prepared to do so.

I was waiting for him to come back to me on this when, in April, Sheila Gore phoned. 'I've just come back from the Birmingham Gift Fair. I don't know if you are aware, but there is a range of sponge bags on display, and I'm not sure how to tell you this, but they are really cheap and nasty. They *are* in the Vantona print, but the make up is shoddy, the binding is poor, the trim doesn't match.'

So far as I knew I had only one licence: with Vantona bedlinen. Sheila furnished details of the manufacturing company and I telephoned at once and spoke to the managing director. He told me that his firm had negotiated a contract with Berlei, and had been on the point of signing when that company went into liquidation.

He had been assured that the contracts would shortly be signed and was ready to go into production. In addition to being offered to the trade at the Birmingham fair, the goods had been advertised in a catalogue. His company had paid a deposit to Berlei's licensing agent pending the final contract.

They were a very respectable company. The fact that they make an inexpensive product is not to their discredit; they give value for money, but that was not the image I wanted. They were perturbed, and rightly. They had understood Leslie Creasey was my agent and acting on my behalf. They were already committed when Berlei went into liquidation, and had taken the decision to go ahead with production. Nobody wants to miss the big selling season, and what manufacturers don't show in April, they cannot deliver in the autumn. Business is pressure; they had gone ahead in all good faith.

I hotfooted it round to Leslie's office, to discover several other 'Janet Reger' products on display and in production. Some manufacturers had even paid their deposit against royalties. One had merely stuck a Janet Reger label on everything in his existing range that seemed vaguely appropriate (or not too devastatingly inappropriate) and was selling it as Janet Reger. I absolutely refused to accept this. I agreed to the sponge bags: the company was too far in to pull out. I stipulated changes in the design over a period of time, but eventually this did not suit their production methods and the contract was not renewed. I subsequently signed with another company to produce the most beautiful range of bathroom accessories, tissue boxes and the like, which now sell very successfully.

To resolve matters I made an *ex-gratia* payment to Leslie for the work he had started, and which I then proceeded with. However, these were not big moneyspinners: there aren't too many blinds sold to match bathmats!

From the moment I regained my trademark, I set about the licensing world with vigour. I needed the income it generated and I wasted no time. First I had to sort through the possibles already lined up and waiting, and then I began to pursue my own ideas. It focused my mind on the positive. Work is a great therapy and I certainly needed that. Now I like to think I have learned a thing or two in the process.

Licensing is a minefield. It is easy to lose sight of the objective as you concentrate on finding a safe path, and the designer can quickly be led astray. It is important always to ensure that the designer's hand is on the design pencil – to what extent, in my case, depends on the product and how good I am at being able to help that product.

When it comes to clothing there is quite a lot of Janet Reger input. With products outside my range of expertise, I make suggestions. For example, I wondered why Vantona didn't make a pure cotton range since I had always bought pure cotton myself. Because it doesn't sell outside London, I was told. Customers don't want to pay the price of pure cotton and certainly don't want to have to iron it, and of course the small polyester content makes bedlinen stronger as well as easier to manage – as I've discovered since by trying it myself.

Licensing is more work than I had believed possible, having imagined I would merely sign the contract, sit back and count the money. This is what everyone thinks, and why manufacturers are so keen on buying designers' trademarks when their companies go under.

You need precise planning; to retain a clear vision; to be very strict with the licensees or they dance on your head. If you are not firm and don't tie them up well; if you don't make sure that they keep to their contract, then you finish up with a disaster. 'Oh well, we forgot to submit,' they will say, and put on the market some product that you can't stand, or deliver something quite different to what was agreed, or do artwork that looks hideous. And this is a continuing battle. The moment you blink, someone has done something *wrong*. And then there's always an excuse: there wasn't time to submit the drawing; we had to get the invitations out; we were late for photography; we forgot. All these excuses are true. The companies concerned are not villains; they are very nice people. But the clothing trade is always under the twin pressures of time and money. You have to sell your collection; you have to be ready to sell; you have to produce and deliver when the customer specifies. You have to be on the ball all the time, and in the mêlée it's easy to forget to submit a design detail for approval. It might seem a small detail to them, but if it's wrong, it's a very big detail to me.

No designer wants to hurt a licensee, but my first experience of a hosiery range was almost disastrous. I had to ask my manufacturer to withdraw the merchandise from the market.

The manufacturer began by presenting various sketches of a motif to decorate the stockings and tights: fine. Empty packaging: fine. We arrived at the launch date and I had yet to see a pair of tights. After a delay, the tights were delivered to the shop. The girls and I had ordered some for ourselves, at the wholesale price, and we eagerly unpacked the first box. So much for the beautiful packaging: each pack was criss-crossed with bits of Sellotape; the edges were loose before we had even unpacked; in the display the floppy edges were turning up.

To my horror when the packet was opened, the tights were scrunched up; some had snags. It had been a lovely design, but it didn't work. I complained at once. The manufacturer was a friendly, helpful, good-natured man, but he couldn't see the difference between one quality and another. He had put a product on the market without my approval because he was in a hurry.

'Don't you worry, Janet,' he said. 'I'll soon sort that out.' Nothing happened. I wrote a formal letter, giving him thirty days to get it right. Still nothing happened. I travelled up north to the factory. Determined to be positive – I was aware that their packaging was expensive, so I wasn't about to suggest they put the whole lot on the bonfire as I was entitled to do – I worked out a way of using it slightly differently, with bags over the original packaging so it would still be clearly displayed, while giving the whole presentation more gloss.

He and his co-director had a big fight with me, but finally agreed. I hadn't finished. 'Now I want to see what's going into the packs,' I said. They prevaricated.

By now we were starting to receive complaints. One of my customers opened a pair of tights and found an odd leg in there. There was the pantie part with one leg attached, and the other leg had been folded and put inside.

I suggested to the manufacturer that the entire stock be offered around the trade at sale price, marked as seconds. It was the only way of getting rid of it without making too big a loss. Then we would start again with a tighter quality control.

'Oh, we couldn't do that,' they said. 'It will damage your reputation.'

'Not half as much as selling the stuff at the regular price,' I said. 'There's nothing wrong with having a sale. I've had a sale in my shop twice a year since I started. In Knightsbridge the stores are full of sale-price Dior tights. It's good for business. If they're marked as seconds and reduced, people won't object if there is a small flaw.' I had the snags and patchy colours in mind, and I wanted the goods sold as seconds or slightly imperfect.

They refused. They preferred to take everything out of the packages, inspect and re-pack in new packaging, which was a ridiculous waste of time and money in my opinion.

One day a customer in Beauchamp Place bought a pair of tights to wear at once, and went into the changing room calling out that if she liked the colour, she would buy several more. After a long interval she asked for assistance and the manageress went to her aid. They struggled together. 'I can't seem to get them straight,' the customer was saying, and the manageress agreed there seemed to be a problem.

The tights were removed and held up for inspection. It was hardly surprising they wouldn't fit: the right leg faced forward, the left leg faced backwards! 'No problem, Madam,' said the assistant, taking a replacement from the hosiery display. 'Have this instead.'

The whole pantomime was repeated. One foot forward, one foot backwards. The staff began feverishly opening the packs and could not produce a single pair with both feet facing the same direction.

'Well,' said the customer, trying to ease our embarrassment, 'they *are* marked slightly faulty.'

It was the last straw. Do it my way or cancel the contract, I told the licensee. We parted company. His business later went into liquidation.

The Janet Reger logo now covers bedlinen, window blinds, lampshades, slippers, hosiery, bathroom accessories such as tissue boxes and toilet bags, leisurewear, daywear, costume jewellery and precious jewels, underwear other than my couture collection, and swimwear, sunglasses, spectacles, handbags and a perfume.

I go into battle over items I cannot in all honesty endorse. I take the view that I have to like the merchandise. I don't care if the manufacturer says: 'It will sell well.' Lots of things sell well, but that isn't to say they would sell to me, and it isn't to say I should put my name on something I don't like. I know it is important to be commercial. It is equally important for me as a designer to hang on to my integrity. For instance, I might approve something as a sketch. If I next see it made up, ready for delivery to the stockist and it's nothing like the sketch, then I have to put my foot down and get tough.

I introduced a system of regular licensees' meetings because it seems a good idea for them all to know how the trademark is being used elsewhere, and how they might benefit from any spin-off. The slipper licensee looks at the leisurewear and suggests a line of matching indoor shoes. The licensee making sponge bags can see the scope for beach bags to match the swimsuits.

Peter's solicitor, engaged after we split up, reminded me when we were sorting through Peter's affairs not to forget to take up my option to renew the lease on Cadogan Gardens.

How could I forget? Especially as Aliza and I had now settled so comfortably there. It was cosy, secure, convenient for the shop and, above all, we felt close to Peter. We spent a little money decorating the apartment and making it more suitable to our new way of life. It was as if we had taken a huge breath of relief to be home at last.

My major preoccupation had to be the survival of the business. Repayments on the loan which enabled me to buy the trademark were to cost £32,000 a year and, since there was no way that could be found out of the shop takings, I was pursuing possible licensing outlets with zeal and consequently spent hours in meetings with manufacturers and lawyers.

I was also very tired. I was bound to make a mistake. And I did.

Aliza was stopped on the stairs one day by Mrs Regal.

'So you are moving out in June,' said Mrs Regal.

'No we're not,' said Aliza.

'Yes you are, my dear, you ask your mother. Perhaps she hasn't told you but you're moving out at the end of June.'

Aliza said: 'I don't know what you're talking about, Mrs Regal. What do you mean?'

'Well,' said Mrs Regal, 'your mother hasn't taken up her option on the lease, so I presume she is moving out. She'll tell you about it when she comes home, I'm sure.'

Aliza said: 'Mrs Regal, there is a mistake. Of course my mother wants to renew her option. You know she does. Do you think we would have done all this work on the flat, and gone to all the trouble of moving in just to move out again a few weeks later?'

'It's none of my business what you would or wouldn't have done,' said Mrs Regal. 'As far as I'm concerned you are going at the end of June.'

Aliza repeated this conversation to me on my return from a business trip the next day, her little face white and pinched with anxiety. I hastened at once to Mrs Regal. There was a misunderstanding, I told her. Of course I didn't want to move out.

'You should have renewed the lease,' she insisted. 'I have someone else now, who is interested.'

'I'm really sorry. You know what I've been through these past months,' I said. 'It was sheer absent-mindedness on my part and I've been away on business. Of course I want to stay.'

She was adamant that she would not renew our lease. It was obvious she did not want the flat for herself, as it occupied the third and fourth floors, a steep climb for anyone and hardly suitable for Mrs Regal who was well into her seventies. She insisted on her right, according to the lease, to show prospective tenants around. I felt it was crazy that she should be going to all this trouble when we, the incumbent tenants, wished to stay on, and were prepared to pay the going rate, for it was implicit that lease renewal gave her the opportunity to increase the rent.

Peter's words came back to me.

When we first viewed the flat we had been looking for a property to buy. Mrs Regal, born in Romania, had no strong ties in England and told us that eventually she planned to sell up and go to Australia, where she went each year to visit her brother. When the time came, she promised, we would have first option to buy, and that clinched it for us.

The flat itself at that time was hardly an inviting prospect. There was old wallpaper on the walls, which had been painted over with hairdresser blue (a horrible shade) hastily applied as a freshener, the paint making the paper pull away from the walls. There was sad-looking, murky beige carpet of cheap quality; a bathroom with a stained old bathtub; and a kitchen dating from the forties.

The only detail of any merit was the period drawing-room fireplace – not my colour, blue – and we concealed and protected this *in situ*, installing a log fireplace in front using stone from Derbyshire. We decorated, carpeted, changed cheap plastic door-handles and doorknobs for brass (storing the plastic ones), fitted cupboards and shelves and effectively transformed the grottiness into homeliness.

As a landlady Mrs Regal kept herself well informed of everything that went on in the house. She knew each time anyone came in or went out, and observed every delivery, every visitor. Aliza would tiptoe up the stairs holding her breath until she felt she was safely past Mrs Regal's door, and the click of the latch which signalled that Mrs Regal 'wanted a word'. She was obsessed with the water tank, which was accessible through the loft in our flat, and demanded and was given access for frequent inspections of it. In vain did I tell her that all over London multi-occupied houses have tenants sharing the water system without mishap.

'Be careful, Mrs Regal wants this flat back,' Peter said once after one of her visits to look around.

That now became clear. Mrs Regal indicated that, for certain considerations, she might allow us to renew. Never mind that we had installed a beautiful tiled bathroom, a working kitchen, well-built cupboards. Now she wanted it written into the lease that she would own my specially woven, forest green Wilton carpet; my brass doorknobs; my Gaggenau oven and refrigerator and Miele dishwasher; my hand-painted, pure silk drapes. We had had nothing but the best in those days; now we might never see the like again. 'No, Mrs Regal,' I said. 'That is quite unfair.'

There was continual stress. She made appointments for prospec-tive tenants to view on Sunday mornings when Aliza and I wanted to sleep; she demanded frequent access visits to the water tank. Our burglar alarm went off one evening. Fortunately it wasn't too long to wait before Aliza and I came home. Mrs Regal was standing on the stairs in her dressing-gown and with her hair in curlers.

'You terrible people, we have to listen to this noise because of you. No wonder your husband killed himself, having to live with a person like you, having a daughter like you.'

We were shaking with distress and anger. And the fight went out of me.

It would have been possible, according to my solicitor, to put pressure on Mrs Regal by quoting the irregularities of her insistence that Peter form a company for the express purpose of the lease, because personal tenants had protection in a way not provided in law for company lets. She had nevertheless occasionally accepted Peter's personal cheque for the rent. But it was all very messy, and I didn't see why I should spend time and money on litigation in order to continue to pay Mrs Regal for the privilege of living in her house. We settled for an extension of a few months and began flat-hunting in earnest.

It made sense to buy rather than rent, and I heard of a flat going at rock-bottom price because another link in the buying chain had broken. It was also very basic, very neglected, had the lavatory at the end of the kitchen and was four storeys high. But it was bright and sunny on the day I saw it, and the price was right if I could manage to find the money.

Peter came to my aid. He had, unknown to me, a picture at auction in Germany at the time he died. A few weeks afterwards a very large cheque arrived: £17,000 (it must have been one of his better deals) and, as the bank had frozen his account pending probate, this went straight to my accountant.

Was there any way I could use Peter's £17,000 when buying the property? I asked. Strictly not, but I could borrow against it since it was, in effect, my money. By August the deal was done and we said goodbye to Cadogan Gardens and all its memories.

24

Although I am still running the same business I started in London nearly twenty-five years ago and I don't have Peter working alongside me, I do have Aliza (taking on an ever-increasing role in the business) and we are a formidable team. I'm certainly older and, I hope, wiser, and I can't, for the life of me, understand why it is still as frustratingly difficult to run a business operation now as it ever was when we began. In the worst respects, nothing has changed.

When, in 1990, Laura Ashley announced its decision to cease making its goods in the UK and to switch to manufacturing abroad, there was a sharp intake of breath as if the shining example of Britishness had committed some frightful indiscretion. But the Laura Ashley move makes sound commercial sense.

When we first took over the factory in Wirksworth, there was a dispute because the machinists could not see that the wage we were offering was better than the piecerates they had been accustomed to. Twenty years on, things are no different. Every innovation sparks off a surge of rumour and gossip. As a freelance designer I have worked in many countries, and noticed the difference in staff attitudes.

In my factory at the end of the break a bell is rung and the workers start to drift back to their machines, the supervisor ushering them along: 'Come on; bell's gone; tea break's over . . .' And they go back and start work. This is common practice.

In Germany and various other countries I have noticed that when the bell rings people are already sitting at their machines, and as it sounds they start work. I think that shows everything about the difference in attitude, and why this country is not successful in production. We have the brains, the creativity, the inventiveness, but production problems at home are a nightmare. Laura

Ashley is doing what most of us are planning or have already done, and that is to look for production abroad. In the UK it is too expensive. I had a factory manager who summed it up in a nutshell. She used to say: 'They expect to be paid for attending, and a bonus if they do some work.'

The attitude is that 'they' are doing you a favour working for 'you', and because they are doing you a favour you must be falling over yourself to make sure they are over-the-moon happy. This is nothing to do with 'rights'. Of course they have rights. So do we all. I never ask for something for nothing; whatever I ask, I pay for. But always there has to be negotiation and even blackmail.

Every year, at Christmas, I need overtime. There is no way I can run the business without it, because I cannot afford to stockpile all year. Why didn't we make more in May or June when we didn't have so much work? the workers demand. And always I explain that I cannot afford to invest in cloth and labour and have the goods sitting on the shelves for six months. In three weeks leading up to Christmas we do one-third of our annual turnover. Every garment is handmade, the intricate lace work undertaken by only the most skilled operators. Add to the making up time my factory costs and the price of pure silk and lace, and it is clear that I cannot afford to carry stock of this value for any period of time. Each and every Christmas we have the same dialogue, when I ask for someone to do overtime. In the factory they speak as one voice. It's all or none.

The Christmas of 1989 was particularly irritating. At the beginning of the rush, the factory supervisor came to me. 'The girls say they will only do overtime if it starts at thirty-eight hours.' Regulations say that overtime starts at forty hours, but I always pay overtime from the time they would normally stop work, which in most cases is thirty-eight hours. Then they came back to demand time-and-a-half from the first hour of overtime. Customarily, the rate is time-and-a-quarter for the first two hours, and then time-and-a-half. However, I said yes – as I do every year. Then they came back and said: 'We want to agree our new hourly rate for next year now, and we want to agree a shorter working week.' To which I replied that we always agree our next year's rate in January when I know what sort of Christmas I've had. I was not willing to agree to anything else before Christmas.

These are not militant women. Were they militant, we would never get anything done. As it was, the negotiations I have outlined took two working days in the pre-Christmas run-up, my busiest time of the year and with customers waiting, and the women lost a week when they could have been doing overtime and earning the extra money.

Yet the Christmas I was burgled at Beauchamp Place and eighty per cent of my stock disappeared overnight (the thieves couldn't quite manage it all), the girls at Wirksworth rallied unhesitatingly to work round the clock to replenish my rails and shelves. They were motivated by loyalty and anger at the injustice of our hard-earned potential profit disappearing without trace, for eighty-five per cent of my annual sales are clocked up from 1 December. I can only assume the blood was up and it was a case of everyone pitching in. Their hearts are in the right place, but one year later we were still back to the same old dispute.

I made up my mind at Christmas 1989 that I must find less troublesome production and Christmas 1990 found me back in the old CMT routine which Peter and I were doing twenty years ago. Cut Make and Trim covers a range of factories, large and small, and outworkers who service the rag trade. I deliver my cut pieces; they put it together and I collect or they deliver to me, depending on the size and scope of their organisation. It is an elaborate system but without CMT I couldn't have kept the retail business going.

25

I answered a telephone call in Beauchamp Place one day and after nearly thirty years, I recognised the voice at once. Not the surname; he had changed that to Hebrew.

Jonathan. He had read about me in the *Daily Telegraph*, and had decided to check whether Janet Reger was one and the same with the Janet Phillips he had known many years ago in Israel, last seen in hot pursuit of Peter Reger.

He hadn't rushed to contact me. Jonathan has turned out to be the sort of man – he wasn't like this in Israel in 1959, but life changes people – who's afraid of rebuff, who assumes that he won't be remembered, who is hesitant and nervous of the outcome, a mass of maybes, perhapses and possiblys.

I was ridiculously happy that he had made contact with me again, and we arranged to meet. He was living in London and working for the Israeli government. His curly hair had thinned; his skinny frame had thickened but only slightly; he still had the same attractive face. I thought he had aged quite well and told him so, and he said the same of me.

It was pleasant over lunch to relive old times. I assumed, simply because he didn't talk about it, that he was not entirely happy in his marriage. He spoke of his three children. He borrowed a book (later returned with a note), and I hoped it was the rekindling of our friendship. I was disappointed when I didn't hear from him.

Months passed. Then he wrote to say he was sorry he hadn't been in touch. There were problems at home; he wouldn't be good company right now. I wrote back that sometimes to talk to old friends helps, and to call me if I could be of any use. 'But don't leave it another thirty years,' I said, 'or I might not be capable of meeting you for lunch or anything else.' I deliberately kept it light.

Jonathan did call, eventually, and I cancelled another date I was toying with. I looked forward excitedly to seeing him, even though the only commitment he had made was for Saturday afternoon tea.

We ended up in bed together and he stayed the weekend. He told me his wife was thinking of going to live in South America and he would be alone, although I doubted very much that a mother would put herself at such a distance from her children. I could see that his problems were a major preoccupation, and it explained why he had felt harassed and not inclined to get in touch with me. This was nine months after the initial overture.

And so our affair began. Sometimes the candlelit dinners out, or at my home, once or twice he arranged to be away overnight. There was once a casual ring at the doorbell on a Saturday morning. His wife and family were shopping at Harrods and he had time to kill: 'Just thought I'd drop in.'

I once saw him with his family. I had introduced him to my favourite Chinese restaurant, The Red Pepper in Park Walk. A week later I went to the same restaurant with a friend, Carlos. 'What a coincidence,' I said as we were shown to our table. 'This is exactly where Jonathan and I sat last week. He's in Paris right now.' And I looked up to see Jonathan, sitting directly ahead of me, half-risen from his table in shock. He had seen me arrive. He was dining with his wife, who was no more than a tuft of blonde hair, the rest hidden by a pillar. There were two young men at the table, one clearly his son as he looked exactly like the Jonathan I had known as a young man. We were both acutely embarrassed. Jonathan came to our table to say good evening. Today was Anna's birthday, he said. He had brought her here because he had so enjoyed it on our visit the previous week! Carlos and I left at once.

'If I left Anna, would you have me?' he asked.

'That's unfair,' I replied, 'making me responsible for you leaving your wife. Only you can make that decision.'

Although I professed not to mind, his habit of making arrangements and cancelling at the last moment – due no doubt to the inherent complications of leading a double life – was inconvenient to say the least.

Because Aliza was living in Paris at that time, Jonathan and I had my place to ourselves. I loved him and appreciated his companionship. He was easy, undemanding, interested in everything. And although we progressed far beyond the stage of stirring over old memories, perhaps there was also in our relationship the sweetness of nostalgia for a time in our lives when everything was just beginning.

He planned to leave his wife as soon as he found a flat, he said. But he never seemed to get around to viewing any. He admitted that when she asked, point blank, if there was another woman he lied because he didn't want to hurt her; or because it was the day they had friends to dinner; or because his wife had been in a particularly happy, or sad, mood. It was all very inconclusive.

Fortunately I could immerse myself in the business and let his problems wash over me when I didn't want to get depressed about him. After each development he would ask me what he should do.

'There's only one way to leave, Jonathan,' I said, 'and that is to say I'm going, and go. It's very hard. I know because I've done it. Once it's over, you must move on.'

I never wanted to be his reason for leaving her. But we had grown very close and it seemed entirely feasible, once he and his wife had settled things amicably, that Jonathan and I should marry and buy a flat between us. His solicitor advised as a preliminary to divorce that he should establish his own address.

Three weeks before Christmas I announced I was thinking of visiting Christina in Venezuela. He begged me not to go. He dearly wanted the two of us to spend Christmas together in London. This was his moment to pack his bags and leave home; he had made up his mind.

I hesitated. Christmas is not the time to sit alone at home. But Jonathan was adamant. So I ordered the turkey and invited my family. Aliza said she would come home from Paris to complete the gathering. Then suddenly it was the week before Christmas and I'd yet to hear from him. On Christmas Eve word reached me: his name on the answering machine. Just 'Hi.' No message as to his imminent arrival. Aliza's French boyfriend, Richard, elected to return the call, and spoke to Jonathan's daughter. Idiotically, he left my number. He wasn't very bright.

Wives have a sixth sense in these circumstances . . . I should know. Within seconds of Richard putting the phone down, it rang.

Aliza answered. 'Who are you?' demanded the angry voice. Aliza had no idea it was Jonathan's wife.

'Who am I? Who are you?' she said. This exchange went back and forth a few times, then Aliza capitulated. 'My name is Aliza. Please tell me who you are.'

The voice demanded to speak to Richard. By now Aliza had guessed the identity and we held our breath. Richard took over. Anna began firing questions at him. Who was he? How did he know her husband, in what connection? Why did he want to speak to him? Richard barely spoke English. Their conversation was frustrating for her, while he sounded like somebody giving a very bad impersonation of a foreigner. Eventually, he managed to bring the exchange to an end. We laughed hysterically, although not because it was funny; it was really quite sordid.

Jonathan called to placate me.

I was furiously angry. I was landed with a turkey and a whole Christmas arranged in his honour, and he hadn't even bothered to tell me he wasn't coming. 'Which you're obviously not at this late stage,' I said.

He insisted he would definitely be with us for Christmas lunch.

A thought struck me. 'Where are you calling from?'

His study.

'Your wife must be having the rottenest time of all and I feel really sorry for her.'

'It can't go on like this, Janet,' he said.

How right he was. His wife had listened on the extension to every word. When he called back after ten minutes it was to say: 'You've got me now whether you want me or not.'

He had wanted one of us to make the decision for him, and his wish was granted. He also wanted always to be Mr Nice Guy. I used to say, 'There's no way a husband walks out of a marriage after all those years without the wife feeling angry.'

At this point, Anna believed Aliza was 'the other woman'. She warned Aliza that she could expect to be cited in the divorce, which made us laugh although it wasn't very funny.

Jonathan arrived, bag and baggage. Christmas passed happily. We celebrated Aliza's birthday together, then she and Richard left for Italy and it felt strange having a man around all the time. Much as I enjoyed his company, I had the odd fleeting doubt that perhaps this was not such a good idea after all. He intended finding a flat of his own, and I offered to help.

When he suggested I meet his children, right now seemed the ideal opportunity as we weren't working, but he backed out: 'It's a bit early yet.'

We had been looking forward to spending New Year's Eve with a party of friends at Langan's, but when the day came he was plunged in gloom and guilt, thinking of his wife. He knew she wouldn't go out alone. And his children, too, must be suffering.

Through Insight I knew a lot about guilt. I tried to say the right things about how it is implicit that somebody's feelings are hurt in any decision, but that doesn't mean it is the wrong decision.

The party had been arranged by Giselle and Stuart and included Giselle's mother, a wonderful much-married lady, full of *joie de vivre*. 'He's a lovely man,' she said to me. 'Take care of him.' They were all aware he was suffering. When I got up to dance, Jonathan began telling the others, 'Here am I, in this wonderful place having the best New Year's Eve party of my entire life, and all I can think about is my wife, sitting alone at home. What she must be going through!'

Giselle's mother patted his hand and said in her sharp New York accent: 'Jonathan, I thought you left your wife because you were unhappy with her. You left to be happy. If you're still unhappy, go right back to her. We don't want you being unhappy with us! Janet doesn't need that either; she's had enough unhappiness.'

In January he went to the airport to meet his eldest daughter on a visit from Israel, and without warning he was incommunicado for the next week. I was at a loss to know why he couldn't pick up the telephone. Eventually he contacted me to explain that there had been a temporary truce with his wife, and he had stayed at home with her.

I asked him to collect his things. I regretted the affair hadn't stayed as it had been for most of a year: dates, dinners, the occasional weekend together. He called to say goodbye. After he left I noticed his raincoat over the back of the chair and I threw it down to him from the window. No hard feelings.

We had reached the end, I thought. But a week later he came back. He missed me; he missed the companionship; he missed talking to someone who listened without putting him down. His wife complained that he monopolised the conversation. He missed my cooking.

And I missed him, his enthusiasm, wit, knowledge. Aliza always used to say Jonathan knew everything about everything, and it was true that he could hold forth on any given subject without ever being boring or hogging the conversation. The companionship was more important than the sex, although it was nice to have a man to cuddle up to in bed.

He stayed. The following day he moved into a friend's flat in St John's Wood as a lodger, and we went back to the way we were, except that now his life was even more complicated. His guilt was more persistent although it was clear to me from the way he described it, that his wife, far from being helpless with depression, was actually making quite a good job of getting on with her life.

Financial negotiations regarding a divorce settlement occupied him, as did his daughter's impending marriage. He was seeing a psychiatrist, whose advice was that the end of his marriage was a possibility, but that he should not immediately go into another. He needed *space*. I agreed with that. 'Spend more time alone,' advised the psychiatrist, and Jonathan did. In his room at St John's Wood, thinking, he said. Often when I phoned him there, he was out. The friend offered to pass on the messages, once adding, 'But we don't see too much of him, you know.' Strange. One day I realised that the stock of clothes he had left at my flat over the many months of visiting and staying had dwindled. There was almost nothing of Jonathan left.

I managed to get him at the office. 'You've moved back home, haven't you?'

There was a brief silence. For once I got a straight answer: 'Yes.'

'Would you mind sending back my keys, please.'

My keys arrived the following day. I never saw or spoke to him again.

But I spoke to Anna. Many months later she telephoned me. She wanted to talk about her husband and their problems. Not aggressively. Was he still seeing me? We talked a little, both, I think, realising that we were equal participants in a dilemma created by Jonathan's inability to face facts and make decisions. She said it would be nice for us to meet. 'No,' I said firmly. 'You have your own life to lead. It has nothing to do with me.'

Recently I took a wrong turn on my way to Wirksworth and found myself in Kirk Ireton, where once we owned the house that Peter and I planned to settle in. Converting and restoring the derelict farmhouse was one of Peter's great new concepts that never happened. I parked outside the village church and looked at the house. Sheep grazed in the paddock, newly planted saplings defined a driveway sweeping up to the front – or was it the back? – door. You never know with old farmhouses. It had such a 'family' look. Peter and I made wonderful plans for the house. I would love to see how it turned out, just out of interest.

I could have called this book *With Hindsight*, and certainly now that it is written I intend never again to look back. My priority right now is to get out the sketch pad, sharpen the pencil and begin on Aliza's wedding dress.

JANET REGER, *May 1991*